Bein

Being Love

Creating Beautiful Relationships...

AWAKENING with BRAHMA KUMARIS

Sister
BK SHIVANI
in conversation with
Suresh Oberoi

AMARYLLIS

AMARYLLIS

An imprint of Manjul Publishing House Pvt. Ltd.
• 7/32, Ansari Road, Daryaganj, New Delhi 110 002
Website: www.manjulindia.com

Registered Office:
• 10, Nishat Colony, Bhopal 462 003 – India

Being Love – Creating Beautiful Relationships

Copyright: Brahma Kumaris
Created and Authored by: Sister BK Shivani
Transcribed and Translated by: Muskaan Kapoor
Edited by: Arathi B Narayan

ISBN 978-93-89143-87-4

Cover design by Neha Behl

Printed and bound in India by Thomson Press (India) Ltd.

Contents

Being Love

We come into relationships to give love and be loved. Love is a source of emotional fulfilment, a directional compass to hold, to progress along the journey of kindness, happiness and harmony. But despite earnest efforts, we seem to run out of love for ourselves, for other people and for the world. This book aims to re-connect us to an infinite source of love so there will never be a deficit again.

When we think of love, we think in terms of familial, friendly or romantic relationships. But the exploration through these pages transcends these variants. It gives an exhaustive account of the nature and power of love. So that by eliminating whatever stands in the way of love and by not peddling limiting beliefs around it, we become radiators of true love. Thereafter, feeling love will be a natural way to be.

Being Love is a conversational adaptation of the television show that spanned over 40 episodes as part of *Awakening with Brahma Kumaris*. It has *Sister BK Shivani* taking on questions by

Suresh Oberoi. The discussions progressively throw light on the foundation of relationships, perceptions of love, beliefs blocking it and our quest to reignite it. Ultimately, the journey is not about 'falling' in love, but about 'living' with love.

This is not a word-for-word transliteration of the conversation. Through this book, an account of Sister BK Shivani's thoughts and insights about love are captured.

Introduction

The international spiritual and motivational flagship show *Awakening with Brahma Kumaris* has continued to change millions of minds for over a decade and has been spreading its wings far and wide across the planet. Even if only for 30 minutes a day, the daily talk show has answers to life's probing and insightful questions. At the helm of the show is the globally acclaimed authority figure in spiritual and emotional empowerment, Sister BK Shivani, whose profound and practical wisdom has made millions of viewers think, understand, introspect, experiment, take positive steps forward, and experience self-transformation. The peace, love and compassion that she embodies reflect in her timeless messages shared through the platform.

With over 2,000 episodes between 2007 and now, the *Awakening* programme has explored more than 20 wide-ranging series themed around upliftment of human consciousness.

Not just a household name within India, the show has left prominent footprints in USA, UK, Europe, Asia, the Middle East,

Africa, Australia and New Zealand. Viewers have been successfully overcoming self-defeating behaviours leading to mental stress, depression, addictions, low self-esteem and troubled relationships. They have realized their inner power, become resilient, feel good about themselves, and have taken responsibility for their everyday life.

The essence of knowledge shared on the platform is an offshoot of the teachings of the Brahma Kumaris, a spiritual organization headquartered at Mount Abu, India, and the largest to be led by women. The seed of service was planted in 1937, and today has sprouted into as many 4,500 centres in over 140 countries across 5 continents. The institution is accredited with General Consultative Status with the United Nations Economic and Social Council (ECOSOC). It also holds Associate Status with the Department of Public Information (DPI), Consultative Status with United Nations Children's Fund (UNICEF), and Observer Status to the United Nations Environment Assembly of UNEP. It supports UN programmes on a wide range of developmental, humanitarian and other issues.

The teachings of Brahma Kumaris are derived from the ancient spiritual wisdom of Raj Yoga but perfectly relevant in today's times. Everyone explores their own spirituality and learn skills of reflection and meditation derived from Raj Yoga, which will help develop inner calm, clear thinking and personal well-being. With a commitment to make spiritual education accessible to everyone, Brahma Kumaris welcomes people from all walks of life, irrespective of age, faith and background.

Anyone can simply walk into their nearest centre and fix a time convenient to them to learn Raj Yoga meditation. The foundation course is a 7-day programme of 1 hour per day, offered free of charge. People are also welcomed to attend the spiritual study class conducted worldwide every day. Several other courses are offered to individuals and corporates through dialogues, community projects, inter-faith programmes, lectures, workshops, seminars, conferences and other platforms.

Website: http://www.brahmakumaris.org
Centres in India: https://www.brahmakumaris.com/centers/
Centres Worldwide: http://www.brahmakumaris.org/centre-locator

A Note to the Reader

Dear Loving Soul,

Om Shanti. Greetings of peace and love.

You have spoken about love, read about love, written about love, and maybe sung lines glorifying love. Love is the perhaps first emotion you felt as a child. When people carried, cuddled and comforted you, even as an infant you intuitively knew how to respond lovingly. Growing up, you may have learnt different connotations of love.

You undoubtedly love people in your orbit of relationships. The real question is – do you love them unconditionally? Perhaps not. Today, original qualities of peace, love and happiness are not brought into action consistently. When our mind is disturbed, we don't even respond with stability, so thinking about love would be too far-fetched.

Each time you blame other people or situations for how you feel, each time you are judgmental about someone, each time you are unhappy that someone is not your way, each time you get rejection, or each time you face an adversity – you block the flow of your love. When you stop experiencing your own love, you expect someone else to give it to you. Conversations in this book point you to an infinite source of love within yourself.

Other people love you only 'conditionally' because they are also seeking it outside today. So, your experience of love needs to begin with you. It is not possible to love others if you do not love yourself, it is not possible to accept others if you criticize yourself. The book draws you into love for the self, so that giving it to others becomes natural.

The book examines other emotions to eliminate everything that does not qualify as love: attachment, expectations, possessiveness and control. When emotions are sorted in the mind, the energy carried into relationships is clean. Compassion, co-operation and kindness are gateways to a deeper realm of love are also discussed.

This book will shift you from holding expectations of being loved ... to make that life-changing discovery of BEING LOVE.

Om Shanti
BK Shivani

Acknowledgement

We are thankful to Muskaan Kapoor for transcribing and translating the TV series *Being Love*, from the programme *Awakening with Brahma Kumaris*.

We also extend our gratitude to Arathi B Narayan for editing the book.

Their contribution is highly appreciated.

Relationship is a Connection Between Two Souls

Suresh Oberoi: Love is the basis of any relationship. Love, you've always emphasized, is a quality of the soul. But relationships are on the physical level.

Sister Shivani: A relationship is never about physical dimensions. We are taking up the subject of relationships because a majority of us find it challenging. This aspect of our life once gave us love, happiness, satisfaction and a sense of purpose. But today it has become a source of tension, pain and jealousy. Let us come together to restore the original goodness of relationships. You said relationships are physical. There is a physical label or name for every relationship – such as parent and child, husband and wife – depending on the form of interaction we have. But what really is a relationship and who is it between? A relationship is a connection between two souls.

SO: I thought being love is all about the quality of the soul [internal] and forging a relationship means to talk and behave well with others [on the outside]. I separated the two things.

SS: That's the reason our relationships are not so beautiful today. We always perceive them at the level of words or actions exchanged. Sometimes we wonder why, after investing so much in a relationship, our bond is not as strong as it should have been. We need to check if along with choosing good words and actions, are we also thinking well of the other person?

SO: Are you saying that a thought reaches the other person first? Is it more important?

SS: A thought is not more important, it is the singularly most important aspect in building a relationship. This is because a relationship is essentially an exchange of energy between two souls. However, today we believe it to be an exchange of gifts, words and behaviour.

SO: But we have been conditioned to think that a relationship is based on what we do for each other.

SS: Doing good for others is absolutely important. But despite doing so much we are still struggling with our relationships today because we are putting all our efforts into perfecting the exteriors of the building while paying very little attention to its invisible foundation.

Today we can talk cordially with people despite thinking otherwise about them. We extend our cooperation but internally we are judgmental and critical of them. So, outwardly it appears to be a perfect relationship, but its foundation is weak. The building can collapse in the wake of even a mild calamity. This has been a common scenario.

SO: People routinely shower sweet lies and false praise on others for years. Is that not important?

SS: Have you been in a situation where someone talked very sweetly to you and yet you did not feel comfortable?

SO: At some parties, I felt the need to wrap up a conversation quickly and leave. Though people spoke nicely to me, I felt uncomfortable.

SS: This is because there was something apart from the conversation that was reaching you, which was invisible and inaudible. You could sense the other person's negative thoughts, feelings and vibrations. Those were reaching you and reversing the effect of their kind words and perfect gestures. Let's experiment with the belief that relationships are what we think of others and not what we say or do to them.

SO: I'll give an example of what you just explained so beautifully. I had once changed my hairstyle. I attended a party after that. Everyone appreciated except for one person who said my new hair style did not suit me. But I didn't mind him saying that. We spent a good time together and I even changed back my hairstyle. Your explanation fits into this example. Though he was the only person who disapproved, his clean intention is what mattered.

SS: Yes, it matters not how sweetly we talk, but how sweetly we think of others. First, we have to strengthen the foundation, then we can focus on the building. We usually let the foundation of thoughts stay as they are (weak) and focus on words alone. Since childhood, we are coached only about how to speak and how to behave.

SO: Children are trained to use courtesies like 'please' and 'thank you' while speaking.
SS: Yes, it is good that we are taught the art of speaking, and the art of behaving. We are never taught the art of thinking.

SO: Where can one learn the art of thinking?
SS: We ourselves have to check our thinking because no one else can see our thoughts.

I alone know what gets manufactured in my mind, so I have to set it right myself. I have to be convinced that the thoughts created for people in my mind, form the foundation of my relationships. Till today we believed that our thoughts are hidden from others, so we gave ourselves the liberty to think any quality of thoughts for people, but manipulated our words and actions. But now we understand that the energy our thoughts carry automatically radiates to others, and reaches them much before our words and actions.

SO: But so many people are thinking about me, do I catch everyone's thoughts?
SS: Thought is energy; it radiates. You may not be able to catch the exact thought but you will sense its vibration. So be certain that whatever you think about someone is radiating and reaching them, laying the foundation of your relationship.

If someone is creating negative energy for you, their negative energy will reach you. Now if you are not consciously choosing your thoughts, and believe that thoughts emerge on their own, you will automatically create similar thoughts for him. This is the law of reciprocity. When your negative energy bounces back to that person, his feelings intensify. With this continuous exchange, a loop of high negative energy is created. This then serves as the foundation of your relationship with him.

SO: But why did that person think negatively about me in the first place, when I had no such thoughts for him?
SS: He may have his own reasons to think negatively, irrespective of your positive behaviour. He could have an inferiority complex, insecurity or a sanskar of being critical.

SO: Does distance play a role in this transfer of energy?
SS: This exchange of energy is comparable to an SMS. Even if you are in America and the other person is in India, he is bound to receive a thought that you create for him. Nobody else will receive it because that message is meant for him. Factors of time, space and distance are never a constraint in this exchange. This is communication through thought power.

SO: We feel we can privately think negative about others and put up a nice face in public. But that is not possible.
SS: We give ourselves the liberty to think whatever we want. Since our personal interactions with others are brief, we think we can manage to talk sweetly for a short while. But the number of thoughts we create for others far exceeds the number of words we say to them. Thus, the impact of thoughts is greater. So, we have to take care not just when we are with others but even otherwise.
Suppose I do not think well of my boss. When I meet him, I can block my thoughts and speak politely to him. I meet him only for a short while, but I think negative about him several times at work, at home, while travelling and so on. And there's a general tendency to think a lot about those whom we dislike.

So, how many messages did I send that soul? I can create 1,000 thoughts for my boss in a day. This is easy because we create around 60,000 to 70,000 thoughts per day.

SO: So, we must get tired by thinking.
SS: It depends on the quality of thoughts we create. When the thoughts are negative, their quantity increases.

If we are in a stress-free environment, like when we go on a holiday, we feel very relaxed. This is because number of thoughts reduces as the quality of our thoughts changes for the better. The situations or stimuli that influence us to create negative thoughts are absent, though only temporarily.

So, when I create so many negative thoughts for my boss most of the times and speak only a few kind lines when we meet occasionally, what will be the quality of our relationship?

In today's scenario, relationships incur too much investment but bring minimal returns. We are putting in a lot of effort by talking nicely to others, exchanging expensive gifts, going out for dinners together, but we don't get along well. This is because we are focussing on the building while the foundation is weak. Even one tremor can bring that whole building down, and then we have to rebuild it from scratch. So from today, let's focus on the foundation [thoughts], and the building [words, actions] would be taken care of automatically.

SO: Let's have a meditation on strengthening the foundation of our relationships.
SS: Sure.

MEDITATION AND REFLECTIONS

Let me look at myself ... I am a soul, the power that thinks all day ... from today I will have the awareness that my every thought is the energy that I create and radiate to the world ... let me look at myself ... check what kind of thoughts I create for others through the day ... they may be doing anything, but what are my thoughts for them ... from today I have the awareness that what I think of others is the foundation of my relationship with them ... what I add to this foundation is my choice ... today, throughout the day, I will lovingly check my thoughts for everyone, then gradually change those ... the foundation of my relationships is my choice and creation ... from today every thought that I add to this foundation will be clean, pure and loving ... Om Shanti.

MANTRAS FOR BEING LOVE

- A relationship is beyond labels and roles like parent-child, husband-wife. It is a connection between a soul and another soul.

- A relationship is not limited to what we speak and how we behave with each other. It is about how we think and feel for the other.

- A relationship is an exchange of thought energy between souls.

- Our thoughts are the foundation of our relationships. We cannot hide our thoughts, they will radiate to people.

- The quality of thoughts we radiate, trigger similar quality of thoughts about us in the other person.

7

Thoughts, Words, Actions
Are My Creations

Suresh Oberoi: I assumed it is fine to be angry with others while showing respect to them externally. This training, which we got from childhood and from what we observed around us, has remained with us. Now changing it seems difficult. I read a nice quote: 'Beautiful thoughts are beautiful people.'
Sister Shivani: Let's make this quote the mantra of our life. We all want to be someone who the world accepts and appreciates. But we are looking at it from a physical level. We look at our position, costume, car, and overall lifestyle. We thought they earned us appreciation, acceptance and respect. Now you shared this beautiful quote: 'Beautiful thoughts are beautiful people.' It means if we want to be beautiful and earn everyone's love and respect, there is only one mantra – think beautiful.

SO: It is difficult to hold on to beautiful thoughts. Even after meditation, I return to the old patterns of thinking.

When I even if I come across just a picture of someone who wronged me, I get overwhelmed by angry thoughts. I want to see him punished.

SS: When you see the picture, you create an angry thought: 'he did this to me'. This thought will not stop here.

SO: **The next thought I get is, 'If God is unbiased, why is this person happy despite having wronged me?'**

SS: So you put a question mark even on God.

SO: **'I want to see this person punished' – such angry thoughts go on continuously.**

SS: You get this chain of thoughts – 'he was bad to me', 'if Karma philosophy works, he should also suffer' and so on. This is how many us think during the day. Such thoughts trigger an endless chain of similar thoughts and generate negative feelings.

SO: **By creating these thoughts, we become 'anti-God' and 'anti-law of karma'.**

SS: Most importantly, such thoughts make us 'anti-self'.

SO: **How do I become 'anti-self'?**

SS: Who felt the pain while creating these thoughts? Who created the anger inside?

SO: **That person's past behaviour made me angry. I got angry with him and felt the pain.**

SS: But who is creating anger now due to his past action?

SO: **The anger was created due to his behaviour. I will not call**

it my creation. **The thought automatically came to my mind.**
SS: Is it possible to create some other thoughts on seeing the same photo? The thoughts did not come from an external source.

SO: **These thoughts were first created in the past due to certain situations then. Later, they were repressed in my memory. Today, when I see that person's photo, they resurface.**
SS: But who first created the thoughts that were repressed?

SO: **They were the creation of the situation.**
SS: There are things that come to us from outside, and those that we send out. Situations and people come from outside. What we get from them is not in our control. But what goes out from us – such as what we think of them – is in our control, right?

SO: **No, what we give out may also not be in our control. Just as a blessing is automatically evoked in our heart, negative feelings too get generated on their own.**
SS: A blessing is a good thought you have for someone in response to his good behaviour towards you. But who creates that good thought?

SO: **The thought 'happens' inside me on its own.**
SS: Okay, let's not talk about thoughts. Whatever you speak, whose creation is it?

SO: **Mine.**
SS: Can we choose our words, or are they automatic?

SO: **They are an automatic response to a situation.**

SS: This means we are living in an unaware mode. Being unaware means doing something without realising it. If something is automatic, there is no room for choice. If we feel our words are automatic and we don't create them, then we would not have the power to choose what we say.

We are aware of what is happening outside, but are we aware of what is happening inside our mind? We are aware of what others are doing to us, but are we aware of what we should be doing? Most importantly, are we aware that we are creating our words?

SO: Most of my words are my creations, but others are involuntary, plain reactions.

SS: But whose reactions are they?

SO: They are an automatic reaction to others' actions. It is similar to the eyes closing involuntarily if an insect is about to enter them.

SS: Your words could be a reaction but they are not automatic. Let's take your example. If an insect is about to enter your eye, your body creates an automatic response. Now you create a thought: 'The next time I am in the same situation, I will just sit stable.' Can that happen?

SO: Yes, I will be able to do it.

SS: This means we have a choice. When we operate in the 'unaware mode', we repeat a pattern that we have used several times. This is like the body responding with a reflex action when an insect is about to enter the eye. The same happens when someone says something unpleasant and we react. This is a habitual way of thinking, behaving and living. When we repeat an act several times, it becomes a habit and a part of our automated mode. Then we feel it is happening on its own. But if I consciously decide today that instead of reacting I will deal with the same situation differently, then I am using my choice of action. First, I become aware, and then I exercise my choice to respond differently. This is how we take responsibility for the self. When repeated over time, this new choice will become a habit or an automatic response. This means we are choosing to create our habits. If, however, we think that habits exist on their own or things happen automatically, then we will not have any choice to exercise. We would then not be able to change anything.

SO: Yes, then we will feel that nothing's our fault. So we will stay the way we have always been.
SS: This means we will never change the habits we once created.

SO: In fact, those habits will be reinforced due to repetition.
SS: When we understand that our habits are our creation, that they are our own choice, it means we can change them if we are not comfortable with them. So who is creating your words?

SO: I am.
SS: This is always the case, irrespective of the stimulus.

SO: Yes, we choose what to speak with whom, depending on who they are.
SS: So our words and actions are our creation. Suppose you

spoke rudely to someone yesterday, remember that it was your creation. If today that person does not talk properly to you, can you speak nicely to him?

SO: Yes I can.

SS: This means we can choose to alter our creation. The moment we realise that our words and actions are our own creation, power comes back to us. On the other hand, if we think our thoughts and words are an automatic reaction to other people's behaviour, we give our power away to them. Until we realise this truth, we will continue to reinforce our old habits.

So our actions are our creation, our words are our creation. What about our thoughts?

SO: Our thoughts are our creation.

SS: Absolutely. If we do not hold on to this truth, we will feel overwhelmed by similar, old emotions time and again.

SO: Along with the thoughts of the past, those feelings also emerge. Everything from the past is relived.

SS: Now we can consciously create the thoughts: 'When I see the same photo now, my thoughts will be of a different quality irrespective of what happened years ago ... I will not allow that person or memory to make me go through those feelings all over again.'

SO: I feel so small imagining that just anything, even a photo, could elicit such a strong reaction from me.

SS: That is it. The more we react, the more depleted we get. Nobody else is responsible for creating our emotions or making us feel a certain way. We create our own emotions in response to their words/actions, but mistakenly think that they are responsible for how we feel. We are in the habit of justifying our emotions. We think 'if he did something like that, it's natural for me to be angry'. Every time we relive the memory, we justify that emotion and get caught in a habitual way of thinking. The more we create such thoughts, the weaker we get. The weaker we get, the more reactive we become to people's behaviour.

SO: Yes, by doing that we become a puppet in the hands of people and situations, and lose our originality.
SS: True. If we do not use our originality, it will start to fade away. In your profession (as a movie actor), if another actor is not performing well, what would you do?

SO: I will focus on my role.
SS: Yes, that is power. But some actors blame their co-actor's bad performance for their inability to give their best. Similarly, we blame others in life for our bad performance. We don't have the courage to accept that we are not good actors, so we point a finger at others. And the moment we do so, we give them the power to bring out the best or the worst in us. Who do you call a good actor in your profession?

SO: Someone who does not get disturbed by what's happening around him.
SS: A good actor is one who can give his best performance irrespective of any external constraints. Do we find such actors?

SO: Yes, I've done that myself. One of my co-actors tried to distract me but I performed my role well. Whatever she was doing did not matter to me.

SS: How did you manage to do that scene?

SO: I just kept the awareness on myself.

SS: Now you have to do the same in every scene of life.

SO: But she was playing a prank on me, it was nothing serious.

SS: It was your power. The other person was disturbing and distracting you, yet you remained focussed.

SO: Can we, in real life, keep the focus on ourselves if someone gets angry with us or swears at us?

SS: If you are a good performer, a powerful soul that does not blame others for its performance, you will be able to manoeuvre through the scene creatively.

We have spent many years blaming others for our responses, and because of that we have not used our original qualities. Anything that remains unused for long will fade away with time.

SO: But there is a difference between real life and reel life.

SS: Yes. But you can use the power you gained while enacting that film scene in real life.

MEDITATION AND REFLECTIONS

Today, throughout the day, let me look at every scene of life as part of a drama ... everyone around me – whether in family or at workplace – is my co-actor ... keeping the focus on the self ... I am a powerful, beautiful actor ... irrespective of how my co-actors perform, my thoughts, words and actions are my creation ... let me look at myself through the day ... whatever other actors may say, my performance would be unaffected, stable, focussed, concentrated on my role ... my performance, thoughts and behaviour are my creation ... Om Shanti.

MANTRAS FOR BEING LOVE

- People's behaviour towards us is an external force and not in our control. The thoughts we create in response to that is an internal energy, which is completely our choice.

- Thinking, speaking and behaving in the same manner repeatedly becomes a habit, and it soon becomes an automated way of responding.

- We are the creators of all our habitual responses and we can choose to change them.

- When we blame people for the way we respond, we give away our power to them.

Be Love in Action

Suresh Oberoi: I am reminded of a couplet that fits in with our discussion:
'Umr bhar hum yehi galti karte rahe,
Dhool thi chehre par, aaina paunchhte rahe'
[I made a mistake all my life – there was dust on my face, but I kept wiping the mirror.]
Sister Shivani: Yes, that's what we have been discussing. We must take responsibility for our thoughts, words and actions, irrespective of how others behave with us. From today, we should make sure that words such as 'the thought just occurred to me', 'the words slipped out of my mouth', 'I happened to hit him' should not be part of our vocabulary.

SO: There was dust on our mind.
SS: Because we were unaware.

SO: When there's too much dust, we can't see.
SS: Yes. The dust has been there for several years and we

have been unable to see the reality because of it. We have been in this state because we repeatedly blamed others for our condition/behaviour. The more we did this, the more we reduced our power and made others powerful. Each time, we allowed situations and others to overpower our state of mind.

SO: But when I react to someone's behaviour, I do not realise that he is overpowering me or is becoming mightier than me. At that moment, I think I am just being right.
SS: Let's take an example. You are sitting comfortably in a chair. Someone comes and shakes it. If that person is more powerful than you, he will be able to shake you off the chair. But if you are more powerful, however much he may try, you will have control over your position. So the question is, who is more powerful of the two? Just as you can be physically strong, you can be emotionally strong.

SO: Does it mean that I was weak in all those situations – such as when I got angry with a member of my staff because he gave me black tea in the morning, as he had forgotten to get milk?
SS: Whenever we say 'I did this because of them', we weaken further.

SO: So, does it mean the whole world is controlling me?
SS: It means we are not in control of ourselves. When we wake up in the morning, we are peaceful. We want to remain so for the rest of the day. But then comes a situation which is not to our liking – such as you being served tea without milk. We

then get irritated and annoyed, and raise our voice. We thus shift from our natural state of peace.

SO: But this means I am never in my natural state.
SS: You were in your natural state of peace in the morning, prior to that incident.

SO: But I might have slept after having a fight at dinner, and might be annoyed with others the whole day. So, when was I natural?
SS: We are not living naturally, which is why we are looking for peace, happiness and love outside. We seek peace from temples and saints, happiness from things, and love from people. So we are seeking all the time. Being love means to be in our original state, not seek any emotion from outside.

SO: What we are doing is begging for love.
SS: We are begging for peace, love, respect and happiness today. We are looking for them outside because we are unable to experience them within, all day long. They are our property, but we started to lose them gradually, and then came a point when we thought we did not have them at all.

The kitchen shelf, for example, is full of bottles of various ingredients used in cooking. The ingredients we use often are typically placed in front rows, the rest are pushed behind. Peace, love, happiness are the original qualities or ingredients of all souls. But they are not put to use throughout the day. So the bottles of these 'ingredients' are pushed to the back shelf. What are the ingredients we use the most through the day?

SO: Anger, criticism, blame and judging others.

SS: So these ingredients got shifted to the front row while peace, love and happiness – the original qualities of the soul – were pushed behind. They were pushed so far behind the rest of the ingredients that we forgot we had them. So one day we went to the market to buy them. Doesn't this happen often?

SO: Yes, it happens many times.

SS: If we want peace, we think we know where to go. We can go to the mountains, religious places, or seek it from people. We look for happiness in things, achievements and success. We ask people for love. We think when we get these from outside, we'll experience them. But being love means to stay in the original quality of the soul.

SO: So being love is the same as – 'I am love'?

SS: Yes, it's the same thing.

If being refers to the soul, and love is its original quality, how should we be the whole day? We will be love in action. So being love has two meanings: first, to 'be' love; second, the being's, that is, the soul's nature is love. Every morning, we must remind ourselves that we have both sets of ingredients – peace, love, happiness, and also anger, irritation etc. We have to decide what ingredients we would use in scenes during the day.

In the morning, if your staff brings you tea without milk, you can use an ingredient [your quality] of your choice while responding to the situation in a different way. You can choose the ingredient at that moment or prepare yourself beforehand for it. If you use one of your original qualities such as love, you will be in control of the situation. Then the situation will not overpower your state of mind.

SO: I could respond by saying, 'It is okay if you do not have milk. Get lemon, I can have lemon tea today.' This would resolve the issue without us arguing over what went wrong.

SS: The main thing is our state of mind at that moment. We become weak when the situation overpowers us.

SO: When we were born, we had within us all the good qualities of the soul – bliss, love, purity and power. What happened to them later? If a vehicle runs on diesel, we can't fuel it with petrol. So, if we are beings of love and bliss, why don't we stay like that all the time?

SS: If health is the original state/quality of the body, where does disease come from? We fall ill only because we do not take care of ourselves. So, the disease does not come from outside, it is manifested when we do not take care of our health.

SO: We were taught to take care of our health by our parents, and at school. But nobody taught us we are bliss, love and purity. We always observed around us that things are set right only by complaint and punishment. So, who is to blame for our misunderstanding?

SS: It does not matter if we didn't have an opportunity to learn something earlier, or if we got conditioned by how our elders behaved. We can learn things today because we have the bottles of both the ingredients or sanskars with us. For example, I may have been eating spicy food from childhood and may have developed a taste for it, but if I get to know that it's damaging me, wouldn't I change my habit today?

SO: Yes, you do. But even in films, we see that the protagonist becomes a hero only when he follows the policy of 'an eye for an eye'. The whole world believes in it. Does it mean that everyone has forgotten their original qualities?

SS: Let's not talk about other people, we will just focus on ourselves. We used certain ingredients according to what we learnt from our surroundings. What was the result we got? You said we are begging for love today.

Suppose I've been eating spicy and fatty food from a young age, it may not be my fault. Everyone was eating it so I picked up the habit. But when I see its impact on my health today – if I have developed high cholesterol, if there is a blockage in my heart, and if something is wrong with the functioning of my liver – I know it's time to change. It is fine that I had followed a certain diet for fifty years, but will I not bring about changes in my diet from now on?

SO: Certainly. I like the phrase 'it's time to change'. It's time to change our thinking. In my previous question, I was trying to blame the world for my state.

SS: Now we've seen the result – the body became ill by using the old diet pattern. We need not look at others because we will find people who are sick because of eating spicy food, and yet they will continue with it. They declare that they can't change.

SO: Yes, many people who suffer from oral cancer continue to chew tobacco.

SS: If someone is unable to change a harmful habit despite suffering its consequences, it means the soul is very weak.

So it is immaterial whether we got the sanskars of anger and irritation genetically or we picked them up from our parents, teachers or surroundings. The result of using them is – we remain stressed and sad, we do not have control over ourselves, and even trivial scenes disturb our mind. This means we are not healthy. Now we need to stop and ask ourselves: 'Is it time to change or do I continue the same way?' This is the need of the hour.

SO: Once, my driver stopped at the airport for a few seconds because he wanted to confirm an address. The driver behind us did not stop honking for the entire duration.
SS: This is a reflection of our state of being today. The being which was originally peaceful and loving has become impatient and agitated now. It has become so sensitive that even the slightest stimulus can disturb it.

Let's take the example we discussed earlier. Initially, if someone shook the chair we were sitting on, we did not move. That was a state of health. The second stage was – someone shook the chair hard and we experienced a small shift from our original position. This means we had become slightly weak. Now we have arrived at a stage where even if someone touches the chair slightly, we fall off.

SO: There's another relatable example. The owner of this area, where we are shooting, told me that if I drove around here in the evening I should not honk or switch on the headlights, as the locals would get offended. Instead, he said, I should stop the car and politely ask them to give way, and they would let me go. Just look at the two instances.
SS: When we realise that we cannot honk here and need to request permission to pass, we accept it and become willing to do it. It's a matter of choice at every step.

SO: And we can do it.

SS: Yes. Congratulations for saying this, instead of thinking that it's difficult to do something new because of our past conditioning. The first step to change is – to know that we can do it.

SO: Just like it is illegal to throw trash on streets, so we don't do it.

SS: Because we tell ourselves that it is not allowed. Similarly, we can tell ourselves that anger and irritation are not allowed in our interactions.

SO: Yes, and the mind accepts what we tell it. To say that we can't convince our mind is a mere excuse?

SS: It has become a habit to blame others. We think someone else is responsible for our anger. The second reason for blaming others is that we are not aware that the emotion of anger is our own creation. Third, we justify our action.

Now we have to go backwards and look at the results of following this pattern. The first result is that there is uneasiness in our mind and we become sad. We keep seeking love and happiness from others. Second, our physical health is affected. Today we have a rich diet, we exercise and use good medical facilities, yet our well-being is not ensured. The third and most important effect has been on our relationships. There is growing conflict in relationships due to the weakening of souls and exchange of negative energy. Today, let us ask ourselves if all this is okay for us.

SO: Can we do so through meditation?

SS: Sure.

MEDITATION AND REFLECTIONS

Let me look at myself, the soul ... in every scene the situation comes from outside ... but my response to it is my choice ... my own state is my choice and creation ... from today I will stay in the consciousness that I am a powerful soul ... no person or situation can shake me off my state of peace ... I am a powerful being ... today I will keep attention on myself ... I look at myself in traffic, at work, with family ... there will be unpleasant situations, but I will stay stable ... nobody can shake me ... my original qualities are peace, love, happiness ... whatever be the situation, I use these three ingredients in all scenes ... Om Shanti.

MANTRAS FOR BEING LOVE

- Every time we blame people for our reaction, we are reaffirming that we are weaker than the other person.
- When we lose control over our stable state of mind, we shift from our original quality of peace.
- Our original qualities of peace, love, and happiness are not being used repeatedly in action, and hence we forget that they are our own sanskars. We then start looking for peace in silent places, happiness in objects and achievements, and seek love from people.
- We need to make a conscious choice of responding through our original sanskars, instead of reacting through our habitual negative sanskars.

Forging a Relationship
with the Self

Suresh Oberoi: If I am weak, and I get constantly angry and irritated, does it weaken my relationships?

Sister Shivani: Wouldn't that happen automatically? I, the being, am the seed that creates each thought and action which is vibration. The first effect of the seed is on my emotional health. The second effect is on my body. Every thought I create impacts every cell of my body. As the seed, so the body.

When I interact with other people, as is my state of mind, so will be my thinking and behaviour towards them, the energy I radiate to them, and also my mental state when others behave with me in different ways. If I am weak when I interact with you, the slightest disagreeable behaviour by you will irritate me and I will not be able to tolerate it. I will want you to act as per my desire. If you don't do so, I will be easily disturbed and often react. Won't all this affect my relationships?

Until a few years ago, people from across a village or an entire neighbourhood lived harmoniously, as though they belong to one family. Even then, there were differences in their thinking and behaviour, but they had far greater power to adjust, tolerate and cooperate with each other. So, even a hundred people were able to live as one, united family.

SO: I want to know if they had no choice but to live in harmony or did they really have the power to be loveful?
SS: It was soul power. They were more soul conscious then. Which means, they stayed connected with their original self, so situations or people did not influence them a lot.

SO: People were not weak in earlier times?
SS: We were emotionally healthy then, had greater power to let go of things and forget the past. We could adjust with each other. So even a neighbourhood of a hundred people lived as a family. Over a period, we became weak and narrowed down our circle to say, a joint family, where around 15 people co-existed. Subsequently we became even weaker emotionally, as we did not take care of ourselves. So we started to live as a smaller family. Then even that seemed a great effort, so we shifted towards nuclear families. But we now find it hard to adjust even with our parents, and we live separately. Today, even couples struggle to live together. Why is the divorce rate so high today?

They say the divorce rate is high because of the stress of both the partners working. But that is not the case. The reason is that both partners are not taking care of their inner self. And when they come home stressed each evening, they transmit that negative energy to each other.

SO: Even earlier, both the partners were working equally hard. In villages, while one partner took charge of the fields, the other took charge of home, kitchen and cattle.

SS: Challenges have definitely increased today, but the basic difference between then and now is that we are not taking care of ourselves while carrying out our responsibilities. Suppose while achieving targets at work, I ignored my physical health for days – I said I was too busy to eat, sleep or exercise.

Would it not take a toll on my physical health? By the end of the journey, I would achieve targets, but I also would succumb to illnesses. Similarly, if I do not take care of my mental health on my journey – if I get angry, create feelings of jealousy and competition, stress, worry and anxiety – I may professionally reach the highest designation, but my power would be so depleted that I would lose out on good relationships.

SO: Which power is depleted?

SS: The power of the soul is depleted. When we get angry or sad, hate someone, or replay negative memories and relive those emotions repeatedly, what happens to our state of mind? Our mind shifts from its natural state of emotional health. If the soul shifts from its natural or original state of ease, several times during the day, it weakens. As its immunity goes down, a weak soul will not be able to keep up with the relationships it was once comfortable with.

This is similar to our body's immune system. When it weakens, even a small stimulus such as a change in the weather or food will make us vulnerable to diseases. We will fall ill more often.

SO: This is an illness of the mind?

SS: This is about the soul, the one that creates every thought and feeling. The soul is the seed of the tree. The tree is represented by our relationships, work and achievements. Today, most of our time is spent in taking care of the tree, while the seed is weakening inside. So now it's time to take care of the seed. Until we make the seed healthy, the tree can't flourish.

SO: But the mind feels pressurised while making any positive inner change. When, despite all my efforts, I am not able to do what I decided to, it becomes an additional source of stress.
SS: Even when we take care of our physical health, we do feel some pressure initially. Suppose our bodily parameters are not healthy and we are advised to go for a daily walk, the new routine will seem taxing to us.

SO: Correct. We experience body pain.
SS: Yes, and that too for quite a few days. Initially, we will even look to make excuses and struggle to follow the routine.

SO: And then, a day will arrive when we cannot resist going for a walk.
SS: When will that happen?

SO: When the body will be healthy, muscles toned up and proper blood circulation restored in the body. We will then want to go for a walk, even if the weather is not conducive.
SS: But till that stage is reached, we will have to go through that initial phase of struggle, isn't it? That phase is experienced because we are trying to move out of our comfort zone.
Likewise, if our 'comfort zone' is in reacting impulsively to situations, and now we choose to be calm all the time, it won't be that easy in the beginning. When we make a positive inner

change, we go against our old belief system. It's a big shift we are making, so it is normal to feel some pressure inside.

SO: That is the reason I wonder if I would be able to do it.
SS: But haven't you ever experienced the result of your efforts?

SO: Yes, I have. But sometimes I get disheartened when I progress so slowly and when I compare with others.
SS: A fair comparison can only be made with our own self. Appreciate and motivate yourself whenever you make progress, no matter how small. Do not look at others, whether they are ahead of you or behind you in the journey. Always check – 'Where was I yesterday, where am I today, and where will I reach tomorrow according to my capacity? If I got angry ten times yesterday, did the number go down to eight today?'

SO: But people around us don't look at our improvement; they focus on our shortcomings.
SS: It is their sanskar to look at the negative side, but you are improving yourself and so you need not be affected by it. You must see only yourself, because nobody truly knows you and the internal change you are making. Hence you evaluate your own self.

SO: So we are our own teacher, our own examiner and also the one to make corrections. We must also pat our own back.
SS: Yes, it's very important to appreciate ourselves every day. If we want to make our relationships beautiful and harmonious as they originally were, the first step is to forge a beautiful relationship with the self.

SO: If I criticise myself when I make a mistake, does it mean that I do not have a good relationship with the self?
SS: Criticism is negative energy, so we need to avoid it. Suppose you see a person making a lot of effort to stand, yet he is falling down and losing. What will your response be? You will appreciate him. If you criticise him, you will deplete the energy he was using to make that effort. Similar is the case with us. If we are trying to improve ourselves but it's taking time, we need to give ourselves positive energy to accelerate our progress. We cannot be critical of ourselves. If we have a beautiful relationship with the self, our soul power increases. When the empowered soul interacts with others, its relationships will be strong.

MEDITATION AND REFLECTIONS

Let me look at myself ... each thought is a seed ... from this seed emerges the tree of my body, relationships, work and each role that I play ... this seed – my each thought and feeling – is my creation ... for a healthy tree, I make the seed healthy ... my each thought is pure, clean, loveful, powerful, in control ... rising above the impact of the situation ... such a seed creates my healthy body and relationships ... from today I make effort not towards the tree ... but I pay attention to the seed ... Om Shanti.

MANTRAS FOR BEING LOVE

- The soul is the seed. The energy that it creates has an effect on our emotional health, physical health and relationships.

- When we are emotionally weak, our thoughts and behaviour towards others become negative. We radiate negative vibrations to others. We are unable to respond with stability to their unexpected behaviour and our relationship starts becoming weak.

- If we are unable to accept the behaviour of one person and we react, it depletes our energy. This depletion has an effect on other relationships which were beautiful.

- Our journey of self-transformation has to be checked in reference only to ourselves, no comparison with others. Let's appreciate ourselves for even the smallest change made.

From Blame Game
to Self-Responsibility

Suresh Oberoi: Building a loving relationship with the self seems difficult because I am critical of myself. I feel I will improve only if I am strict with myself.
I would like to share with you a beautiful quote that changed my thinking – 'Be careful when you talk to yourself because YOU are listening.' Could you explain it?
Sister Shivani: It's a powerful line. We are very careful while talking to others because we don't want to hurt them. But we talk to other people much lesser than we talk to ourselves. Verbal interactions happen rarely. But there is an inner conversation we are constantly having with ourselves throughout the day. We are listening to our self-talk all the time and so that affects us first.

SO: I used to think that if I create negative thoughts about someone, they reach him.

SS: Yes, your vibrations reach him. But the impact of those vibrations on you is far greater than on him.

SO: And the same energy will return to me later.
SS: Yes. Suppose you are thinking negatively about me and your vibrations are reaching me. Now, I have a choice. If I am living in the 'unaware mode', I too will start thinking negative. But if I am living in the 'aware mode', I will recognise that it's not good to have negative thoughts, so I will change my thoughts. So what you think about me can have either a great impact, a slight impact or no impact on me. It is a variable factor. But it will definitely impact you far more than anyone else. You cannot escape your own thought vibrations.

Let's understand this at the level of words instead of thoughts. Suppose you tell me 'you are no good'. You speak these words, but what I do after hearing them, is a power that lies completely with me. I can ignore them. Or I can accept them and feel bad. Or I can even hit back at you in the same tone. All these choices lie with me. So when you speak to me, I can shield myself from the impact of your words. But nothing can save you from what you are telling yourself through your thoughts.

SO: Suppose I am criticising myself again and again for not being able to give up smoking, then I am subjecting myself to an energy loss.
SS: Who will save you from the negative energy you create for yourself? The first impact of your thoughts will be on your state of mind. The second will be on your body. Nobody can save you from that either. That is why the words you shared

are very beautiful: 'Be careful while you are talking to yourself because YOU are listening.'

SO: This means we need to love ourselves.
SS: We speak sweetly to others while thinking otherwise about them because we do not want to hurt them. But we get hurt inside by thinking negatively about them because we are 'listening' to those thoughts. Others hear what we speak, we listen to what we think.

SO: That's right. You also said that anger affects every cell of our body.
SS: It affects our state of mind, body and relationships – in this order. We share a beautiful relationship with those who love us because they send us the energy of acceptance and comfort. That makes us feel empowered. We can't be sure about receiving this energy from others, but we can surely start giving it to ourselves. One by one, we must change those old thought patterns and habits that deplete us. Look at the soul as a battery. We need to plug the leakage of energy and make ourselves powerful. This way our relationship with the self will be revived.

SO: How do I make myself powerful? I have always associated power with control. It is said *'mann jeetey jag jeetey'*, which means one who conquers his mind rules the world.
SS: This line is self-explanatory – one who knows how to manage his mind, and is not subservient to it, is able to rule the world. Our world is that tree – which encompasses our state of mind, body and relationships. We, however, have wrongly believed in the opposite – that the one who has good health,

good relationships and and a good career is happy. Now, let us start taking care of the self first and find ways to recharge our battery. The simplest way to deplete our energy is to blame others for the state of our mind.

SO: Since we are already in the habit of criticising ourselves, we start to blame others too.
SS: Criticising is different from blaming. To blame means to hold someone else responsible for the state of our mind.

SO: If someone acts wrongly, it is natural to get disturbed. Isn't it so?
SS: Someone can harm me financially, even physically, or interact through his negative sanskars. But what is created in my mind in response to their behavior is my creation. Within my mind, only one person can shake me – I, myself. The moment I point the finger of blame at someone else, I give him the power and deplete my own.

SO: So we must not blame others.
SS: We have a choice: blame others or take personal responsibility. In the first case, 'they' are responsible and in the other, 'I' am. If we get angry, our power is depleted. On top of it, if we hold others responsible for it, getting angry becomes our habit.

SO: Blaming others is a never-ending game.
SS: Yes, and this means our battery will keep draining. To blame circumstances, our past, destiny, God or the world for how we are feeling today makes us weak. Yes, things may not be favourable, but responsibility for the state of our mind is still ours. We may

feel angry or hurt, it's okay. But we need to claim responsibility for our emotion so that our power is not depleted further by blaming others and thinking about it again and again.

SO: Earlier, I found it hard to accept someone who had wronged me. But now I find acceptance a beautiful thing.

SS: And acceptance is a prerequisite to bringing about a change in the self. If I get angry and blame others, I would want them to change, because I believe they are responsible for my suffering. When I understand that anger is my creation, my focus shifts inwards. So it becomes easier to change my sanskars. Now my power is depleted only for a limited time as long as I create anger or hurt. There is no further blame game so I don't wait for someone else to apologize or change. This means my power will start to increase sooner and I will be able to change my sanskars. If we blame others for our condition, our old sanskars will not change and the same patterns of behaving and reacting will continue day after day. So, the first sanskar we have to change in order to love ourselves is that of blaming others. It needs to stop.

SO: When someone says something hurtful to me and I keep quiet, it troubles me later. Eventually, I have to vent it out in front of a friend.

SS: You may not talk back because you wish to maintain your best behaviour, to keep good relations, or may be due to other reasons. You are troubled within because you keep quiet only externally, and your mind is not quiet.

SO: And it stays on my mind for years.

SS: Be careful of what you are saying to yourself because YOU are listening. Since you do not answer back, you maintain a good relationship with others. But as you keep replaying that incident in your mind, your relationship with yourself is spoilt. Who is responsible for repeating it mentally? You.

SO: I feel it would have been better if I had spoken back at that moment. The matter would have ended then and there.
SS: The matter wouldn't have ended, rather it would have been prolonged because you would have initiated an argument. So it's wise not to answer back. It means you had the power not to react.

SO: If I stay quiet, maybe the other person will realise his fault.
SS: There's another powerful way to make others realise their mistakes. In addition to keeping quiet, we can think well of them and send them good vibrations.

MEDITATION AND REFLECTIONS

Let me look at myself in a situation where someone behaved in a manner ... which was not right according to me ... how did I think, speak and respond in that situation ... now I visualise the same scene again, paying attention on the self ... the other person behaves in the same way ... but I keep quiet, I do not react ... even if I speak, I am sweet and peaceful ... now let me check my thoughts in the same situation ... what quality thoughts could be created for the other person ... I am aware that what I think is what I hear ... my thought impacts my state of mind ... whatever they did, they were responsible for it ... how I am feeling now, only I am responsible for it ... I shift from blame to self-responsibility ... Om Shanti.

MANTRAS FOR BEING LOVE

- Like we take care of what we speak to others, we need to be careful about how we speak to ourselves. We are constantly listening to our inner conversation.

- When we think or speak negatively for another person, the extent to which they get affected is their choice. But we will not be able to stop our own negative energy from affecting our mind and body.

- Blaming people, situations, past or the world for how we feel is the prime reason for depletion of soul power.

- When we take personal responsibility for our emotions, we conserve energy and also take responsibility to heal.

- Even if our thoughts are negative, let us first stop reacting in words and actions.

Self-Criticism Versus Self-Motivation

Suresh Oberoi: This beautiful quote says, 'At the end of the day, tell yourself gently that you have done your best.'
Sister Shivani: We have discussed that, in order to nurture a beautiful relationship with others, I – the soul – must be very pure inside. It is my purity that radiates to others. If I keep criticising myself for anything that has happened in the recent or distant past, my state of mind and energy field will be of pain. And that will reach others.

SO: When I was trying to give up an addiction, I used to compare myself to those who were able to easily give it up. I hated myself for my inability to do so.
SS: When we hate ourselves, our aura becomes negative because we have been critical of the one with whom we spend all of our time – the self. Any thought we create repeatedly will leave an imprint on the soul and become a habit. We may be

careful with our words and behaviour towards others, but they form a very small part of our daily interaction. Since we talk constantly with ourselves, what we say to ourselves leaves a much deeper imprint on us. Self-criticism depletes our battery. If we then interact with others and say motivating and loving words to them, our goodness will be limited to our words. As our energy field is negative due to self-criticism, its vibrations would radiate to others too, sending them conflicting qualities of energy.

SO: I created the vibrations of criticism for the self, not others. So could you clarify this point?
SS: When you are critical of yourself, you feel depleted, low and depressed. Suppose I come meet you at that moment, you are careful about how you talk to me. You appreciate me through words, but your vibrations will still radiate your mood of self-criticism. Your vibrations are a perfume that you have already rubbed on yourself. In the morning, you wore a perfume of self-criticism, self-hatred and guilt. When I meet you later in the day, your words are sweet. But what fragrance will I receive?

SO: Self-hatred?
SS: Not self-hatred, it will be of criticism. Criticism is now in your vibrations and thought pattern. A soul's sanskar or habit is formed on the basis of what it does repeatedly. In this case, you talked to others politely a few times during the day but criticised yourself repeatedly. So your resultant sanskar would be of criticism.

SO: I have often seen that when a husband scolds his wife or when a mother reprimands her daughter repeatedly, that wife or that daughter end up accepting and internalising their flaws.

SS: Yes, it all starts with that. Most of us developed the habit of self-criticism in childhood. At that time, our thought process had not matured. We did not know how to differentiate between what was good and what was bad for us. So we accepted an image of ourselves which our parents or elders created for us. Whatever a parent says about his child is the introduction which the child gets about himself. For a child, the parent is always right.

So, if a daughter receives a negative message about herself from the parent, she accepts and believes that to be the truth and forms a self-image based on that negative message. Even if positive messages that are contrary to the negative self-image are given to that individual later in life, they may have very little impact on her as she would have already internalised her shortcomings since childhood. However, another fact is that one cannot spend one's entire life in a state of victimhood.

SO: But very strong negative beliefs have already been fed to that individual and confirmed by others time and again.
SS: True, but we cannot change the past. Now we have set out on a journey to change ourselves. One way to live is to submit to our past conditioning, continue with our old thought patterns and be self-critical.

SO: Many children blame their parents for their shortcomings.
SS: We have already discussed that blaming others depletes our battery. We have to understand that the past is no more in our hands, and now is not the time to think about it. It is more important to now do what we can, to improve the self. If we continue to blame others, we will continue to deplete our energy. Earlier, others were responsible

for our loss, now we will become responsible by back-referencing.

SO: My mother would always tell me that everything will turn out to be good.
SS: We must first use those words to motivate ourselves, then pass them on to others. Unless we do the right things with ourselves, it is not possible for us to change others' thoughts. If we try to motivate others without working on the self, it will not leave any impact on them, because it will just be superficial appreciation through words.

Today, we have become too critical internally, at the level of thought. We need to change this sanskar – the imprint or the groove that has set into the soul.

So, we need to follow a few mantras. First, stop the blame game. Remember, our response to anything is our creation. Second, stop self-criticism. If we have done something that is not right, it is better to accept it and do it differently in future rather than be self-critical.

SO: It is a beautiful realisation – what we do to ourselves is what we do to others.
SS: The energy that we create for ourselves is what we will automatically give to others. We do not have to make any effort for that.

SO: Yes, it is like the fragrance of vibrations you talked about.
SS: The perfume we wear automatically reaches others. The perfume of vibrations is the thoughts we create for the self. It is not possible to love others while we hate ourselves. Likewise, we cannot be critical of the self and appreciate others. And we cannot disrespect the self and respect others. It is not possible that

we wear one particular perfume and spread another fragrance to others. This is the biggest illusion we need to overcome.

Let us not retain the negative self-image we created using the colours given by our elders or the people around us. We can choose our own colours and repaint that image as we want.

SO: Many people advised me against becoming an actor. They told me that I could never become one. Why did I not accept it?

SS: Because your focus was clear. Others gave you colours to make your painting. But you refused to accept those colours or the information they gave you. You took charge of creating your own image. The powerful thought you used when choosing your career can be applied anywhere else too.

Whether our parents said something in the past or people are criticising us in the present, we need not accept their energy of criticism. We must move on even if everyone around is critical of us. We must at least ensure that we do not treat ourselves, the way others have treated us.

SO: But everyone is not powerful enough to rise above such an environment.

SS: It is possible that even when we were right, our parents or teachers criticised us may be because they had a habit of criticism. We accepted their version, but did not evaluate ourselves. How long do we want to live with the criticism they showered on us years ago?

To let go of it, we have to sit back and make a list of things we criticise ourselves for. We actually need to write it down: 'I criticise myself for such and such attributes.' Then we must counsel ourselves as we would do with a loved one who is losing himself to self-criticism. We must ignore public opinion about the self and remind ourselves of our special qualities.

Remember, we have to change our painting by using colours of our choice. We need powerful energy for bringing about this change. Self-counselling increases the energy of the soul and enables it to set things right in future. On the other hand, self-criticism depletes the soul's energy. That makes it even harder than before to change, making us more prone to error. Constant self-criticism is the reason we are not able to change ourselves.

SO: Beautiful!

SS: Our homework now is to list out whatever we criticise ourselves for. Then counsel the self as a detached observer, as we would do it for another person, and write down our advice for the self on paper. We must remember to talk to ourselves lovingly. The way we treat ourselves also forms a pattern for our behaviour with others.

Sometimes people ask: 'Should we appreciate ourselves even if we have gone wrong?' The answer is 'yes', because for bringing about any change we need the soul's battery to be more charged than it previously was. And that will happen only through self-appreciation. Self-criticism will only decrease our power, so it is not the answer even to our biggest blunders.

SO: We can't reach our destination of self-transformation if our car's fuel tank is empty due to lack of self-appreciation.
SS: Yes, and the more number of times we fail to reach our destination, the more we will give up. Then we will feel like a victim and spend our lives in that mode. So, from today, let's put an end to self-criticism and appreciate ourselves lovingly.

MEDITATION AND REFLECTIONS

Let me look at myself ... I am originally a pure and beautiful soul ... whatever others told me about myself, I accepted that ... I thought this is me ... till now I have been living my life believing the things told in my childhood ... as my truth ... from today I change ... let me look at the self as a detached observer ... I check what image I have created for myself ... do I want to change the painting ... to change the painting, I change the colours ... I use only colors of appreciation and encouragement... from today every thought I create is of appreciation of the self ... I have many qualities ... I take colours of my qualities, guide myself gently ... I speak to myself carefully ... choosing pure and powerful words only ... I, the soul, empower myself ... I love myself and I can do whatever I want to do ... Om Shanti.

MANTRAS FOR BEING LOVE

- We interact less with others but we constantly interact with ourselves. The way we think about ourselves becomes our habitual way of thinking.

- Our thoughts become the energy field we carry around, like the perfume we use. People receive our vibrations even before they receive our words and behaviour.

- What parents say about their child is an introduction the child gets about himself. The child uses the opinion of the parent to create.

- Self-criticism depletes our energy. Let us appreciate and motivate ourselves and create a new, positve self-image.

Befriending the Mind

Suresh Oberoi: There is a beautiful quote: 'If you had a friend who spoke to you the way you sometimes speak to yourself, how long would you allow him to be your friend?'
Sister Shivani: We like friends who appreciate us, motivate us and push us forward, and those who accept us despite our flaws. We cannot be friendly for long with those who criticise us or deplete our energy.

SO: But what if that friend wants us to understand something?
SS: We would not like to receive negative energy from others even if their intention is good. We would not feel good in their company if they criticise us, and we would start to drift away.

SO: Is this why people hide things from their parents, and move away from their siblings, teachers and bosses?
SS: We can hide from others, but not from ourselves. What people do to us is not so important, because we have a choice

to accept or reject it. We can protect ourselves from their criticism, but not self-criticism.

SO: Can't we fix a particular time for talking to ourselves? Can't we tell our mind that we have an appointment with it later, just like we schedule other tasks?
SS: When there is something on our mind, it is followed by a rush of thoughts. If we tell our mind 'let's talk later', that might not really work because those thoughts are dominant. If we did something wrong yesterday, it will be on our mind today. We may not be able to, and should not, suppress or avoid it. It is a priority and is a very important thing on the mind right now. This thought is like a restless visitor who wants his issue to be sorted out urgently, and he keeps coming in again and again. So it's good to deal with it immediately. To resolve it, it is important to talk to the self with love and acceptance.

SO: When I was in the process of giving up alcohol, many times I was unable to keep my promise. If I had addressed myself kindly after each such defeat, wouldn't I have been postponing my decision?
SS: That is not how to go about it. Self-counselling does not mean avoiding self-transformation. After every mistake, we have the choice to interact with the self in two ways. One way is to question, scold and criticise ourselves, telling ourselves that we can't do it.

SO: Such talks are, in a way, a validation of our weakness.
SS: In a subtle way, we allow our mind to continue with that weakness. When we identify with our weakness, we give ourselves the liberty to repeat that pattern of behaviour.

SO: So what should we tell ourselves?
SS: Thoughts of determination.

SO: But why doesn't my determination work everywhere?
SS: You have to remind yourself – 'I have achieved great things that once seemed impossible. This means I am not weak. I am a powerful soul.' You have to motivate and empower yourself, and this motivation is not false. It is meant to reaffirm your original nature of power. If we were not powerful, we would not be able to achieve anything until now. Are we not powerful?

SO: Of course, we are. For example, during Navratras [a festival of nine nights], people observe fasting and sacrifice their temptations, and they do so willingly. But the day the festival ends, they return to their routine habits.
SS: This proves it is all in the mind.

SO: It means that I can do it when I want to, and can't do it when I don't want to.
SS: Exactly.

SO: But what about my habit of getting angry? That is not something I want.
SS: Yes, but you don't get angry with everyone. You get angry only where you are allowed to get angry. For example, employees in the hospitality or airline industries know they cannot afford to get angry with their customers. But the same people may be getting angry with their family at home. They are aware of where they can get angry and where they can't.

SO: But isn't this a suppression of thoughts?
SS: This is not suppression, but a choice we make. If we exercise self-control, if we do not let our angry thoughts interfere with our work, it means we have the power to regulate emotions. If people in the hospitality industry can do that, why can't others? We are not keeping calm for others, but we need to do it to save our own power. So when we say 'I get angry because I got this sanskar from my parents', it is an excuse for not making an effort to change.

SO: I have met women who could not adjust in their marital homes in the initial few years. Later, they made certain changes in their mindset, and today they are happy.
SS: It's always a choice we make. Sometimes we set limits for ourselves by saying 'I cannot do this'. This also depletes our battery because we restrict ourselves to a level below our potential. Now let's change our thought and tell ourselves 'if I can do everything else, I can do this too'.

SO: Do we make excuses or is there any truth in our limits?
SS: We have created our comfort zones through self-conditioning. Some comfort zones are harmless but others might be giving us discomfort. So we need to break the barrier and come out of it.

SO: Is it a mental block?
SS: Yes. When we think 'I cannot do that', the thought blocks our energy. These days, in corporate workshops, there is tremendous focus laid on 'making our mind our best friend'. It is being said that the mind is our friend and foe. When we direct negative statements at ourselves, our mind becomes our

enemy; when we encourage and motivate ourselves, our mind becomes our friend.

SO: How should I befriend my mind?
SS: Just talk to your mind the way you talk to a friend.

SO: Why do we remember negative things but not the many positive ones?
SS: If several nutritious dishes and a few unhealthy snacks are laid out on the dining table, it is for us to choose what to eat.

SO: But why does the mind go where it must not?
SS: It's an old habit. Our taste buds will attract us to the unhealthy food. But if we decide not to consume anything unsuitable as the doctor has advised us, will we not take care?

SO: Yes, we will.
SS: Just like we decide what to eat and what to avoid, we must tell ourselves what to think and what not to think.

SO: But why aren't we able to apply this easily?
SS: We need to make a choice and be determined to act on it. For changing any sanskar, we must have the will to do it. All of us already have the power to change any sanskar we want to; it is innate.

SO: Did I not have the will to give up my alcohol addiction?
SS: Superficially, you did want to change, but your subconscious mind was not ready for it.

SO: I even went to dargahs and temples, and requested saints to help me overcome it.

SS: You thought they could bless you and do some sort of a magic, but it does not work that way. Others can give us positive energy, but we have to make the change ourselves. Even if others bless us, until we bless ourselves, we will not be able to bring about any change in us. On the contrary, even if everyone around us says 'you can't do it', we can achieve what we want because of our desire to do so. So, with whom is our relationship most important?

SO: The self. But sometimes we have faith in someone and think that if he has said it, it will happen.
SS: That is temporary. When you have faith in someone, you may think 'now my sanskars will change because he has said so'. But that thought will stay with you only for a few days. After that, you will have to live with your own self. That is why spirituality teaches us to bless ourselves.

Whenever we want to change something in ourselves, we should not indulge in self-criticism. Just check if we have a strong desire to do it. We already have the power to do it. We can also create the desire to change by talking to ourselves about the benefits of that change.

MEDITATION AND REFLECTIONS

Relax ... let me identify one of my sanskars that gives pain and sorrow to me and others ... this sanskar is damaging me ... I need to change ... it's time to change ... if today I change this sanskar ..., I analyse what transformation will it bring in my life ... I visualise myself with the new sanskar ... I see the benefits I get in my life ... with this change ... I have both the will and the desire to change ... I have a clear understanding of the benefits of this change ... I make a decision that I, the powerful soul ... will put a full stop to things of the past ... I am ready to come into action with this new sanskar ... Om Shanti.

MANTRAS FOR BEING LOVE

- When others criticise us, we can reject their opinion and protect ourselves. But when we criticise ourselves, the mind accepts that criticism. We cannot protect ourselves from the depleting energy of self-criticism.

- When the mind creates critical thoughts about the self and others, do not suppress or avoid them. Address every thought and change it with understanding. Shift from self-criticism to self-motivation.

- When we make a mistake, criticise ourselves and re-affirm that we are weak, we are giving ourselves the permission to remain weak and repeat that mistake.

- Self-criticism depletes soul power. We need power to not repeat our mistakes. Irrespective of all our faults, we need to remind ourselves 'I am a powerful soul and I will do it right the next time'.

I Am the Creator of My Sanskars

Suresh Oberoi: How can we love ourselves when we are bound to make mistakes and remember our past negative karmas?
Sister Shivani: If we have hated someone for long and focussed on his weaknesses for years, it will not be easy for us to love that person.

Look at yourself as another person, with a detached perspective. Though we had good qualities, we focussed only on our flaws and failures, so we could not respect or love ourselves. Over a period of time, we started to hate ourselves. Now we realise that when we hate ourselves, we block our energy of love. This forms a barrier in loving others as well, as we create hatred in abundance.

SO: When I am angry and irritated with myself, and my family members sit in my room, will they feel uneasy?
SS: When we enter some homes, don't we sense the energy of the place to be very heavy? It's another thing that people get

used to that energy, just as people around you may get used to the perfume you wear, even though they may not like it. But again, our vibrations have more impact on us than on other people. And their own vibrations have more impact on them.

Let us suppose that your energy is heavy due to self-criticism. Your wife, on the other hand, has the sanskar of being kind to herself, so her abundant perfume or energy is that of love. So, even if you have been staying together for years, your energy will have only a little impact on her because her perfume is stronger. Your heavy energy would impact her more if she too is self-critical. We automatically get a sniff of our own fragrance much more than the fragrance of those around us, because our perfume surrounds us closely.

SO: If my original quality is love, why doesn't this natural perfume suppress other fragrances?
SS: It is because the soul's journey is much longer than one lifetime, and so a lot of factors influence it and its fragrance.

For example, I – the soul playing my part wearing this bodily costume – develop a habit of self-criticism. This sanskar leaves a deep imprint on me. When I leave this body and take another one, I will carry along the sanskar of self-criticism. If the parents I am born to in the next birth are also critical of me, my old negative sanskar will be reinforced. In this manner, the soul acquires several new sanskars that cloud its original sanskars. Suppose I am born to parents who appreciate me, then my old sanskar of self-criticism would slowly fade away and a new, positive sanskar would be created.

No doubt others influence us, but we influence ourselves the most. That's why we cannot blame others for how we are feeling.

SO: But I may become what everyone says about me or does to me.

SS: When someone gives me criticism or appreciation, I get a result only when I use it. His role is limited to giving me that 'gift'. The way the gift is used and the result it brings are not in his control. That power lies completely with me. Some people say that another person's criticism became an inspiration for them to achieve something in life.

SO: I have experienced it several times.

SS: Suppose someone told you 'You can't do it'?

SO: Then I make sure that I prove myself to him.

SS: But there are some people who will accept that statement and believe they really can't do it. So the role of the other person is limited to giving that gift, but how I use it is up to me. I can't ask, 'You gave me that gift, so what should I do?' Similarly, if you inspire me, it's not necessary that I will achieve something because of that.

SO: As you said, we can receive blessings from saints, but they will bear fruit only when we bless ourselves.

SS: What the saints give us is a gift of pure and powerful energy, but we may choose not to use it, by not creating the same quality of energy for ourselves. The power lies only with ME.

So let's put a full stop to whatever others have said in the past or are saying today. My energy is my own creation, and I have the power to create my thoughts irrespective of what I receive from outside. Always remember that the thoughts I create are completely independent of the influence of the outer world.

The remote control of my mind needs to be only in my hands. This is something I must remind myself each day because it is very easy to succumb to the old and convenient sanskar of blaming others.

SO: When someone close to me hurts me, it naturally impacts me. Is my remote control still in my hands?
SS: Who creates that hurt? We have to take responsibility for it. Others give us a 'gift', but we wrongly blame them.

SO: This is not blaming them, it is a fact.
SS: The fact is they betrayed us or did something we did not expect them to do. But another fact is that we created the hurt inside us and have continued to do so for years. Yet another fact is that we blame them for the hurt that we created.

SO: When I was young, my father ran a business. One of his trusted partners at work was like a father figure to us. But one day we realised he was cheating us.
SS: One fact is that there was a person whom we trusted as a family member. The second fact is that he cheated us. But the third fact is – how bad we feel about it, how much hurt and hatred we create in our mind, and how long we live with all that, is in our control.

SO: Each one of us are sensitive to different extents. How can we then apply this spiritual knowledge? For example, if my wife loses jewellery, I may not worry much. But someone else can may feel devastated.
SS: There are two situations here. First, someone cheated you

and you were hurt. Second, you lost expensive jewellery but were not affected by it. In the second case, whose power allowed you to remain unaffected by the situation?

SO: It was my power.
SS: Someone else in your place probably would not have overcome the pain for days. It is thus our quality that determines whether we stay stable or feel disturbed in any situation.

SO: But this quality is inherent since birth.
SS: It's a sanskar which we have created. Whether we got it at birth or created it in this lifetime or a previous one, this sanskar is now our property. If situations were responsible for our feelings, they would create the same response in everyone.

SO: So, the situation is not responsible for our disturbance.
SS: Who is responsible?

SO: But it just happens. I get disturbed because that is how I am. Am I the creator of it?
SS: You have programmed your mind with this sanskar.

SO: It's in my nature.
SS: Nature means our sanskar. We are on a journey of changing our nature. The first step is to accept our sanskars as our own, and not blame anyone for having them. A sanskar is deep. Once it is created, we respond through it automatically. It is like installing a program on a computer. Thereafter, the software works as per the programming. Since we have been operating through that 'program' for years, we don't realise that we are

consciously creating something, as that program is running inside automatically.

But who first created that program? I did. The most important question is – can I change the programming today?

SO: Could I say that I forgot after programming myself?

SS: The programming was done a long time ago, so I do not realise it when I am operating through that sanskar. I have to first accept that my sanskars are my creation. Most importantly, I must know that I have the power to change any of my sanskars.

SO: Is it in my hands to change my sanskars?

SS: Yes, no one else can do that. 'I' was the one who created 'my' sanskars. It's just that, I don't remember when I created them. It's easy to change our sanskars once we understand how to do it.

SO: So it's my choice and decision.

SS: If I have a sanskar of criticising myself and others, I will not criticise consciously, but the sanskar will play by itself. But I can decide to put a full stop to this sanskar. I can decide that whenever I have a thought of criticism, I will counter it and change it through self-talk. We have to change our programming step by step.

There is another deep sanskar that depletes our energy, and a majority of us have it. It is the habit of complaining constantly. It is so subtle that we do not realise that we complain all day.

SO: Complaining is like blaming.

SS: Blaming means holding people or situations responsible for how we are feeling. Complaining means finding fault with everything and everyone and thinking 'why is it like this'... 'he should not have done that' ... 'why is the government like this' ... 'why is the world like this' ... 'why is the weather like this'. We keep thinking about things that are not in our control.

SO: Today, social media has become a platform of complaints.
SS: We consider it normal and continue complaining without realising the impact it is having on us.

SO: What impact does it have on me?
SS: If I keep complaining about you in my mind, and think 'why are you like this, why are you wearing this, why are you sitting like this' and so on, it is a futile inner conversation that will not produce any result. But my battery will continue to discharge because I am creating thoughts about things that are not in my control. If I can set things right, let me do it. But to complain about them constantly is a waste of energy.

SO: What is the difference between complaint and concern?
SS: We can fix something or ask those in charge of it to set it right. That is a positive approach as it does not deplete our energy.

SO: Many people habitually crib and discuss it with others.
SS: Yes, so you already know the difference between the two. Concern is solution-oriented.

MEDITATION AND REFLECTIONS

Let me look at myself ... I, the soul, am the master of my mind and body ... that is all which is in my control ... whatever is outside of this – people, situations – nothing is in my control ... today I have the awareness of what is in my control ... what is not in my control ... I save my energy, keep intact my power ... I don't to blame others, I don't try to change them or desire to do so ... I don't deplete my power ... today I pay attention to changing what I can ... not think about what I can't change ... with this understanding, I do not complain ... for the next 24 hours – no complaints, no criticism ... Om Shanti.

MANTRAS FOR BEING LOVE

- If we criticise or hate ourselves, it blocks our energy of love. To radiate love to all, we need love to flow through us, and for that we need to first love ourselves.

- People can protect themselves from our vibrations, but we experience them constantly. Our vibrations are the fragrance with which we live.

- People's thoughts, words and actions towards us are like a gift we receive. What we do with it is completely our choice. People can criticise us, but we can use that criticism either to dis-empower ourselves or to motivate ourselves.

- Complaining depletes our energy because we are thinking about what is not in our control. Complaining means focusing on the problem and concern is focusing on the solution.

Re-Programming the Mind

Suresh Oberoi: Over the years, the habits of blaming and complaining are so deeply ingrained in us that we have lost awareness. And we thought we were getting exhausted due to work or due to playing our roles.

Sister Shivani: How did you realise today that you were indulging in that habit? It happened because you paid attention to yourself. Our battery was getting discharged earlier also, but we did not realise it or check the reason behind it. We thought we were exhausted because of situations and people. This means we were blaming others for our weakness. But just because we have realised it today and decided to do away with the habit, it does not mean things will be perfect tomorrow. In the beginning, we will have to keep this awareness consistently, because until now we were not aware at all. We are now changing a sanskar. Self-transformation is a journey. It is not a time-bound goal that we decide today and achieve tomorrow. After all, our sanskar of blaming others was not formed overnight.

SO: It could have developed over a few births.

SS: Possible. But that does not also mean it will take more than a lifetime to change the sanskar. Sometimes we think transformation can be a very long and indefinite process. It is not so. We need to have awareness and attention, and be conscious of the change we are trying to bring about. If today we decide not to complain, and are able to adhere to it even a few times during the day, we have made some progress.

SO: When I was young, I used to swear at others in anger. But while enacting an angry scene on a film set, I would not swear. Why?

SS: Because on the film set you paid attention to yourself, and you were aware that you had to use the right language while working. Now you can use the same programming at home. Tell yourself that you can't do certain things there at home.

SO: But there is a difference between home and office.

SS: We decide what behaviour is allowed where. Who programmes the mind for this?

SO: I did not programme my mind, it happened automatically.

SS: You did your programming. You decided what is allowed in your room, in your extended family, in the outside world and in your inner world – your mind.

We are strict with ourselves while dealing with the outside world, but we become relaxed while interacting with our family members. When we enter our room, we lose attention on the self. In our mental space, we even lose that attention completely and allow ourselves to think anything.

SO: Because we are alone in our mind, it is our inner space.

SS: Because nobody can see what goes on in our mind. We feel no one is looking.

If we decide to make a shift, we should tell ourselves: 'I talk nicely and respectfully with others. Can't I do the same when I am alone? When I can do it outside, I can also do it in my mind.' We are careful about being on our best behaviour while interacting with others but despite that we make mistakes. If we pay as much attention to our mental space, we will create miracles.

SO: But we need a good enough reason to pay attention inside.

SS: What better reason do you need than the fact that our thinking affects our mind, physical health and relationships?

SO: But we were never trained to think in this manner.

SS: We at least knew that 'as we think, so will be our feelings'. We also knew that a majority of illnesses start in the mind.

SO: I had heard as a child that if we dig a pit for others, we will fall into it. We knew morals but still erred, probably because these lessons did not get registered in the mind.

SS: We did not take it seriously.

SO: There are many people of my age who still don't take them seriously. These things matter only to those who want to learn.

SS: That is okay. It's not about others, it's about me. I have to ask myself: 'Do I want to make my life better than what it is today?'

SO: We usually don't change until fear is instilled in our

mind – like when a doctor warns us, 'if you smoke another cigarette, you will die' or when we are told, 'if you commit a sin, you will go to hell'. There is no other motivation to change.

SS: Understanding, not fear, should be our motivation. We must realise that unless we work on ourselves, we will not be able to experience happiness, our health will not improve, and our relationships will not become as beautiful as we want them to be. Whether we understand this or take it as fear, it is our choice. Now we have gained this knowledge, and that is more important than any other motivation. We don't have to change for others but for our own sake, because we want happiness, peace and love.

SO: I had learnt since childhood that to gain peace and happiness in life, one needs a car, a bungalow, social status, fame, family etc. And the list was so clear.

SS: We have achieved all of those and seen the result.

SO: We experienced both happiness and sorrow.

SS: The experience did not come from outside, but was created by us. When people and situations were as we wanted them to be, we created happiness, and when they were not to our liking, we created sorrow. Now we are creating a shift and deciding: 'I have to create happiness and be stable irrespective of the circumstances and others.' This is because in future, situations can be more challenging. Day by day, people will behave in ways that are not expected of them. Things are not going to be as we plan.

SO: We are heading towards a world of zero tolerance.

SS: Situations are going to be more challenging. It means they are not a constant but variable factor. If we make our state of mind dependent on something which is variable, our mood will fluctuate throughout the day.

SO: But I experience several different emotions even while watching a movie.

SS: This means the remote control of your mind is with others.

SO: Am I that weak?

SS: A majority of us are weak today.

SO: I think it's natural to feel so, I don't think it's a weakness.

SS: If we are not able to bring our mind out of the influence of the situation, it means we have no control over our mind. If we are watching a movie, we should have the power to detach our emotions from the on-screen emotions. Till now our emotions used to be similar to what was being shown in the movie. But since it is my mind, I should have the power to take charge of it whenever I want. As we lose control of our mind, we lose control over our words, and even our hands. Look at the increasing incidents of road rage today. People have hit, even shot at others on the spur of the moment. Then they claim it just happened.

SO: I have seen people getting so angry during a live interview, that they hurled furniture at each other even when the camera was focusing on them.

SS: They choose to call such behaviour as natural. When our mind, words and hands are out of control, can we call it natural?

SO: Even if it is unnatural, this is what happens in the world.
SS: Yes, but just because everyone is weak, we cannot say that weakness is strength. Simply because everyone around is unwell, we cannot describe being unwell as a state of health. If everyone is in pain, we cannot call it the normal way to be.

SO: Yes, if there is outbreak of a disease, we cannot say it is natural.
SS: If we say the disease has spread and we can treat it, that is fine. But if we call the disease to be natural, then we make it acceptable, and then we say it is right, and finally the disease will only grow. First we called stress natural, then we called anger natural, then we started to consider even high blood pressure natural, just because it is common these days. We called diabetes, depression and even the rising divorce rate natural. When our children started to be drawn into addictions, we said it was natural these days for kids. So we labelled everything unnatural as natural. On the other hand, we started to seek peace and happiness outside, though they are our original qualities. So whatever was natural to us, and should be our nature, has become a rarity today.

SO: People are taught to laugh in laughter clubs. Is laughter something to be taught?
SS: We have reached this scenario because we are no longer connected to our natural self.

SO: But the indisputable fact is that humans have always sought peace, love and happiness.
SS: We are looking for them because, even though they are the soul's original qualities, we are unable to experience them. We will experience love when we use that energy in our interaction

with others, and when our every thought, word and action is filled with love.

When we started to get angry in our thoughts, words and deeds, we stopped experiencing love. It was not flowing through us. But we needed love in our lives, so we started asking others for it. Every quality of the soul – purity, peace, love, power – must first be experienced inside. We are the first to experience the energy we create. Only then we radiate it to others.

SO: When I used to be self-critical and hated myself, I would go to sleep in that state of mind and wake up unhappy. I would not feel like talking to anyone and looked for excuses to stay away from others.

SS: Because we experience what we create inside.

SO: But how should I come into a state of being love?

SS: Pay attention to changing the quality of every thought you create. If your thinking does not change, you will not be able to experience the feeling you want to. Suppose you are creating self-hatred, but everyone around you loves you. They are all giving you the energy of love, but what is the energy you are creating?

SO: I will still think that everybody hates me.

SS: The first energy you receive is of self-hatred.

SO: Also, I do not believe that others love me.

SS: Why are you not able to believe them?

SO: Because I am indulging in self-hatred.

SS: You are unable to feel their vibrations of love because you are surrounded by your own vibrations of hatred. Suppose you enter an air-conditioned room. If you are wearing several layers of warm clothes, you will not be able to experience the cool environment, even though others can.

This is so interesting – people love us, but we don't trust them, yet we continue to seek love from them. We don't feel loved because we block their energy of love with our own thoughts.

SO: While we are shooting for this episode, I can hear music. People are walking around and it's a distractive environment. Earlier, in similar situations, I would have lost my temper. But today, I am fine with everything and want to complete the episode. Do you think this change is temporary?

SS: No, it's not temporary. Just tell yourself 'I did this'. This is self-appreciation. Note this down. Remind yourself that you have done something differently. This means you have the power to change.

SO: I want to know if this change will last or will I have to keep working on it forever?

SS: You'll have to pay attention to it for a few days, because it takes time to form a new positive sanskar, just as it took years to form the sanskars of anger and reaction. How long would you have to pay attention if you wanted to stay healthy? Every day.

SO: Yes, people go to the gym daily, or twice or thrice a week.

SS: After a period of time, you will feel like going to the gym. Initially, you will need to push yourself for it. Similarly, for a few days you will need to train yourself with the thought: 'I have to be stable despite any unfavourable situation outside.' Later, you will start enjoying the process because you see positive results.

You will start to experience a change in your feelings and see your relationships transform.

SO: I am happy that the scenes here are not distracting me.
SS: This is because you accepted that things here were not favourable, and you decided not to be influenced by them. Now use the same approach at home. We can all do it. Anyone with a will can do it anywhere.

MANTRAS FOR BEING LOVE

- Blaming, complaining and criticising discharge the soul battery and we feel mentally exhausted. Instead of blaming situations for our fatigue, let us take personal responsibility for the emotions we create.

- We take care of our words and behaviour with others. Let us take the same care in our inner conversations with ourselves (our thoughts).

- While watching television news, sports or any scene, practise creating an emotion different from the emotion created on the screen. Take charge of your mind.

- When we create the energy of peace and love in a situation, only then will we be able to experience it. The more negative emotions we created in situations, the lesser we experienced our original positivity, and then we started looking for peace, love and happiness outside.

- When we create an energy of anger and hatred, we will not feel love and respect even if we are receiving it from others. This is because we are enveloped by our own negative vibrations.

We Are Human Beings
Not Human Doings

Suresh Oberoi: A quote I read says, 'Is your life merely a repetition of repetitions? Do you simply repeat your favourite ways of thinking, feeling and behaving, or are you willing to get off the old treadmill?' Why is it so difficult to change ourselves and return to a state of love?

Sister Shivani: We have been thinking and behaving in the same way for many years, and we are still looking for the same things. The quote asks us a very important question – is our life going to continue like this?

If our life continues with the same patterns of thinking, feeling and behaving, the results will continue to be the same as before. As they say, 'When you do what you've always done, you will get what you've always got.' Now let us add a step before that, 'If you think what you've always thought, you will do what you've always done, and get what you've always got.'

SO: Sometimes a person may say something he does not want to say.

SS: We speak only what we think.

SO: So why do we forget to do what we decided to?

SS: Because we haven't yet decided on it. We aren't determined to do it and are comfortable with the old ways of living. We decide not to get angry, but the moment a situation comes up, we change our stance. We feel that unless we get angry with others, they won't understand or learn anything.

SO: Even the opposite of this could be true – that we can't be comfortable without getting angry.

SS: The reason behind this too is the belief system that others won't improve unless we use anger. We think anger is necessary to get work done. The moment we create such thoughts, that old sanskar of anger gets triggered.

We are not able to change ourselves despite wanting to do so, because we are weak. A weak person can't do as he desires due to the lack of requisite energy. We may have knowledge, but unless the soul is empowered it cannot achieve what it wants to. A mere decision will not yield any result. Even if we pay attention to small things like keeping away from the habit of complaining and blaming, the soul's energy will increase. We cannot increase our soul power just by reading, listening to or sharing good things. Today everyone is exchanging uplifting messages through social media.

SO: We send it and forget the message soon after. We do not apply it in our lives or experience it.

SS: We hear it, share it, but do not use it. When it's time to act, we return to our same old patterns.

We were all taught to forgive others. But when we need to use this wisdom, we create a contrary thought 'how can I forgive their mistake? So what we hear, read and do are not in harmony with each other. It does not matter how many discourses we listen to, workshops we attend or books we read. Today, most books in the market are on self-help. This means the desire to change is there, but we need to start applying what we've heard or read. Otherwise, we will continue to use our old patterns.

We discussed earlier that all of us have two sets of ingredients on our 'kitchen shelf' – ones frequently used are in the front and ones rarely used are at the back. Likewise, we have the ingredients of our original sanskars – peace, love, purity – and acquired sanskars such as anger, irritation, fear, insecurity. We need to use ingredients of peace and love. The soul is a combination of mind, intellect and sanskars. The mind creates a thought and the intellect decides whether to implement it or not. When we bring a thought into action, a sanskar begins to form.

Let's say I read about peace and my mind creates peaceful thoughts. The intellect agrees and decides in its favour. But until I bring peace into action, the sanskar of peace cannot be formed. We are just one step away from changing our sanskar. And that step is to bring the good things we've read and heard, into action the very same day. Otherwise, that ingredient of peace will be pushed behind and the ingredient of anger will remain on the front shelf, as that would be brought into action.

There are two grooves in the soul. The groove of peace, and that of anger. If we create the thought 'I am a peaceful soul', and decide to interact peacefully with others through the day, but get angry even once during our interaction, the ingredient of anger is brought to the front again. The same sanskar is reinforced and that groove gets deeper. We may meditate on positive thoughts daily, but if we return to our old sanskars when it is time to act, those sanskars remain as they are.

SO: Then we think 'I can't do it'.
SS: We become weak by strengthening our old, weak sanskars. Every morning, we must sit with ourselves and reflect on how we plan to be the whole day. Today, all of us have a list of things we want to DO during the day – a 'to-do list'. But we also need to decide on how we are going to BE while doing all those things. We need a 'to-be' list. We are not human 'doings' but human beings. A human being that is doing things.

SO: It would be nice if we could buy love from the market.
SS: That is what we are trying to do. We are trying to buy love, seek love from people and things.
Till today we had reversed the order of things. We thought if we did a certain thing, we would feel good. We thought if we did a 'doing', we would experience the 'being'. But what should we have done instead? We needed to pay attention to our 'being' and bring it into our 'doing'. Bringing 'being' into 'doing' is how we experience qualities like love and peace. If we have achieved a lot on our to-do list but still feel hollow inside, it is because our attention was never on the 'being'.
Let's say you have a meeting scheduled in your to-do list. Now add another column in that list in which you write down how you will be during the meeting. What will be your 'to-be list'?

SO: I will be peaceful and loveful.

SS: Yes. We need to visualise ourselves during the meeting. We can decide: 'I will be peaceful' – this means even if my suggestions are not accepted, I will stay calm, not get agitated even in my thoughts. 'I will be patient' – I will not expect others to accept my ideas quickly, thinking that I am always right. 'I will be loving' – I will listen to others with love even if I do not agree with them because what they say may be right from their perspective.

'I will be humble' – even if my ideas are not accepted, I will not hold a grudge against them. I need to have respect for all. Now our 'to-be list' is ready.

SO: One person may take the decision, but others ought to abide by it.

SS: To have a 'to-be list' does not mean that we allow anyone to do anything, but we need to be patient with others when they are expressing their views. Today we have such little patience that even before the other person can express his views, we express ours in a hurry because we are so attached to our opinion and to the idea of us being right. This is the reason a meeting becomes an argument, instead of a dialogue. What kind of energy will be exchanged in such a meeting? What sort of relationships will be formed? What will be our state?

Even if we are an authority figure in that meeting, whether it is at our workplace or in our family, we need to listen out to everyone patiently, respect their views with humility, lovingly empower them, and inspire them to think for the benefit of the organisation or the family. If our decision is still not in agreement with anyone in the meeting, but we know it is right, we can put it forward assertively yet lovingly. Where is the scope for getting disturbed?

SO: But many people fight, it's so common.
SS: Should we do what others are doing?

SO: All I am saying is this basic nature is very strong.
SS: This is because the ingredient of anger and the sanskar of being attached to the thought 'I am right' are lying on the front shelf of the soul.

SO: But who all could we teach?
SS: We have to teach only ourselves.

SO: Is it practical when I am dealing with people in large numbers, and I alone carry this wisdom?
SS: Even if everyone around you is unwell, will you not take care of yourself? Let's say you are a family of four that goes out for dinner. Next day, everyone except you falls ill. One option is that you take care of your three family members. This is definitely going to involve a lot of effort. The second option is that you say that you too are unwell and need rest. What option will you choose?

SO: I would not want to be unwell.
SS: Would you not want to take care of your family? The desire to take care of others is a human instinct. In fact, in such a situation it is more important to take care of yourself because you can't afford to fall sick when the family around you is unwell. The caregiver cannot afford to fall ill.
Similarly, in a family, three members could be emotionally

unwell. Let's say one is short-tempered, the other lacks patience, and the third one has low self-respect – he feels hurt easily and reacts fast.

SO: If we have low self-esteem, do we become more reactive?
SS: If we do not respect ourselves, we will always expect respect from others. And the moment others do something which we think is disrespectful, we will react. That is why we need to give ourselves what we expect from others.

SO: On the contrary, I had heard that we should give others what we want from them.
SS: Yes, that's a good thought. But we can give only what we have. If we are hollow inside and are seeking from others, and so is everyone else, then who will give? We have heard that when we give respect, we get respect. We thought when we give it to others, they give it back to us. But the reality is, what we give others is what flows through us. So that is what we experience or get. When you get angry, who feels it first?

SO: I do.
SS: Likewise if you respect others, you get it first. In that sense, it is not 'give and take' but 'take and give'. What we first experience ourselves is what we automatically radiate to others. That is why our relationship with ourselves is most important.

Let's get back to our previous conversation. If three people in your family are emotionally weak, not very stable or secure, you now understand that their impulsive reactions are a sign of weakness. So will you heal them by giving love and respect, or will you react like them?

SO: I will try to heal them.

SS: To heal them, how should you be?

SO: Stable.

SS: Therefore, we can't fall sick just because others are unwell. Even if we are dealing with many people, and are part of a big organisation, our equation with them will be the same as that with the three family members. We can't wait for others to change.

SO: People may listen to the captain or the one in charge, but everyone can't be a captain.

SS: One thing is that we obey someone because he is in a position of authority, the other is that we listen to him out of respect. The most important thing is the state of being of the captain himself. Others may obey him because of his position, but what if the captain is not able to control his mind, and does not listen to himself? Can we then call him a captain?

SO: Yes, first we need to be in charge of ourselves.

SS: In the beginning we discussed that today we end up saying things we don't want to. Our tongue does not obey our orders, but we want others to be according to us. How is that possible? Our sense of power in this case will be derived from controlling others. We would get disturbed by their slightest mistake. So it's not about other people; it's about us.

SO: We have five physical senses. Do we have to make an effort to control each of them?

SS: No. We only have to take care of what we think.

MEDITATION AND REFLECTIONS

Let me look at myself ... I, the master of this body, mind and physical senses ... I am the master ... my every thought, feeling and action is my choice ... nothing is happening on its own ... today whatever I do, I pay attention to how I feel while doing it ... how am I going to be while doing things ... today's diary or 'to-be list': peaceful, patient, loving, humble ... let me visualise my day today ... how I, the being, will remain while following my 'to-do list' ... I am working with the same people ... same situations ... a different me ... I remain peaceful, understanding and loving ... being love is my original nature ... Om Shanti.

MANTRAS FOR BEING LOVE

- If we think what we have always thought, and do what we have always done, then we will get what we have always got.

- To change our sanskars we need knowledge and power. Only listening to wisdom or reading good words are not going to create a change.

- The soul consists of mind, intellect and sanskars. Mind creates thoughts, intellect takes a decision, but only after the decision repeatedly comes into action will it become a sanskar.

- We were doing things so that we could experience peace, happiness and all the qualities of the being. We thought DOING could make us experience the BEING. Truth is, we will experience the being only when we express our qualities in the doing.

- When we give energy to others, we are the first ones to experience in. We get while we give to others.

Role Consciousness
to Soul Consciousness

Suresh Oberoi: If the soul is the master of the sense organs, why do we find it difficult to control the senses?
Sister Shivani: If the master forgets his position or is oblivious of it, no one would obey him. Our crisis today stems from not knowing our original identity. We do not have the answer to 'Who am I?'

We will experience the qualities of peace, love and purity only when we are aware of our original identity and nature. In response to the question 'who am I', when we state that which is not the truth, we deviate from our original qualities. Suppose at home you are the head of the family, and in office you are the chairperson of your organisation. If someone does not obey you or reacts rudely, you will feel hurt and disturbed, and believe it's natural to feel so.

SO: Is it not natural to feel hurt?
SS: We will come to that later. When you get hurt, what is your inner conversation like?

SO: 'I am the senior here, how could they behave like this with me?'
SS: Whatever thought you create, a corresponding feeling is generated. In this situation, your response to the question 'who am I' was 'I am a father', 'a father-in-law', or 'the head of the family'.

SO: But I am all of these.
SS: If you are the father, how should your son talk to you?

SO: With respect.
SS: So you had programmed your mind to think that a son should behave respectfully with his father.

SO: Shouldn't it be so?
SS: We want respect to be shown to the position, role or relationship. The moment the other person responds in an unexpected way or in a manner that does not match our definition of right, we create hurt.

What is the thought behind the creation of that hurt? Hurt is a feeling, it cannot be created without first creating a thought. A feeling always follows a thought. The source of this feeling is the thought 'I am a senior' or 'I did so much for them and they treat me like this'. Behind these thoughts is your consciousness that you are a father or a senior. Now, change your consciousness and consider 'I am a soul'. How will you now see the other person?

SO: As a soul.

SS: If a soul does not talk to you in a way that you expect it to, what quality of thoughts will you create? The thoughts will change.

SO: But the other person is not talking soul-to-soul with me. He thinks he is talking to his father. Only I know that I am talking to a soul.

SS: Where should our complete focus be?

SO: On the self.

SS: We have to change our own thinking and feelings so that our love does not get blocked. As will be our consciousness, so will be our thought. As will be our thought, so will be our feeling. As will be our feeling, so will be our behaviour.

Earlier, your consciousness was – 'I am a father'. Your thought was – 'this is no way to talk to me'. Your feeling was that of hurt, and your behaviour was according to that.

Now change the consciousness by giving yourself your true introduction: 'I am a soul playing the role of a father.' What is the original quality of 'I', the soul?

SO: Love, peace.

SS: And also understanding, power, patience. Now you will respond with the consciousness that I am a peaceful soul.

SO: Does it mean that even if I do not like something, I must respond with peace, love and understanding?

SS: It does not mean that anyone can behave with you as they want. It just means that your response will be without any disturbance.

SO: And what if they still do not listen to me?

SS: You can't force them to. It becomes easy to accept this when you know you are interacting with another soul.

When you think 'I am a senior', your belief is 'others ought to obey me'. When your thought changes to 'I – the soul – am the master of myself', then you continue to respond through your beautiful qualities.

SO: I may also realize that just as I have forgotten my original nature, others too must have forgotten theirs. I become non-judgmental of them.

SS: Very true. We now have the knowledge that a soul can have all kinds of sanskars.

So here you are, a peaceful and loving soul, meeting your family members in this awareness. The other soul in front of you may be in the body of a child, but if his acquired sanskar is that of anger, he will talk in that manner. However, if you think that he is a child and you are the father, he is younger and you are senior, and so he must behave in such and such way, then you will create hurt and think it's natural to feel so. Then your behaviour will be a repetition of repetitions, as you will keep getting hurt in every interaction. Instead of 'being love' you will become 'being hurt', and radiate that to others.

SO: Then I will move away from my goal.

SS: Yes. And all this would happen just because your answer to 'who am I?' was not right.

I, the being, can experience love all through the day. We miss this experience only when we forget our original identity and mistake ourselves for some position, role or status. Because we identify with the role, we come up with a list of expectations from others. On the other hand, when we remain aware that we are souls, we will be remembrance of how we must behave with others.

If you are a doctor, you will carry that consciousness. If someone falls sick, you will treat him because your consciousness will trigger a thought, the thought will trigger a feeling, and then a corresponding behaviour. But suppose there is a loss of consciousness and you, the doctor, forget who you are. Then even if someone gets injured in front of you, you will not heal that person. With a false consciousness, everything will change.

SO: But being trapped in a false identity is deep-rooted. It has been carried forward from previous births.

SS: Never mind. At least now we are beginning to change our thinking. Even if we begin by remembering our original identity just once a day, it is an achievement. Otherwise things will continue to be a repetition of repetitions.

What happens on a treadmill? Once we get on it, we keep moving in the same direction and can't change it. Now let's get off that treadmill.

SO: And change the direction.

SS: Yes. We should be able to turn when we want to, instead of continuing to think that hurt and anger are natural. The fact is that peace, love and bliss are natural to us. To know, recognise and meet ourselves means to build a relationship with the self. Many a times, we say that we don't understand others, but do even understand ourselves?

SO: My mother would tell me, 'If you win over your mind, you will win over the world. Everyone will then love and respect you.'

SS: Why would the whole world respect you?

SO: Because I would be respecting myself.
SS: Yes. We thought if people gave us love, we would be able to love others. No, we have to create love and give it to ourselves. We must pay attention to small things to save our soul power, such as stopping blaming and complaining.

SO: These are not small things to me.
SS: Even if we continue to create anger and hurt, the least we can do is to take responsibility for creating those feelings instead of holding others responsible for it.

SO: Correct. And this will save us from cribbing and thinking negatively about others.
SS: That is it. It will save us from discharge of energy. Suppose you get angry at someone. Your battery is discharged for as long as you create anger. But after that if you create the thought 'I created this anger', then there will not be any further energy leakage.

SO: But it could also have the opposite effect. I could feel guilty, get depressed or punish myself.
SS: That's why we discussed about stopping self-criticism. By taking responsibility, we put a stop to further discharge of energy. Otherwise, we are likely to think negatively for days.

SO: I told someone to let go of his anger as the situation had ended. He said his family wanted revenge and retaliation.
SS: In the process of setting others right, we end up becoming our own enemy and carry bitterness in our mind. If we keep blaming others, it will not just remain in our thoughts, we will also spread it around.

SO: Then we will look for those who obey us and endorse our views.

SS: Then our battery would be discharged not just when we get angry, but even afterwards. So we must make sure not to hold anyone responsible for the state of our mind.

SO: We should accept our actions.

SS: We must take full responsibility for what is happening in our mind. If we go to your room right now and find something is not in its right place, who is responsible for it?

SO: Me.

SS: Similarly, in the room of our mind, nobody else can enter or do anything. Only we are responsible.

SO: Then why do we think that others upset our mind?

SS: Because the stimulus comes from them.

SO: But others do enter our mind by getting angry with us.

SS: Others can say something to us, harm us physically or exploit us financially, but their power ends there. They cannot enter our mind. What happens outside can be because of them, but what happens inside our mind after that stimulus is directed at us, is entirely our creation. We have to make this shift in our understanding. Even if someone insults us, we should tell ourselves 'he insulted me, but I created the hurt'.

SO: When I complained about a classmate when I was in school, I was told, 'Sticks and stones can break your bones but words will never hurt you.'

SS: We can hear the words, but what we create in our mind after that and how we respond to them, is our responsibility. If we do not realise this, we will spend our lives like victims. Suppose I insult you and you feel hurt. One choice you have is to try to change me. You tell me that I should not have spoken in that manner. The second choice is that you tell yourself 'I should not have thought like this'. Which is the easier of the two options?

SO: To correct oneself.
SS: Most importantly, which of the two is feasible?

SO: To work on the self.
SS: But what are we doing throughout the day? Trying to change others. This is the easiest way to deplete our energy, because it is an impossible task. We think others should change so that we feel nice. But they don't change and we continue to live in pain. This can go on for a lifetime.

SO: Couples keep waiting for each other to change and end up with divorce.
SS: So, from today we must decide not to blame others, and also not to criticise.

SO: We have heard these things time and again but are unable to do it practically. We've heard the story of a princess with soft feet in a kingdom with hard rocks. The king ordered that carpets be rolled across the kingdom so that she did not get hurt. But the easier option would have been that the princess wore shoes.
SS: Yes, we want the carpet to be laid everywhere so that we

don't feel any pain. But how far can we do this? We think that when everything around is perfect, we will be happy. But the easier way is to protect ourselves, then we can walk on any terrain and nothing will hurt.

SO: Our protection lies in remembering who I really am.
SS: We must remember the truth about 'who I am' and 'what my responsibility is'.

MEDITATION AND REFLECTIONS

Let me look at myself ... this body is a costume that I, the soul, use ... I, the soul, command the senses to speak, hear or walk ... I, the soul, am the master ... this body will work as I want it to ... today, whatever I do, I will remember my original nature ... role, position and relationships are what I have acquired in this life ... but the one doing all of this – is I, the soul ... today whoever I meet, it would not be a meeting of position with position, role with role or status with status ... it will be a meeting of a soul with another soul ... when I, the soul, meet another soul, I will remember 'I am a loving being'... even if the soul in front of me does not behave right, I keep attention only on myself ... I understand the other soul is in pain ... today I have the understanding of what to give ... I radiate love, compassion and understanding ... being love comes naturally to me ... Om Shanti.

MANTRAS FOR BEING LOVE

- When we are in the consciousness of our position, role and relationships, we expect others to behave according to the role. When we do not get what we expect, we get angry or hurt.

- Let us be in our true consciousness of a soul interacting with another soul. Then we will accept the sanskars of that person and radiate our original energy of love, irrespective of his behaviour.

- Role consciousness creates expectations, soul consciousness creates acceptance.

- People can financially exploit us, physically beat us or verbally abuse us, but the emotional creation is completely our choice. No one can get into our mind and create our thoughts. Emotional abuse or a peaceful acceptance – is our choice.

Being Yourself
is an Act of Giving

Suresh Oberoi: I made it a mantra to remember that I am love, I am peace. But my old sanskars re-emerge with full force when I do not find others to be either love or peace. Then I am no longer able to see them spiritually – a servant looks like a servant to me, a master looks like a master, a friend looks like a friend, a thief looks like a thief. None of them looks like a soul to me.

Sister Shivani: To identify people with their role is a deeply ingrained sanskar acquired over several births, so it can't change in a day. We first have to remember that I am a soul, then see others as souls. This is the first lesson of the knowledge given at the Brahma Kumaris. The old sanskars keep coming back, but we have to remind ourselves of this new wisdom. When we say 'I am the master, he is a servant' – it is a role-to-role connection, not soul-to-soul connection. We play several roles in life. For example, you are a friend to someone, a husband, a father, and a master to others. For several births we have been connecting role-to-role, position-to-position and relationship-to-relationship due to which our thinking and behaviour have changed.

SO: But we have never seen the soul, nor do we know about it. So we'll have to imagine it now.

SS: Why do you have to imagine it? Our everyday vocabulary may not contain the word soul, but we do say that everyone is a human being first and then comes the role. For example, if someone does not speak respectfully to his domestic help, we tell him to treat the person first as a human being with dignity. This means we want to practise our basic humanity everywhere, without barriers of position, profession or qualification. Even relationship consciousness creates a barrier. If we think 'I am a parent', then the child ought to behave in a certain way. We believe a father can talk to the child as he wishes but the child must follow norms. This is because here the connection is role-to-role.

Since we have played so many roles and lived in that consciousness, we have become distanced from the original qualities of the soul. This is because our ego has grown. Ego is always related to one's position or achievements. You became an actor at the age of thirty, was there a change of consciousness? As an actor, what were your expectations from people?

SO: To be applauded.

SS: You wanted privileged treatment. You did not have such expectations from others before becoming an actor. Expectations are formed on the basis of what we acquire in life. There is nothing wrong in acquiring though.

Suppose we lived in a one-bedroom flat and today we live in a bungalow. If we do not take care, then can be a simultaneous shift in consciousness. Earlier, we were humble, but now ego can creep in. The more we achieve in life, the farther we might move from our original qualities.

Though we need to achieve certain things, we must have our thinking and behaviour in sync with our original qualities. For instance, after acquiring wealth, name and fame, if one just remembers 'despite everything, I am still a soul', then his qualities would remain the same as before. He would not struggle with expectations from others or feel hurt.

A child is taught to give respect to others. An adult, on the other hand, thinks he must receive it. So the older we are, the higher our position and educational qualification, the more our behaviour shifts from giving to wanting. We must check throughout the day if we are giving good energy to others or asking for it. The original quality of the soul is to give. It is human nature to feel good after giving. But somewhere on our journey, we shifted from giving to wanting and taking.

SO: Trees give us oxygen, water quenches our thirst. Nature is all about giving, but not human beings.

SS: Everything in nature is giving without expectations. We too are part of the same nature.

SO: Sunlight is available uniformly – to a thief and a cop, to the wise and unwise, to life and to matter.

SS: So the Sun is unconditionally and constantly giving energy to everyone. We may choose to water a tree or throw stones at it, but it will continue to give us shade, irrespective of our behaviour. We could, just for an hour, try becoming like the Sun – give light and power to others irrespective of what they give us. In the process of giving to others, we would first receive it ourselves. The truth is, we don't even have to give. The Sun is not giving, it is just there the way it is. It is not giving with the intention of giving.

SO: Just as a flower does not give away fragrance.
SS: Fragrance is its quality, so a flower naturally spreads fragrance everywhere. Even a soul need not think it has to give love to others. We just have to be love.

SO: Like a child – he smiles at and talks to everyone he meets.
SS: This is because a child has no consciousness of having attained anything. He is not even attached to his own body and is pure and innocent. But as that child grows and starts acquiring one thing after another, his ego develops. If we remove our acquired layers, we will reach our original self – the soul. All we need to do is to be original. A flower is both beautiful and fragrant, and all it does is to be itself.

SO: It does not bother if it is apart of a wreath or part of a garland. It does its job wherever it is.
SS: A soul must also be like the flower – beautiful and fragrant – and it will radiate naturally. We go on the opposite track when we think we must receive something from others. We often hear that relationships are about give and take, and this is a belief ingrained deeply within us. We have started thinking, 'I have given so much respect and love to others, I have adjusted and cooperated so much with them, what did they give me in return?' This means it was always about give and take – just like a business.

SO: These days, people even check the price of a gift they have received, so that they can decide on how much to spend on a return gift.

SS: This give and take is still about material things, but now the give and take has gone to the subtle level. We think: 'I obeyed them all the time, but how many times did they obey me? I adjusted, respected and trusted them so much, did they too?' The exchange here is not limited to objects, socialising or courtesy, it has gone to the level of exchange of energy in relationships. If we don't get our due in relationships, we start blocking our own energy and suffocate ourselves.

SO: Rising above this give and take does not sound easy. If, for example, I greet my co-star for two consecutive days, but he does not respond, the third day I would not want to extend courtesy.

SS: But whose loss is it then?

SO: There is no loss. At least this would make the other person realise his fault. Why should I insult myself by greeting someone who does not bother to acknowledge?

SS: But being love is your original quality.

SO: Why should I give love and respect to someone who can't respond to my polite gesture?

SS: We need not bother whether the other person responds. We must only take care that we keep giving. You quoted the example of the Sun. The Sun is spreading its energy, but if even close your window, it won't stop giving you the same.

If you meet someone you know, and instead of acknowledging you that person ignores you, then you have two choices: either you talk to him nicely or you copy him. Today, we are trying to copy each other's behaviours and vibrations, and in the process we are losing our original personality.

SO: I used to greet a senior actor, who would never acknowledge it. One day, I ignored him at a press conference. This compelled him to initiate a conversation with me.
SS: It is not our agenda to improve others or to set them right. By being focused on others, we will deviate from our own path.

SO: But don't I have self-respect?
SS: This is how so many of our equations in life go wrong. If you have self-respect, you will respect yourself for being able to talk sweetly to everyone. You will talk lovingly to them because that is your nature. You will be able to do so without being bothered about others' behaviour, as you respect yourself and are not dependent on them for it.
However, if you are egoistic, you can't talk to others lovingly. This is because you would get hurt when the other person does not respond to you.

SO: At an award function, I ignored a top musician out of fear of getting ignored by him. But I was so embarrassed when that musician came up to me and initiated a conversation, despite my behaviour.
SS: That person exhibited self-respect. You ignored him, but that did not disturb him. Had he been disturbed after you walked past without greeting him, he would not have been able to come up to you.
Ego means to get disturbed. To get disturbed means to bring about a change in behaviour. Self-respect means to be stable. Stability

means our behaviour remains unchanged irrespective of others' behaviour, because we understand others don't have the power to disturb us. So we maintain our original personality. That's what he demonstrated. We can do it too. Everyone can do it. Let's just do this little homework: do not copy others' behaviour, do not react tit-for-tat. By following the principle of an eye for an eye, we actually end up wounding ourselves. So, how should we respond from now on?

SO: With love ... but I still have a few questions to ask.
SS: Sure. Until then, you can try it out.

SO: Yes, I can.

MEDITATION AND REFLECTIONS

Let me look at myself ... a beautiful sentient energy, I, the soul that stays in its self-respect ... knows its qualities ... and brings them into action throughout the day ... my behaviour is not dependent on the respect that others give me ... I bring all my specialities into my actions ... others' behaviour and words do not impact my state of mind ... I do not need respect from others ... I respect myself for my qualities ... today, I interact with everyone through my original qualities ... irrespective of what I receive from them, I give them my qualities ... I talk to them according to my nature, irrespective of how they talk to me ... love and sweetness are my own qualities ... I give these to everyone ... today I give, give and only give ... Om Shanti.

MANTRAS FOR BEING LOVE

- When we connect as a role to another role, there is a barrier of ego. With ego consciousness, behaviour is of anger, hurt and negative emotions.

- When we connect as a soul to another soul, there is equality. With soul consciousness, behaviour is of compassion, love and positive feelings.

- As we acquired knowledge, position and power, we developed ego and shifted from giving respect to expecting respect.

- As we acquired the body, relations, knowledge, position and property, layers and layers enveloped the original self. We then interacted with others through the consciousness of our acquired layers and forgot the qualities of the original self.

Hold On to Your Goodness

Suresh Oberoi: We were discussing that our nature must not change irrespective of how others behave with us. It seems very difficult.
Sister Shivani: Yes, it will be difficult because our ego will block our efforts. When someone ignores us, we have two choices – either we also ignore him or we greet him. When that person ignores us, our ego will be hurt and the mind will create the thought 'if he doesn't talk to me, why should I?' At that time we have to tell our mind 'what the other person is doing is his sanskar, my quality is to greet everyone with love'. We have to change our old way of thinking and behaving.

SO: What if I remain stable when the other person does not respond to my greeting, yet I choose not to greet him?
SS: But why wouldn't you want to wish him?

SO: Because he did not respond to my greeting earlier.
SS: Today, everyone has a sanskar of copying. If you do not wish him, and he has not greeted you in the past, then the

relationship will develop a gap. Your energy will be blocked. Now let's change this pattern – he did not greet you, but you go up to him and greet him. Now will that person greet you or not?

SO: He may choose to nod instead of giving a full response.
SS: Even in that case the two of you will come closer instead of growing apart. But if you also don't greet him, then the next time both of you will not even look at each other. We have to heal relationships and return to our original nature. We will have to keep our ego off our interactions, because it pushes us away from each other. If we are away from our original nature, we will also be away from each other.

If we talk nicely to the other person, that person eventually will copy us. He will talk sweetly, even though he may respond superficially in the beginning. The next time, things will improve further. At least we will be able to strike a cordial relationship. If we give others what we expect from them, and instead of copying them we become the one they copy, our relationships will start becoming stronger.

SO: What is the disadvantage of our energy being blocked?
SS: If we do not talk to someone, we block our quality and keep pondering over the matter for some time.

SO: If the same topic comes up in future, similar feelings might re-surface.
SS: Yes. As a result, the soul battery will keep getting discharged. So it is much easier if we talk at the first instance. Otherwise a simple thing gets complicated, and we will have to spend more energy rectifying it.

When it's time to act, the mind creates two thoughts. It is just like two lawyers arguing with each other. The judge has to remain stable. The two lawyers are our two opinions, which can be completely opposite to each other. The mind will think 'should I do this' and 'should I not do this'. The intellect will be the judge that decides. So if the first lawyer, i.e. the first thought, says 'why should I talk to this person', the second lawyer must respond 'I should do this because it is beneficial to me, my energy flow will be smooth, my negative thinking will be less, I will feel good, my power will increase'. The more we put down our ego, the more we will increase our soul power, and the more victorious we will be. On the contrary, the more we let our ego win, the weaker we will become.

SO: As children, we heard the anecdote about a scorpion that was drowning. A saint rescued it but the scorpion stung him. Someone asked the saint why he had saved the scorpion even though it had repeatedly stung him.
SS: The saint replied, just because the scorpion did not leave its sanskar of stinging, how could he leave his own sanskar of saving others.

If we keep giving up our original sanskars owing to others' behaviour, whose loss would it be? Suppose you like helping others in need even at the cost of your own comfort, you will have to retain that quality. Even when others do not cooperate with you despite your kindness, you need to remind yourself that you help them because that is your quality.

When we understand that we are all unique souls, we realise that others may not have our specialities and we may not have theirs. They will follow their sanskars, we will follow ours. The problem with copying others is that we abandon our qualities, the moment we don't find others displaying them.

Suppose punctuality is your sanskar, but the other person comes late. In response, you may think 'what is the point of being punctual'. You start coming late from the next day. Similarly, you may give up your sanskar of sincerity just because others in the office aren't that honest with their work. Whose loss is it? Others do not lose anything.

SO: I used to think this tit-for-tat behaviour was okay.
SS: We always need to hold on to our good qualities.

SO: If we become a being full of love, then will everyone around us also become like that?
SS: First let us become that. Let's keep following our sanskar, let others keep copying us. Whether they change or not, we will benefit from this exercise. When we bow down, we make sweetness our sanskar. Initially, it may be difficult to do this.

SO: There is a wedding at my wife's relatives' place. I refused to go there because they did not attend one of our functions.
SS: Someone did a particular karma. Why do you need to copy it?

SO: But the whole world does that. People don't go to a social event if its host did not attend their function.
SS: This is why the result today is that everyone is in stress and so are we. Everyone gets angry and so do we. Everyone is getting weak and so are we. We are copying only the wrong things.

SO: There is a gap between spirituality and how the world works.
SS: Spirituality is the right way to go about things in this world. It means using the original qualities of the spirit in practical life. Spirituality does not mean listening to a discourse for half an hour and then doing things that are convenient to us, the rest

of the day. All of us watch, listen to and share good thoughts on the Internet. But when it is time to act, we return to our old patterns. You also exchange messages on social media about forgiveness.

SO: Yes, messages of forgiveness have appeared several times.
SS: There are also messages about being loving, kind and compassionate. These are simple messages that we must have read, liked and exchanged. But if we continue to think that we should not go to a function just because our relatives did not attend ours, then what's the point of exchanging all these messages?

SO: When they are unwell or in need, I meet them and even arrange a doctor. But they did not come to a wedding in our family believing they were superior to me?
SS: But we have to remember to be kind, loving, compassionate and forgiving. This is being natural, this is being love.

SO: Being love does not mean saluting whoever comes your way. What about my self-respect?
SS: To think 'I will not go to their function because they did not attend mine' is not self-respect. It is the ego speaking. It emerged because you got hurt. It is even showing in your vocabulary. 'They think they are superior to me' is the language of ego.

SO: This is not the language of ego, it is their point of view.
SS: You don't yet have an idea about their point of view, because you have not even tried to understand it.

SO: I got to know that they did not want to stay in a place smaller than a five star.
SS: It's fine; it is their sanskar not to be very flexible. Everyone

may not have the adaptability to stay in a place where they do not have their expected level of comforts. Everybody's sanskar is different, isn't it? Where should all our focus be? Only on the self. Just because they did not have the sanksar of adjustment like you do, you activated the sanskar of ego.

SO: My rule in life is clear. When my mother passed away, I noticed who all came to pay their respects. And if someone did not come, we won't attend events that they organize.
SS: This is a very difficult way of living. It is complicated to keep a count of who came and who did not. The simple way is to act according to your capacity. With the equation you have, you will have to do as others did. Sometimes it may be difficult for you to attend their events, but you will still have to, just because they attended yours.

SO: Yes, sometimes we have to do it out of compulsion.
SS: It is difficult to attend a function when you have a constraint. And at other times, when you don't have any constraint, you may choose not to go to an event just because others did not accept your invitation. Either way, you are not functioning according to your capacity but you are just copying them.
Just for a day, instead of choosing ego, you could feel compassion for others and accept their sanskars. If you do not have any constraints, what is stopping you from attending their function? You need not copy them. It will be good to bring in compassion.

SO: We don't attend weddings for the sake of compassion.
SS: Compassion here means to understand and accept why they could not make it to your function. You need to have compassion for their inability to adjust, since we all have our share of negative sanskars.

SO: Even if I attend, it would be only for the sake of my wife, and not for their sake.

SS: Then the intention behind the karma is not right. Never do anything for the sake of anyone else's happiness, do it while being happy.

Today, we take even very big decisions in our life just for the sake of our family's happiness. We meet women who left their job or did not pursue a career after finishing their education, for the sake of their family. Their intention at that time was right – to sustain harmony at home. But they programmed their mind with the thought: 'I am taking this step for the happiness of my family.' Now they feel that even after sacrificing for years, their family is not happy with them.

SO: Maybe the family doesn't even know about it.

SS: Their family is not satisfied with them despite their efforts because while doing it, those women created the thoughts: 'I am sitting at home because of them ... I studied so hard ... I am so capable of having a good career ... look where my friends have reached today ... if I too had the chance, I would do so much ... what respect do I have today?' This means they are not happy and their energy field is negative. They radiate these vibrations to others. So doing something just for the sake of others is not right in the first place.

SO: But I could do something for others even if I may not be happy or convinced.

SS: You will have to change the equation then. Even if you go to the wedding for the sake of your family, you need to programme your mind differently: 'My family wants me to go ... if I go, they will be happy ... their happiness is very important for me ... when they are happy, I feel good ... so I am going for the sake of my happiness.' You have to be very clear about why you are doing whatever you do.

SO: Well, I feel like doing it.
SS: You feel like it – so there is no compulsion. It is important to shift our inner programming from compulsion to a choice. Saying 'I am choosing to do this for them' is okay. But to think 'I am having to do this for them' is not okay. If you do anything out of compulsion, you will keep cribbing inside and feeling negative. Then it's better not to do it.
Now let's rise to the next level and think: 'I am not going there just for my own family, but also for those who invited me … and I will not create a single thought about they not attending our function.

SO: That is not possible.
SS: Can't we improve our energy field? Can't we add power to the karma we are about to do?

SO: So should I lie to myself?
SS: You are not lying. You have to think that you are going to bless the one who is getting married, and to join the host family. There is nothing false about it. To think in this manner is to clean your energy field and change the vibrations with which you go. We all have to broaden our thinking and finish the old patterns.

SO: I agree that we had limited ourselves to a small well. Now we must try to become an ocean.
SS: We have unlimited potential and our thoughts can be as elevated as we want.

SO: I should think big and act royal.

SS: When we do not copy others and we use our original qualities, we leave pettiness behind. 'I won't go because they did not come' is ordinary thinking. Rise above ordinary thinking.

SO: When I think above the ordinary, my ego gets a boost.

SS: No. On the contrary, your ego will get smaller. The above-ordinary thoughts in this case are: 'I am a royal soul and will go to the function with my own dignity ... I will give love to everyone and leave the past here before I go.' If you remember hurt from the past and carry it there, it will radiate to others, they will feel it.

SO: I will carry the vibrations.

SS: Yes, and this is what we don't realise. We think we will talk nicely and people won't know what's going on in our mind.

SO: I understand it now.

SS: So let's forget the past. Remember: 'I am going there because they have invited me with love and have given me respect.'

SO: Yes, they have.

SS: Then why can't we remember the good things? We all have another very old sanskar – to hold on only to negative things in life. We count only those and forget all the goodness we experience in our interactions. If we have to copy, we should copy people's good behaviours.

SO: Now I agree with you. We have to become unlimited.

SS: If you think small, your power will be restricted. If you break the old pattern, forget the past, you will become free and enjoy attending the function.

SO: I am already enjoying myself as I feel so light inside after having this conversation.

SS: You feel light because your relationship with the self has changed. Our own thoughts can lighten us and our own thinking can make us heavy. We have to become our own friend, make our mind our friend.

SO: Thank you, sister, for making my mind my friend.

MANTRAS FOR BEING LOVE

- If we copy an unpleasant behaviour of others, we block our beautiful qualities. Let us radiate our qualities as we come into interaction with them.

- Each soul has been on a long journey, creating different sanskars in each birth. Two souls cannot have the same sanskars. Let us not expect people to have the same qualities as us.

- When we do something for someone, let us not feel we are doing it for THEM. If we have negative thoughts of unwillingness, neither we nor they will be happy. We are doing it because this relationship and their happiness is important to us.

- Sometimes people may not behave as we want. Let us consciously shift our mind to their past pleasant behaviour. This enables us to see them in a positive light and then respond to the present situation in the right manner.

Selfless Acts Empower the Self

Suresh Oberoi: My Guru once told me, 'Your experience is your property and growth. Don't talk about other things, they are not yours.'
Sister Shivani: True.

SO: At a function, I was eagerly waiting to meet a famous person, whose place was reserved next to mine. When he arrived, I wished him but he ignored me. I was uneasy inside. Then I remembered what you had told me about being egoless. I closed my eyes and sat in meditation. I visualised myself and him as loving souls belonging to the same Father, and sent him good vibrations.
After some time, a person sitting in front of this VIP introduced me to him. I told him that I had greeted him but had not received a response. Now that VIP said, 'You may know me, but I don't know you, so how could I respond to you?' During my journey of becoming an

actor I had to bear so many insults, and this was a small one.

SS: True.

SO: So I responded, 'You may not know me, but I know you.' I told him that I had read a lot about him, was impressed with his social service initiatives, and that he was doing a very noble job. He responded by saying, 'You are no less. You are hosting *Awakening with Brahma Kumaris* with Sister Shivani. It is benefitting so many people.'

I was amazed to hear that, as just a minute ago he had refused to even acknowledge me. Later, we became friends and the matter ended there.

SS: The matter did not end there. A new relationship began.

SO: A new relationship developed with myself, not him.

SS: You did something that you had earlier claimed to be difficult, even impossible. How difficult was it talking to someone who had ignored you?

SO: For an egoistic person it is difficult.

SS: All you needed to do was to play with your thoughts. We do so many tougher jobs in life. Our own thoughts create a conflict in the mind by giving contradictory advice. We just have to play with them and sort them out. We can do so just by sitting in silence. How difficult can that be?

SO: It was difficult for me because I have acted in so many films, won several awards. If a person tells he does not know me, it makes little sense to me.

SS: Who was hurt?

SO: I got disturbed.
SS: Who is that 'I'? Here it is not about I, the soul. You were hurt because you were ignored despite having a long list of achievements in life.

SO: The picture that I had made of myself was hurt.
SS: Yes, the acquired image. When we create such an image, we also imagine the way people ought to behave with us on the basis of that image.

SO: Yes, you are right.
SS: When people do not talk in that particular way, we get hurt. We think people must respect and appreciate us and our family must love us because of that image. So we go into the mode of taking from others.

SO: The mode of wanting.
SS: In this mode we ask 'give me love, give me respect'. What you did in that situation was that you used knowledge and changed from the taking mode to the giving mode. You decided you did not need respect from the other person, and gave him vibrations of love and respect instead. Who was the first one to feel good about making this change?

SO: I felt I had gained victory over something.
SS: You gained power. Who did you defeat? This is what we call *mann jeetey jagat jeet* – the one who rules his mind, rules the world. Ruling the mind here means that you conquered your ego, despite it creating an opposite thought. As a result, you were victorious even in that situation. On the other hand, if you had lost the battle with your mind at that moment – that

111

is to say, had you created the thought 'if he does not talk to me, I too will not' – you would have been defeated in that situation. The most important thing is that when you changed from the taking to the giving mode, you felt good. The result was that the other person copied you.

SO: Right. And there could be several reasons for his initial cold behaviour – maybe he was in another mood, or had created a different image of me based on my films or the information he had received about me from others.

SS: Yes, we get this understanding later. This way of thinking creates understanding and compassion – we try to recognise the other person's point of view. But what is crucial is that particular moment when we are in the middle of the scene, and our reaction at that moment. After that moment passes, this understanding does not yield much.

After this experience, you have learnt that IT WORKS. You are now sure that when we use our original qualities, people copy us. It was a bit of a struggle initially – you got disturbed, ego troubled you. After that, you changed your thoughts and vibrations for the other person and talked to him. This change was inside-out. If you repeat this action a few times, it will become your sanskar. You will not need to work on it any longer.

SO: It will go into automatic mode.

SS: Once the sanskar is created, it goes into automatic mode. Just as we cry, get hurt or angry without realising it, this sanskar of giving to others will become natural.

Today, most of us feel hollow inside as we have shifted from the giving mode to the taking mode. The belief that only the fittest survive, was instilled in us right from childhood. According to it, only a constant achiever can survive. So survival became our aim. And what do we need to survive? We have to accumulate more and more. Nobody taught us to give. Everyone taught us to take, both materially and emotionally. But taking is not our original nature. Spirituality teaches us that we don't have to 'survive' in this world, we have to 'serve' here, just like nature.

SO: That's a nice one.
SS: Yes. Survive is not a nice word. It means to struggle, accumulate more, and somehow manage in this world.

SO: Just as they say 'by hook or by crook'.
SS: Yes, and we made survival the basis of our success and satisfaction. We thought the more we accumulate, the more successful we will become, and the more successful we are, the more satisfied we will be. Most of us have accumulated so much but still feel hollow inside. We can't feel the love and happiness that we want to. This is because our original nature is to give, but we have gone against it.

SO: Can you prove that giving is our original nature?
SS: Help another person and see how you feel while doing it.

SO: Of course, it feels good.
SS: But why do you feel so good? It's because the purpose of our life is to give whatever we have.

SO: The purpose of life is to go back to our original nature?
SS: Our original nature is to give. We say we are the progeny

of deities – who were constant givers. They are always shown giving something – whether materially, as Goddess Lakshmi does, or subtly, in the form of blessings.

SO: Even if we give something to others a few times, our motivation may be to earn good karma or gain entry into heaven as a reward.

SS: Spirituality teaches us that the original nature of the soul is to be generous. The more one gives, the stronger one will be mentally and spiritually. This is a spiritual law, but you'll have to try it out.

When we went into the taking mode, we developed a sense of competition, the desire to control others and to pull them down. This created the sanskar of fear in the soul.

SO: Fear and hatred.

SS: Also selfishness. Fear and selfishness became the sanskars of the soul, so we became weaker. When we think 'I want this', a simultaneous thought of fear is created 'what if I don't get it'.

SO: And what if I lose it?

SS: And what if others get it?

SO: And what if others snatch it from me?

SS: We say that the fittest survive, but this belief actually weakens the soul.

Now, let's see what will happen if we change our mode from 'surviving' to 'serving'. If we have a sanskar of sharing, we will not be in competition with anyone. We will be on our own journey. We will achieve according to our capacity, without competing with or copying others. We will develop sanskars of sharing and caring. So fear and selfishness will go away. Will our soul power increase or decrease in this case?

SO: Soul power will increase, but what about our bank balance?
SS: Giving is not just about donating money. We can give in so many ways. We need to check: when we use the sanskars of fear and competition, what happens to our soul power. When we use the sanskars of sharing, caring and cooperation, how much power do we have then? What makes us a stronger person?

SO: Sharing and caring.
SS: Competition will make us weaker as we will be in a state of constant fear, tension and anxiety. On the other hand, if we have the sanskar of cooperation and of pushing others forward in their journey, it will make the soul stronger. Let's finalise that the original quality of the soul is to serve, not to survive.

SO: Beautiful!
SS: When we went into the survive mode, we became stagnant. What happens if water stops flowing?

SO: It starts to stink.
SS: Water flows and nourishes everything in its way. If it stops to flow, it stagnates. Similarly, if we souls keep flowing, and nourish and nurture whoever we meet, our journey would become like that of a river flowing beautifully. On the other hand, if we live only to accumulate things and to receive something from others, we become like stagnant water.

The most basic way of giving is to donate money, do charity. We can give anything, from money to clothes, to blood. But we need to check the intention behind our act – are we expecting anything in return on the pretext of donation?

SO: One could feel sad if, after donating a lot of money, one's name figures at the end of the donors' list.
SS: It means, even if we give something to add to our account of goodness, we are giving with an intention of getting a return. The flow of energy can only be in one direction – either giving or taking.

SO: People think they will be blessed for their act of giving.
SS: It does amount one level of giving, but not the highest one. We may have a subtle desire for recognition, appreciation or to add to our account of goodness. Then the desire to get something in return is already a part of the act of giving.
There is a higher level of giving – we help someone in need, thinking it will be good for both of us. This is a higher level of giving. This is an enlightened way to give. But an even higher level of giving is to give selflessly, without having a single thought of receiving anything in return. This is selfless service – just as a mother cares selflessly for her child. But even she may be able to do it only for a limited period.

SO: As the child grows up, the mother might start to expect his support in old age.
SS: One way of giving that we can try out today, is to share whatever we have, with others. There is great growth for us in this step. Let's not hold on to things for ourselves. It is the

law of nature and that of spirituality, that the more we give of something, the more of it remains with us. But while giving we must check our intention to remove any hidden desire.

Giving means to give and then put a full stop, having no expectations in return. In this form of giving, there is a lot of growth for the soul.

MEDITATION AND REFLECTIONS

Let us sit back comfortably ... look at the self – I, the soul ... my original nature is to give, to serve ... this is my natural sanskar ... the more I give, the more empowered I will become ... today whoever I meet, whatever scene I cross, I keep attention that I don't take from them ... I have to give them because that is my original sanskar ... to think that they should respect me is to take from others ... I shift ... I respect others ... irrespective of their role or position ... I give both in material and subtle form ... I share with whoever I meet ... I cooperate and keep giving ... this is the sanskar of a deity ... the more I give, my soul battery gets charged ... this is my spiritual growth, spiritual power ... Om Shanti.

MANTRAS FOR BEING LOVE

- On the basis of all that we have acquired, we create an image for ourselves and of how people should be with us. When they do not behave as per our expectation, we get hurt.

- When we interact on the basis of our acquired image, we expect love and respect. So we are in the TAKING mode – we want from others.

- When we shift from expecting respect to giving love and respect, we shift from the TAKING mode to the GIVING mode. While giving, we feel light and happy because we are the first to experience the energy of love.

- We wrongly believe in survival of the fittest. But the purpose of our life is not to SURVIVE, it is to SERVE. Everything in nature is for serving others. Our purpose is to serve others with our vibrations of peace and love.

- In the survive mode, we create competition, fear and anger. In the serve mode, we create cooperation, sharing and caring, making us emotionally strong.

Giving is the Art of Living

Suresh Oberoi: Nature gives unconditionally. But we human beings are taught from the beginning that 'if you offer a donation, you'll be successful', 'if a couple goes to a certain temple, they will be blessed with a child' and so on. So every form of giving was about receiving something in return.

Sister Shivani: We need to check our intention while performing a karma. If the karma is motivated by a selfless intention, then the soul performing it will be empowered to an altogether different level. If a soul donates anything with the intention of receiving something in return, it would still be empowered because of the good karma, but the degree of empowerment would be lesser.

You mentioned that we have learnt to expect something in return for every act of giving. But we were also taught that we should give with one hand in such a way that even our other hand does not come to know of it. We were told *'guptdaan mahapunya'* [donation done secretively is the highest form of positive karma].

SO: But how will that benefit me?

SS: The benefit is that the more selfless our karma, the more we are in the mode of giving, the more energy flows from us. Smooth blood flow in the body is a sign of health. If the flow is obstructed or the blood clots, the body becomes numb or painful. Similarly, the qualities of the soul must flow, just like everything in nature does.

If we decide to give to charity, why not elevate our intention while doing it? Today we have expectations even while doing voluntary service. Then it no longer remains service unto others. If we want to be givers, a very simple method is to change our consciousness while going to work every day. Everyone thinks we go to work because we get something.

SO: We get money.

SS: Whether it's a business, job or a profession, we know we are going to earn. This is one intention with which we go to work. The other thought we can create while going to work is 'I have to give something to whoever I meet today'.

If you're an actor, create a thought that you will give something to everyone, right from the spot boy to the director. To give means, to share what you know or have. In the professional world today, the desire to hold back our knowledge, talents, skills and wisdom with ourselves is a concern. Even if we ask someone 'how did you cook this dish', instead of revealing the recipe, the person shows hesitation. But we do not realise that there is no progress in keeping things to ourselves. We don't want to share because we fear that others might get ahead of us. So we restrict ourselves and become stagnant.

We all have the opportunity to share something at our workplace. Let's go to work with an intention 'today I am going to forge good relationships', or 'I have to talk respectfully with everyone'. Let's not go there with the only intention of earning money or promotion. That return is anyway certain. We need to check what we gave others throughout the day. Our inner flow of goodness must be maintained – that is the natural way to be, that is life. If we block this flow, life will be stagnant.

Let's create the thought 'I will share something good with whoever I meet today, whether at work or on the way there'. We can give just a smile, if not anything else. When we give something, we are the first ones to get that vibrant energy. It touches others later.

SO: I read in a book that if we go to someone's house empty-handed, we should give them blessings the moment we enter. We should say 'God bless this house', 'may you be happy and peaceful'.
SS: How beautiful!

SO: And a blessing is so much better than a gift.
SS: We can give blessings all day.

SO: As you said, when I go for a film shoot, I can at least create positive thoughts for everyone.
SS: It would be so nice to greet everyone with a smile, and along with it create a beautiful thought for them. If you can stop and talk for a bit, that would be even better. All these small gestures through which we let our energy flow from inside out make a big difference. Another way to be is to look cold and stern while crossing others, not bothering to give anything.

When we give something to others, it touches them. They then give it to those they meet subsequently, and the vibrations of the place undergoes a complete change. It is nice to at least smile at others, give them blessings, appreciate them and, most importantly, share with them our knowledge, skills and talents. We need not fear that they will surpass us, because it is a spiritual law that he who gives something to others will progress much beyond his own capacity and imagination.

SO: Some people don't appreciate others. If someone performs well, they don't even pay a compliment.
SS: Our ego and insecurity stop us from appreciating others. We can't tolerate it when others do well, that's why we are unable to give them something. But the more we refrain from sharing with others, the more we restrict our own capacity.

SO: Then the world will also not appreciate us when we do something good.
SS: That is secondary. What the world gives us is not our focus. Our focus is on what we can give to others. It's so beautiful to appreciate and motivate others. It is so simple too.

SO: We open up inside when we give freely.
SS: Yes, that's the benefit of giving. By giving to others we let our own energy flow. This energy would otherwise get blocked and we would become stiff. So keep giving.
Another simple practice is to give others responsibility. Today we are insecure about handing over responsibility. Whether we are the head of our family or leading an organisation, we want to keep power to ourselves. Hand over responsibility to others and give them the freedom to do things as they want. When we do this, we empower them. Accept the possibility that they might make mistakes while carrying out the task.

SO: Even at home, a mother-in-law does not delegate tasks to the daughter-in-law. She tells her 'you won't be able to do it'.
SS: When we don't hand over responsibility, we are not being fair to ourselves and others. When we do it, we benefit both parties.

SO: Maybe we are afraid of losing power.
SS: Yes, but we don't realise that if we don't let go of one branch, we will not reach somewhere new. If we leave the branch, we will fly and scale new heights.

SO: Once, a king bought two birds. One bird would keep sitting on a tree branch all day, while the other would fly high. The king sent for a renowned farmer from a village who was an expert on birds. When he intervened, the first bird too started flying. When the king asked him how he had managed to make it fly, the farmer confessed that all he had done was to cut off the branch.
SS: We lose out on doing so many better things that we are capable of, just because we do not entrust responsibilities to someone else. We keep holding on to the branch and telling ourselves we are busy. We must delegate responsibilities.

SO: And do so with full faith.
SS: We also need give them the freedom to do things their way. Then accept that that might err, because that is a part and parcel of learning.

SO: We too made mistakes when we did things our way.
SS: When we empower others and push them ahead on their journey, power flows through us. We have to try this out as we won't understand this completely, in theory.

SO: I did this. When my nephew was growing up, we started seeking his opinion on financial investments. So he began to study about it and gave inputs. This empowered him and today he runs his own office.

SS: Sometimes we hand over responsibility to another person, but keep taking it back by interfering.

SO: We even tell the other person 'I knew you would not be able to do it'.

SS: Sometimes we say 'it would have been better if I had done it myself instead of getting such a result despite guiding you often'. But we have already done it so many times, and now it's time to give others a chance.

It is human nature to encourage others and push them ahead in their journey. We can experiment with these small things at our workplace. When we empower others, we earn so many blessings automatically, without even trying for it. Those blessings lift us to a level beyond our imagination.

Another way to give others is to share our opinion without imposing it on them. When we have experience and wisdom, and see something incorrect happen in our surroundings, we must definitely express our view on it, even if it gets rejected. But the guidance must be given lovingly and in a very subtle way.

SO: Earlier, my tone was harsh. I would say, 'I told you not to do this.' Now, after doing this show, I politely say, 'If I were you, I would not do it this way, but you decide for yourself.' I no longer impose my views on others.

SS: But you do give your opinion.

SO: Yes, I do.

SS: So giving is not just about doing charity. There are many forms of it – to smile, to give blessings, to appreciate others, to share our knowledge, to delegate responsibility, and to share our experience and wisdom with others.

SO: We too have received all this from others.

SS: Yes, and when we pass it on, the flow is maintained. When water flows, it touches and nourishes everything in its way. This is the purpose of our life – to nourish and nurture everyone we meet, in any way we can. This is the way to keep the energy flowing.

Another way to give is to show gratitude for whatever we have received. Today, we spend most of our time focusing on things we do not have, or on those that are not to our liking. We remember that long list but never ever express gratitude to people, nature or the Almighty for all that we have received in life. We always seek from these three, but don't pause and check how to give back in return. If we feel gratitude, what sort of energy will be created within us? We should express gratitude to everything and everyone we touch on our way.

SO: My mother used to tell me that we should thank the Earth when we first place our feet on the floor in the morning. Our guru used to treat his pillow as kindly as he would treat a baby. I found all this funny. But once, I was unwell and nearly fainted and would have fallen had I not held on to a door. I was taken to a hospital. There, I realised that the needle and the medicine injected into me, the door that I held on to, the bed and the blanket that protected me from the cold, and the phone I had used to call the doctor were all lifeless objects,

but had saved my life. We keep distinguishing between life and matter, but from that day onwards, I thank everything in the morning – for example, my pillow and my quilt for keeping me comfortable and warm. I do this by folding and and placing them properly and keeping them tidy. When I leave a hotel room, I thank the walls, the fan and the AC. To others it may seem a crazy thing to do.

SS: We should also thank nature.

SO: Yes, I thank the sun for giving us so much.

SS: How do you feel while doing all this?

SO: I feel very good.

SS: This is the attitude of gratitude. When we thank everything – God, people, nature and matter – then a sanskar of gratitude is created. Check the energy that is created inside. The vibrations in our mind are very powerful and affect everything – the state of our mind, our body, people, the surroundings and nature.

SO: Nature and matter have always protected me. In an accident, while others in my car died or were injured, I escaped without a scratch. This is because I used to thank my car, treat it lovingly and keep it in good shape.

SS: We develop a relationship with both nature and matter. If we scatter things around and waste them, we are not forging a good relationship with them. How we treat things in our surroundings decides what we get in return.

Similarly, we need to thank everyone we meet. Even if someone is creating challenges for us, we need to thank him for being instrumental in our inner progress, and for increasing our inner power. If someone is good to us, we should thank him anyway. By showing gratitude for everything, our attitude becomes one of blessing everyone. Otherwise we keep thinking about what we lack, and how things should have been. This depletes our energy.

We have discussed five forms of giving – charity; sharing talent, skills and knowledge with others; delegating responsibility; sharing our wisdom and experience, and expressing gratitude. Another way, which is the highest form of giving, is to serve others through our spiritual vibrations. Our being radiates vibrations to everyone around us. We don't have to do anything for it – who we are, automatically reaches everyone.

MEDITATION AND REFLECTIONS

Let's sit back … let me look at myself … I – the soul – original, beautiful, pure … all day today whatever object I use, whoever I meet, I first express gratitude … this is a pure and powerful thought for every interaction with souls, with nature and with matter … to give everyone, to thank everyone … to cooperate with everyone I meet … to share what I know … to propel them forward … to empower them … keeping attention on my thoughts and vibrations … because they impact people and nature around me … I am giving everyone automatically … selflessly … I am the child of the ultimate bestower, the progeny of deities … I keep giving … Om Shanti.

MANTRAS FOR BEING LOVE

- The intention behind the karma should be pure and selfless. When we do charity, let there not be any thought of getting recognition in return.

- When the karma is selfless, the energy flows from inside-out because we do not expect anything in return. The energy of giving flows through us and empowers us first.

- Let us go to work with the intention of giving – of sharing our knowledge, talents, skills and giving cooperation, appreciation and delegating responsibility.

- Based on our wisdom and experience, we should share our opinion with people. Even if they reject it, our role is to continue to given our opinion. We should not expect that our advice will always be implemented.

- Let us create an attitude of gratitude towards everyone we meet and everything we use.

Healing Relationships

Suresh Oberoi: Last time I mentioned about what I had read – if we go to someone's house empty-handed because we don't have money to buy a gift, the biggest gift we can give him is our blessings. Could you elaborate on it?

Sister Shivani: Our thoughts and vibrations, which make up our energy field, enter their house along with us. Our energy field is not something we can separate from the self. We usually consider giving blessings to others as situation-specific or person-specific. But another way of giving blessings is by keeping our thoughts beautiful and clean, thinking good about everyone, so that we naturally radiate blessings all day. To bless does not only mean to express a specific wish, such as 'all the best', 'do well', or 'have a long life', but we also need to check the quality of our thoughts for others in general. Even if we usually think negatively about a person, but for one moment wish him 'all the best', then we do create a good thought for him. Several other thoughts of ours are also reaching him.

We spoke about being givers. The easiest and most powerful way to constantly give to others is through our vibrations. We can't stop our thoughts and vibrations from reaching others even if we want to. This is an automatic mode of giving. Relationship means exchange of energy. What I think about you reaches you, what you think about me reaches me – this becomes the foundation of our relationship. If I don't think well of you but I do good things for you, then however much I try, the foundation of our relationship will never be strong.

SO: When I think negatively about others, what impact does it have on me?
SS: If we continuously create thoughts such as 'he is like this', 'why did he do this' and so on, it disturbs our state of mind. Our happiness and peace vanish, and our energy of love is blocked. It will also affect our health.

SO: Is there so much loss.
SS: If we don't think well of another person, we tend to think it's fine because we have an issue only with one person. We feel that way as our relationship with others is fine. But our mind gets soiled by thinking negatively about even one person, as impurity is created there. So our energy field will remain the same even when we meet other people too.

SO: As you said, the perfume we wear spreads its fragrance.
SS: If we create negative thoughts about a person repeatedly, it influences our energy field. It will disturb not just our state of mind and health, but also our other relationships. We tend to think more about those we are in conflict with.

SO: We will also get into the habit of negative thinking.

SS: This habit of criticising another person mentally depletes our energy. So when we meet someone else, we will not have the power to withstand any disagreements or their unexpected behavior. Our relationships automatically get complicated as we weaken.

Suppose we got into such a serious conflict with someone that we had to brake up with him. This means we lifted a rock with our hand, but it pained, so we dropped it. Now that weight is off our hand, but the hand is still wounded and paining. Now we will find it difficult to lift even a pencil.

Bitterness in one relationship affects other relationships because the pain remains in the mind. We think a relationship exists externally, but it actually exists in our mind. What I think about you, creates a relationship in my mind. And what I create in my mind is completely my choice.

If we are in conflict with someone, we must attempt to change the way we think about them. When we try to change the relationship outwardly – if we change only the way we speak or behave with each other, or discuss the past and try to resolve it on the surface – it gets complicated instead of getting simplified. The easier way out is to check the quality of our thoughts. The obstruction in a relationship exists in our mind, not between us. This exercise may seem untypical but we need to experiment.

SO: What if we are unable to forget the person we are in conflict with? Give us a mantra to let go of those thoughts.

SS: If I am in conflict with you and am thinking of you, then I am creating powerful negative energy. This energy will reach you. Since you are in conflict with me, besides receiving negative energy from me, your thoughts will also become highly negative. Next, your thoughts will reach me and I will become even more negative. This goes on. It is like we are throwing a ball of powerful negative energy at each other.

SO: It is an exchange of hatred.
SS: We are throwing it continuously at each other.

SO: How should we resolve it?
SS: We will start to feel heaviness in the relationship. However cordial we try to be, we will keep getting hurt in the relationship because the vibrations being exchanged are negative.
Suppose the negative energy is of blue colour. I am throwing that blue ball at you, then you are throwing it back to me and this exchange is going on. How should we break this exchange of heavy negative energy?

SO: We can stop it from our side.
SS: What would we need to do for that?

SO: We can stop throwing the ball back, which means that we do not think about each other.
SS: That is not possible.

SO: We could send a positive ball.
SS: Yes, that is the only option we have. We cannot stop throwing the ball because it is not possible to stop thinking about someone with whom we have a deeply negative karmic account. Even if we try not to throw a ball [thought], they are throwing one at us. That will trigger our thoughts and the exchange will continue. Only if we, with great attention and effort, change the colour of the ball we are sending to the other side, a positive result will start getting created. This can happen even if one of the two starts to make this change.

For example, I send you a blue ball, and you too send me a black ball. I again send you a blue ball, but this time you send me a white ball of pure, positive energy. I may be continuously sending you blue coloured balls, but the moment I receive one white ball from you, I will experience a little lightness.

SO: The blue colour will start to get diluted if we add more white to it.

SS: Yes, that's all you need to do. You need not wait for me to send you a white ball. If I keep sending you blue coloured balls, but you keep sending me white ones, the colour of the balls I throw at you will eventually undergo a change. Even if I take a long time to change, the important thing is that the colour of the balls you throw [thought pattern] will change.

SO: Right.

SS: You would at least be saved from the huge loss you'd otherwise incur, due to negative thinking about me. The small step you take – thinking well of me even when you are not convinced about it – will lighten and improve your energy field.

SO: I will also be doing the good karma by thinking positive, so my karmic account will improve.

SS: Yes, everything will change when the quality of energy being exchanged improves. The significant result of these efforts will be that you will feel light, your health will be better, and you will find it natural to throw white balls in your other relationships.

SO: Once we get into the habit, it will become easier.

SS: Suppose in one relationship you are exchanging blue

coloured balls, so the colour of your mind is blue. In another relationship, the other person might be sending you white balls, but your creation will still remain blue because that has become your colour. Usually there is conflict only in one or two of our relationships, not all. But if we are able to work on those, the rest get sorted out automatically, and the soul's battery becomes powerful.

It is like, if we come home in a bitter mood, it impacts the mood of others in our house.

SO: Our family members' behaviour then starts to change.
SS: Because a turbulent energy has entered the house.

SO: Even pets at home feel uncomfortable and they tend to hide.
SS: This is how our vibrations impact others. When fear and negativity enter the house, it impacts even children. Though they are not at fault, they get scolded repeatedly just because we elders carry negative energy. When we do not take care of ourselves, our relationships become complicated. Now we have to change this pattern and understand that the state of our mind impacts our family.

If we ask someone 'why do you work so hard despite difficulties, what are you sacrificing your health for...'

SO: They will reply 'we are doing it for our children'.
SS: What do they want to give their children?

SO: The best of everything – good education, clothes etc.
SS: But why do they want to give them that?

SO: So that they are happy.

SS: We think if we give them the best of education, clothes and comforts, they will be happy. If we give them everything they need, but enter the house with a negative energy field, will the children be happy?

The parent may enter the house with a gift, but he also brings along the energy of irritation. His tolerance power is nearly zero by the time he comes home in the evening, because he did not take care of himself during the day. Now if someone at home is not his way, he will become irritated. No doubt he will give the gift to his child, but he also gives an energy of irritation. Can the child be happy?

SO: No.

SS: Today a majority of parents complain 'look at this generation of our children – they are emotionally weak, do not listen to their elders, talk back, get hurt easily, get angry and depressed'. Many children suffer from high blood pressure, and they even contemplate suicide. Is this the result of happiness? Today we are giving more comforts to children, wanting their happiness index to improve. But why is their tolerance level so low and stress level so high? Words like stress and anxiety should not even apply to children.

If you ask parents 'why are children so stressed today', they blame competition, or pressure of school and exams. But even our generation went through those challenges, and we neither had so many comforts nor access to technology. It wasn't easy then. But we were never stressed or depressed.

SO: We used to even share books.

SS: We used to walk or cycle to school. Today a child steps out of an air-conditioned house into an air-conditioned bus or car, and then into an air-conditioned school. Today the comfort level is much higher and the examination system has changed – actually there is lesser pressure. Now, after each exam there is a gap of a couple of days so that children get time to prepare. When I gave my Class X ICSE board exams, it went for five consecutive days – Monday to Friday – and a total of ten subjects.

SO: Two exams in one day!
SS: Yes. We used to go at 8 a.m. and return home at 4 p.m. We put in a lot of hard work as our syllabus included everything we had studied in classes VIII, IX and X. Now the exam is only for the syllabus studied in Class X, with one exam each day, and there is a good gap of a day or two between exams. This means we are making life easier, but there is still a question mark over children's emotional strength. Since we have the sanskar of blaming, we say the reason for kids' stress is exams, competition, pressure.

SO: The reason actually is the parent?
SS: A predominant factor. The sooner parents accept it, the earlier they can start to work on this aspect. Till the time parents take responsibility and stop blaming other factors, they will not be able to address the root cause of the issue. Today, there is stress in the atmosphere of the house.

SO: We keep scolding children for not studying well.
SS: Even if the parents do not say anything, they enter the house with the energy of stress caused by things that happened with them during the day.
If parents really want to give their children the best of everything,

they must know that it depends on their best energy field, not the best facilities. These days, we meet children who have received the best education, but their emotional intelligence is low and ego is high. Any small incident can hurt them and they struggle with teamwork.

An individual's life stands on four pillars – physical, mental, social and spiritual. We take care of the physical aspect by providing our children the best diet, home, clothes etc. We also give them the best education for their mental and intellectual growth. To take care of the social aspect, we ensure that they have good friends, and enrol them into hobby classes or co-curricular activities. We even take them on vacations.

So it is like having a table with three strong legs. But the fourth pillar – of our children's emotional or spiritual strength – has not been our focus. They experience stress, fear and anxiety. We think if the other three pillars are strong, the fourth pillar will be taken care of automatically. But since one pillar is weak, their life is always going to be unstable. If we want a balanced and stable life for ourselves and our children, all the four pillars have to be equally strong.

If parents enter the house without a gift, it doesn't matter. But they must bring home the energy of happiness, love and peace.

SO: When I return home from work, how should I leave my tension and negative energy outside the gate?
SS: You cannot separate your energy field from yourself. How will you separate your perfume from yourself? You need to pay attention to the quality of your thoughts throughout the day, at home and at the workplace.

SO: So we must remember all day long that I am love.

SS: Yes, I am peace, I am happiness. We cannot be in a race to accumulate more and on the way, create anger, irritation, stress and fear. Otherwise these emotions become the 'gifts' we take home in the evening. Today a majority of homes get these gifts. We need to remember that we earn two things every day – money and energy. We give our children both these things – facilities and vibrations. If we give them fewer facilities, it is fine since our spiritual and mental energy will compensate for it. But if children lack the virtue of tolerance, their life will never be balanced. Whatever we want to gift our children, we have to earn it through the day. And for that, we need to pay attention on the self.

MANTRAS FOR BEING LOVE

- Our thoughts and feelings create our energy field. This energy field has an effect on our body, other people, nature and matter. Our consciousness vibrates into the universe.

- If our energy field is pure and powerful, everyone will get influenced by our pure vibrations. This will help them to emerge their own purity and power. This is the true meaning of blessing people.

- Conflict in one relationship depletes our power and this affects our other relationships.

- In conflict, there is an exchange of negative energy between them and us. Let us not look at what they are sending us. Our focus needs to be on sending them pure energy of good wishes. This will heal us and heal them.

Children Absorb
Parents' Vibrations

Suresh Oberoi: Once, we were in a lift and I was worried that my grandson's hand might get stuck in the door. I scolded our maid sensing she was not being careful. My grandson started crying. Later, my daughter told me that he had cried because I had shouted at the maid. The child was not even a year old. Do children absorb energy more easily?

Sister Shivani: Energy gets transferred from one soul to the other; it has nothing to do with the body. But with kids the impact is greater, because as we grow, our own thinking develops and we may choose to accept or reject others' messages. We have our own energy field then. But for an infant, he is not yet attached either to his body or to the family he is born into. He is soul conscious at that time, as he is in a detached state. The more detached we are, the more we are able to catch others' vibrations.

SO: But I thought just the opposite. Does a little child, whose brain is not yet fully developed, understand these things?

SS: He may not understand things but he feels everything. When we learn meditation and practise detachment or soul consciousness – we try not to get entangled with things – the noise in our mind starts to subside. The mind becomes silent and is able to catch others' vibrations, just as saints are able to. When we go to a saint with something on our mind, they give us an answer even before we have said anything.

SO: Correct.

SS: They are able to do so, as their mind is silent after several years of meditation. We think it's magic, but anyone can do this. If our mind is silent and we come across another soul, we will be able to catch its vibrations. Some of us can feel the vibrations. Others, who have meditated for years, are able to understand specific vibrations and respond accordingly. Kids have the same level of purity, innocence and soul consciousness. A small child does not have a clutter of his own thoughts. He neither has an ego nor many feelings. So his power to catch vibrations is very high. A soul has the highest catching power when it is in the mother's womb.

SO: Really?

SS: In the mother's womb, the soul is in a completely detached state and so, can catch everything. Thus parents should take care right from the beginning, when the soul enters the womb. When a child is about to be born in our house, we should welcome the soul with very pure vibrations. Spiritually we understand that we already have a karmic connection with that soul. We have met that soul earlier [in a previous life], so we can start sending welcoming energy. These days, parents create a lot of stress and anxiety by worrying whether they would have the resources to bring up the child well and give him a good life.

SO: It's as if you invite me to dinner, but keep wondering whether you would be able to host me well.
SS: Right. So if you are coming to my house as a guest, and I am creating such energy, what message will you get?

SO: I would think it is better not to go.
SS: You will receive unwelcoming vibrations. You don't know exactly what I am thinking about you, but my vibrations will trigger your thought about postponing the dinner meeting.
When a child is about to be born in our family, our every thought should be pure and powerful. There should not be a trace of anxiety. Otherwise we will, in a way, subtly resist that soul's arrival. We want to welcome it in our life, but if we are also sending it a message 'we are not equipped to receive you', then the soul will feel unwelcome.

SO: It is said that every child brings along his own fortune, and every grain of food he eats is predestined for him, so we should not worry about him.
SS: Very true. This is because the child is actually a soul that has left a bodily costume and taken a new one. In its previous life, when it was part of another family, it formed karmic accounts and sanskars, which it has now carried with it. This is like the closing balance at the year-end becoming the opening balance for the next financial year, on the next day. A child is not a clean slate but has a lot recorded on

him. The closing balance of that soul in its past costume is its opening balance in the new costume. All of us must remember this, because many times we take the consequences of our actions lightly. Every action we perform leaves an imprint on the soul.

When we go to a funeral, we say we were born empty-handed and will leave empty-handed. But neither is true – we neither come nor go empty-handed. Every soul comes with its sanskars and karmic account. Whatever a soul achieves and accumulates in its lifetime – wealth, position, body and relationships – is left behind. But the karma it performs, the karmic account it creates, and the sanskars it forms, travel with it.

Death is a very painful process for most souls because they are compelled to let go of whatever they had acquired in that life – the body, family and attainments. So a soul that has recently left its body is most likely in pain. Some souls struggle more, others less. If someone met an untimely death, or left the body in an accident, or the soul has not been able to achieve what it wanted to in that life, then it experiences greater pain.

So the new parents-to-be must realise – that while for them a new addition to their family is a cause for joy, the soul who will be born as their child is in pain. Their responsibility as parents is to give it so much love, power and welcoming energy that it heals all its pain. However, if that soul receives pain from its new family, it adds to its pain.

The expecting mother cannot afford to have any kind of stress, anxiety or fear because it directly affects the soul in the womb. Even the rest of the family has an impact on the soul but the mother affects the soul directly. That is why it is said that an expectant mother's room should be adorned with nice pictures, and she should read something good, such as the scriptures, so that her thoughts are pure and powerful.

I met a lady whose pregnancy and a year after that were spent in constant anxiety because her mother was in the terminal stage of cancer during that time. Now her son is 18 years old, but even today, fear and anxiety are his predominant emotions. He received these emotions from his mother when he was in a very detached state and was most receptive to her vibrations.

Today, expectant mothers are told to eat properly and exercise for the health of the child. But no one tells them to think right. Mothers must think right not just for the health of the baby, but because their thinking is going to be their child's thinking.

SO: I have seen several cases in which a carefree and playful child goes into a shell after some time. The parents make him wear religious symbols and charms in the hope that he will recover. People say somebody cast an evil eye or did black magic on him.

SS: The intention of the parents is good – they want to give the best of everything to their child. But for that they need to have the best energy. If, in the process of giving the best to their child, they are always worried and stressed, the child receives those vibrations.

SO: And if the parents think that they don't have the means to give the best...

SS: Then the child receives the energy of rejection. We must make sure that when the soul is in the mother's womb, we don't create a single thought that gives it the energy of rejection. It takes a lifetime to heal someone's feeling of rejection; it becomes a very deep sanskar on the soul. It is possible that the soul felt rejected even in its previous birth. If it receives even a single thought carrying that emotion in this life as well, that sanskar would be reinforced.

When a child is about to be born, sometimes a few family members might express a preference for a particular gender, and choose a name, clothes and toys accordingly. But if the child inside the womb is a boy and they are preparing to welcome a girl, what vibrations will that soul get?

SO: It feels it is going to a place where someone else was invited.
SS: Even if the parents accept the child later, the thoughts created during pregnancy will affect that boy. Conversation about a preferred gender is damaging.

SO: My friend said he had invited someone as the chief guest for a function, but that person had declined at the last moment. So he requested me to fill in for him. I was hurt because I felt like a replacement. I still obliged and attended that function, but I felt that if he really wanted to invite me, he should have called me earlier. So now I can imagine the child feeling a lot of rejection if he is not his parents' first choice.
SS: A child feels the rejection far more intensely because he is completely soul conscious. You felt hurt, but then you used your logic and understanding, you were able to steer your mind out of it and attended the function. But the child cannot do all this – it can only catch the vibrations. So we must not have even a casual conversation about gender preference because the child is listening.

SO: Discussion about gender preference happens in many homes. If there is already a boy in the family, parents wish for their next child to be a girl and vice versa.

SS: We have a lot of discussions that we call 'normal'. We have to change this because the child is able to hear that the entire family wants a girl, while he is a boy. This is a very acute form of rejection for that soul.

Our only wish for the child should be that he or she is healthy and happy. This sends a positive message to that soul. Even if we create a thought of doubt, such as 'will the child be healthy or not', and worry about it repeatedly, each thought of ours will affect the soul and its body. Our body receives our thoughts. The child's body is still in the formational stage, and so is more vulnerable. It is good to send him positive messages, such as 'you have a healthy heart, good lungs', and so on. We should not create thoughts of stress by comparing our situation with that of others, or with our own past.

SO: People get stressed about the date and time of their child's birth, as that decides his zodiac sign. These days they even fix the time so that the child is born at an auspicious hour.

SS: What is the underlying thought behind all these actions? We think if we can control the date and time of birth, we can decide the destiny of the child. Now we understand that thoughts lead to feelings, which in turn shape our attitude, personality and destiny. So the destiny of the child is dependent on his thoughts. And that should be our focus right from the beginning.

SO: As the mother's thoughts, so the child's.

SS: Yes. So far we have discussed this spiritually. Latest scientific studies also confirm that as are the emotions of the mother, so will be the emotions of the child. This means the mother is creating a photocopy of her emotions.

SO: We have two grandchildren at home. The doctor says he won't treat them because children take after their parents.
SS: Right. And the doctor is saying what medical science says. If the child is having trouble, the parents will have to check themselves. They must do this right from the time the baby is in the womb.

Parents have their child's health and destiny in their hands, to a great extent. They make lifelong efforts for the good of their child. They should start today and work towards changing their thoughts and lifestyle.

Most people begin their day by reading the newspaper. Since the child absorbs all the thoughts that the parents create, they cannot afford to take in information about violence, terror and pain early in the morning. Such lifestyle changes should be brought in not just by the mother but by the couple. They should start their day together, by reading something pure and powerful. In fact, it would be good if they meditate together in the morning and decide to remain peaceful, patient and light throughout the day. This is because their thoughts will create the thoughts of their child. If the parents visualise every morning that they are receiving power from the Almighty and transferring it to their child, they will start protecting him with pure energy.

SO: It is said that a mother should herself cook the food she feeds to the child, because her love goes into the food.
SS: Yes, it is all about vibrations.

MANTRAS FOR BEING LOVE

- When a soul is in the mother's womb, it is detached from the body and family. In this detached state, the soul consumes vibrations of the parents.

- The soul entering the womb of the mother has just experienced death and is carrying sanskars of pain from the last birth. So the new parents' responsibility is to emotionally heal the soul by creating only pure vibrations.

- The mother should not take any negative information through TV news, violent or horror movies or loud music. The parents should meditate together to create healthy vibrations for the child.

- If parents create thoughts of anxiety about their capacity to bring up the child or about gender preference, they send vibrations of rejection to the child and the child feels unwelcome.

Nurturing a New Life
with Pure Energy

Suresh Oberoi: I mentioned the incident wherein I scolded our maid and my 11-month-old grandson was upset for long after that. Why did the child get so affected when I shouted at someone else?

Sister Shivani: A soul that takes birth in our family brings along its own sanskars. We will not find the same level of disturbance in all children. Vibrations have an impact, but the level of disturbance felt varies from soul to soul. Some children are more emotional than others, so they have the sanskar of getting hurt easily. The moment such a soul senses conflict among elders, it gets hurt and starts to cry.

SO: That child does not even want to sit in the lap of an elder who is tense.

SS: It means his power to catch vibrations is very high. We must make this soul powerful because it will have to face a lot of things. It lacks strength, and so is easily affected by external influences.

SO: It must have got the sanskar from within the family.
SS: Doesn't matter where the sanskar came from. As the child is small, he has most probably carried it from the past. Maybe the child was earlier [in the past life, when the soul was in another body] living in a very quiet and peaceful environment where he was not exposed to too much noise and anger – like this place in the hills. Here people are very simple. They live in harmony and have a sweet and soft disposition. If a soul from here leaves its body and is born in a city like Mumbai or Delhi, where there is too much noise and commotion, it would be a complete cultural change for it.

SO: It might be a cultural shock.
SS: Yes. It will take some time for that soul to adapt to its new environment.
Another possibility is that the soul experienced something bitter in its past life. Suppose it was, in its previous life, the wife of a loud and abusive husband. The soul could have faced violence. When born in a new home, it would be very sensitive to similar negative energy.
So there can be a lot of reasons why a child behaves the way he does. The sanskar could be there due to a cultural change or a past experience, or the soul could have received it from the family it has been born into. We have to accept that the soul has that sanskar and then help change it gradually. The way to do it is to make sure that, as far as possible, it does not receive any more vibrations of pain and anxiety.

SO: You said parents should remain stress-free.
SS: The house should not have the energy of stress and anxiety. It is easiest to empower the soul at this time, as a child easily absorbs the energy of his parents and environment.

SO: Who is it easy for?

SS: For the child.

SO: But it's not easy for the parents, because they may be used to living in stress.

SS: But they have a responsibility.

SO: Will they have to change their nature? They might be bound by the deep sanskars they got from their family.

SS: If they decide, they can pay attention. Parents take care of so many things concerning the child – his diet, timings, sleep, clothes etc. A mother spends all her time around him. So they can surely take care of their own sanskars. Remember that sanskars formed in the initial years of a child will be difficult to change later. A child has no ego of his own, and so it is very easy to change and mould his sanskars in the early years.

It can also happen that some children are very peaceful by nature but the energy they receive in their new environment is very disturbing, of conflict or turmoil. Then their sanskars will change for the worse. So it is the responsibility of the family to give good sanskars to their children. We think giving sanskars means to teach them how to talk or to be truthful etc. But the sanskars of the parents and their thinking directly influence the child – this is the most subtle way of transferring sanskars to anyone.

Every soul has five sets of sanskars. First are those it carries from the past – this is a very powerful factor. Second, those it gets from its present environment. This includes genetic factors and the sanskars it gets from its family and extended family. Third, those it gets from society including school, religion, country etc. Fourth, those sanskars it creates using its will power. This is what we are learning in this series – how to overcome our old negative sanskars and create new positive ones by choice, and with determination. The fifth set are the original sanskars of the soul – wisdom, purity, peace, love, happiness, bliss and power. The soul that has arrived in our house as a newborn, has these five kinds of sanskars. We have to see what sanskars it has come with and ensure that we empower it. For doing so, we elders have to take care of ourselves. There is no other way. If there is constant conflict and stress in the house, it will have a direct impact not only on the sanskars of the child, but also on his health. Today, a lot of children fall ill frequently. The doctors say their immune system is weak. But why is it so? We know that stress affects our immunity. But children have no stress of their own. The parents' stress gets transferred to the children and affects their immunity.

SO: This means as the parents, so the child.
SS: Right. If parents do not pay attention to correct their own sanskars from the beginning, they will keep complaining their whole life about the sanskars of the child.

The other day I met a lady who was expecting her second child. I explained all this to her, and asked her to stay calm and not get angry. She said it was not possible for her to do so because it was not a matter of a few days – it was nine months and a couple of years more. This, she said, was too long a period to not get angry. Then she said that her first child was extremely short-tempered, and that she had never realised that he had received the sanskar from her. I told her that she now had the chance to make efforts at least for her second child. So all parents have to do it.

Another thing parents need to take care of, is food. As is the food, so the mind. If the parents consume sattvic food when the child is in the mother's womb or in infancy, it becomes easier for the child to have a pure mind. Whatever the mother consumes definitely has an effect on the mind and body of the child. So she should not consume tamasic food, i.e. food with negative energy.

SO: Doctors tell parents to avoid drinking and smoking. But they may not know about sattvic food.
SS: Even if the doctors ask them to consume non-vegetarian food, they say so purely from a physical perspective.

SO: But now even scientists tell us that much more nutrition can be found in vegetarian food.
SS: Even if the parents are not convinced about it and want to have a non-vegetarian diet, they must realise the kind of energy they are consuming along with the food. Non-vegetarian food has the least spiritual energy. In captivity, the animal experiences extreme fear, anxiety and much more before it is slaughtered.

SO: They give the animals little food because they want to feed more animals at the same cost. They don't let the animals move so that they don't lose fat.
SS: It's all torture. We get to know these days about the miserable conditions in which these animals are kept. We must realise that an animal is also a soul, and it creates fear, anxiety and hatred.

SO: You told us that every thought we create affects each cell of our body. Even an animal has thoughts, feelings and emotions. So all the negative emotions must be affecting each cell of its body too.

SS: So we must understand what all we consume along with non-vegetarian food.

SO: People do not build a house next to a graveyard.
SS: Because the vibrations of that place are not good.

SO: When someone was asked why he did not consume non-vegetarian food, he said his stomach was not a graveyard.
SS: How beautiful! When we are ready to do anything for our children, we cannot give them this negative-energy food.

After a cremation ceremony, the first thing we do is to wash our hands and feet. Why do we do that? We clean ourselves of those vibrations. It is a custom not to cook food for a day in a house where someone has died. Cooking is done only after the body is taken away and the house is purified through certain rituals. The logic behind all these rituals and rules is that the environment at that time is toxic. So what about the fact that we ourselves consume a dead body of an animal? Is that not toxic? We must realise that by consuming non-veg food, we are using the energy of death to create life.

SO: And that too a painful death.
SS: Yes. What will be the result? We should eat food high in life-force, such as sprouts. But what do many parents do instead? They consume 'dead energy' themselves and even use it to create the foundation of the new life. They must give their child food high in spiritual energy. As you said, parents should not consume alcohol or anything else which is even slightly harmful for their child. There's no need to ask the doctor or to surf the internet to know if they can consume it within certain limits. Why should they consume even a drop of something

which is harmful for their child? Can't they make even a little sacrifice for a few months?

They should consume sattvic food and also take care that it is prepared with good vibrations. The food should be cooked with love by someone who is peaceful. One could even play a devotional song while cooking, so that the meal is prepared in a temple-like atmosphere amid pure vibrations.

We may be unsure about whether such subtle things make a difference, but they have a long-term impact on the child. It is like serving prasad to the child every day. If this food is prepared in remembrance of God and offered to Him first, then it becomes prasad. So just imagine: one option is that parents nurture the body of their child with prasad, the other choice is that they give him 'dead energy'. There can be no comparison between the two. Remember that at this time, the parents have the power to write the destiny of the child, as his body is still getting formed.

SO: Now we have the paint brush and canvas in our hands.
SS: Right, the colours that parents use now will make a deep impact. So they must consume sattvic food and make sure they don't listen to, read or see anything negative – whether on the Internet, in movies or in the news. They should not consume any such thing because it not just affects them but also the child, whose catching power is highest at that time, as he is in a soul-conscious state. They should read pure, powerful and enlightening content. If they listen to music, they should choose soft and soothing music. They must neither take in anything loud and disturbing, nor go to a place which has turbulent energy. All these efforts will nurture that soul. So the parents need to take care of their food and mind.

The third factor is money. Parents should not bring home money earned by cheating someone even a little. Such money should never be used to buy food for the child, because it brings with it pain and misfortune. If we cheat in our business, or are loud and dominating over colleagues at work, then others will create negative thoughts about us, we will earn negative energy along with the money. This energy affects the child. As is the parents' money, food, mind and body, so will be the child's personality.

SO: As the money, so the food, and as the food, so the mind.
SS: And as the mind, so the body. All these four energies are in the parents' hands. So parents should make no excuse at this crucial time. The mother, especially, should not get entangled in petty issues in the family. The health of her child being her first priority, she should not come into conflict with anyone. The entire family has a responsibility to keep the mother light and free from stress, to give her both physical and emotional rest. Emotional rest means that her mind is calm and silent.

SO: Spirituality is not taught in schools. You've described it so beautifully that when a child is in the mother's womb, that is his most crucial schooling period. The parents, at this time, can teach the child whatever they want.
SS: Whatever stories they tell their child at this time, he will imbibe all of that. It is the right time to teach their child values. Never think that the child is not listening. He is both listening to the parents and absorbing their vibrations.

MEDITATION AND REFLECTIONS

The health and happiness of our children and family members is our responsibility ... this is our most important priority ... we take care of ourselves for the child's well-being ... we earn by clean and pure means ... bring home the money that brings along blessings ... food we eat is saatvik, high energy ... mind is clean, pure, positive ... body is healthy ... we take care to have these four energies for ourselves ... and have a direct positive impact on our children ... this is our responsibility ... the efforts made now will write the destiny of our children ... this is the responsibility of every parent soul towards the new creation ...Om Shanti.

MANTRAS FOR BEING LOVE

- A baby is an old soul in a new body. The soul has been on a journey for many births. A baby's present behaviour is because of the conditioning and experiences of the previous births. In a few years, past memories will fade and present conditioning will take over. So parents need to take care of the present environment and vibrations.

- Every soul carries five types of sanskars. First is sanskars carried from the past birth. Second is sanskars of the family. Third is sanskars from environment and friends. Fourth is sanskars created due to our own will power. Fifth is the original sanskars of purity, peace, love and bliss. Each soul is a bundle of these five types of sanskars.

- The food we eat has an effect on our mind. Non-vegetarian food has vibrations of hatred, fear, anger and hurt. When we consume non-vegetarian food, we also consume these vibrations and they have an effect on our mind and body.

Parenting with Love

Suresh Oberoi: In the last episode, you used the word 'priority'. If we remember that I am love, and that is our first priority, we will hold on it in every situation in life.

Sister Shivani: This will have an effect on every aspect of our life – health, prosperity, well-being. So we need to remember our priority. We have discussed that our well-being impacts our children. When a family is about to welcome a new soul, whatever the parents take in through their sense organs – what they see, read, listen to, eat – and even what they think, has a direct impact on the new being taking shape inside the mother.

SO: If parents think of themselves as 'being love', they can give maximum happiness to their child. And that's what they want to achieve. But it's not simple always, because there is a big extended family and relationships can get complicated.

SS: We have to remember that the soul coming into the family has a karmic account with everyone in the house.

SO: The soul has an account with its paternal and maternal grandparents. All of them have their own views on how the child should be brought up. This creates a lot of confusion.

SS: There will be a difference of opinion on many things concerning the child. It is bound to be so, if there are four people in the house.

SO: It's not just four people. Now there is the Internet as well. And to decide what's best for the child, parents read the views posted online.

SS: India is a country with rich spiritual and cultural wisdom. Everything that our elders did was according to that ancient wisdom, which has been passed down the generations. We must see things from the scientific as well as spiritual perspective. We have to understand that if we ignore the spiritual aspect, we suffer a great loss. When we search anything on the Internet, we are actually searching globally. The information on any website is based on the background and culture of those who have created that content.

SO: We don't know who has provided that information, and on what basis. Maybe they intended to sell their product.

SS: Quite possible. Today the difference between our parents' advice and the information we receive from other channels is growing. We tend to see our parents' opinion as obsolete. We forget that their wisdom is based on our environment and culture. There is great benefit in the wisdom that has been passed down the generations.

SO: These days parents hire maids to help in raising their children. But it's better to follow our intuition.

SS: The most important thing is to understand the role of vibrations. Sometimes the staff employed is well-trained to bring up the child, and the grandparents may not have the physical stamina needed. But to bring up a child, to nurture a soul, more than external perfection, we need perfect vibrations.

SO: Vibrations of love.
SS: What is the difference between the food that a mother cooks and an employee cooks at a restaurant? Vibrations. The mother prepares food at home with vibrations of love. The food we get outside is cooked with the intention of earning money, and it carries those vibrations.

SO: I saw a maid feeding a child strapped in a chair. The child was continuously crying and wanted to be free, but she would not let him go. She feared that the child's mother would scold her for not feeding him properly. So the maid's intention was only to obey her employer. So at that moment she neither felt love for the child nor did she understand how the food would affect him.
SS: Staff may be needed for assistance. But tasks like feeding the child or putting him to sleep need good vibrations. That's what the child needs the most. There is no comparison between the vibrations of parents or grandparents and those of a hired maid. The maid works for money or to please her employer. None can provide the love, power, wisdom and vibrations that a child receives from his family. Just the presence of grandparents nurtures the child with good vibrations. A child is fortunate if he is in a joint family during his childhood because, he will receive vibrations from so many family members, which is not the case when one is brought up by a maid or left in a play school.

161

SO: The maid just leaves the child to watch cartoons on TV when his parents are gone.

SS: Because of all these small yet crucial factors, many children today are emotionally weak. When we were children, the atmosphere at home was very different from what children get today. Now the focus is a lot more on being perfect externally. External perfection is good, but the more we are going in that direction, the farther we are going from inner perfection. This is similar to our moving away from intuition and using only logic. We moved away from our wisdom and based everything on scientific calculation. Earlier, we used to remember everything, now we are so dependent on gadgets. We are distancing ourselves from our innate qualities, so what will we give to our children? We are making them dependent on physical comforts. If we want to give them something, it should first be pure vibrations.

A child has karmic accounts with the entire family. If the mother does not share a good relationship with her mother-in-law, that will impact on the child directly. Then the mother will not even want the child to go to his grandmother because of their strained relationship. The child has a very beautiful karmic connection with these two important souls in his life, but when he senses that they are in conflict because of him, he does not get good vibrations.

SO: He will feel guilty.

SS: He feels it even if he is just a few months' old.

SO: The child feels it even when he is in the mother's womb. We read about Abhimanyu in Mahabharata, who was able to enter the *chakravyuh* [circular battle formation] because he had heard how to do it while he was in his mother's womb.

Scriptures talk of a child who knew *shlokas* [verses from religious texts] by heart as his father used to recite them when he was about to be born. We also see that children of musicians find it easy to learn music at an early age.

SS: That's because there is a direct influence of vibrations. All these examples illustrate the impact of vibrations. We have to remember the word 'priority'. Our first priority is to keep the vibrations in the house in harmony. We cannot create conflict with each other on issues related to the child's upbringing. Such conflict can arise between the mother and the mother-in-law and even between husband and wife.

SO: If we think 'my priority is the child and being love', then we can check ourselves.

SS: Sometimes mothers think 'he is MY child'.

SO: They feel the child is their property.

SS: They feel they should bring up their child as they want, without interference from others. But one must not think that way because the child is a soul having a connection with all the other souls in the family. Always remember that the child will benefit if he receives good vibrations from everyone.

SO: Many grandparents complain that their son and daughter-in-law do not let them have a say in the child's life. That child is actually everyone's child.

SS: Yes, he has a connection with everyone in the family, that is why he was born there. The more love he gets from everyone, the more nurtured he will be. That soul left so many relationships in its past life. Now it needs to bond with many people. Thus the mother should not think that she alone can take the best care of her child. The child will feel most cared for when he receives everyone's loving vibrations. And for that, the elders' priority must be to keep their relationships in harmony so that the house has good vibrations.

SO: The child should receive love from his grandparents, uncles and aunts, neighbours – this is good even for the mother.
SS: Yes, because it benefits the child. The child is a soul that recently left a body and went through a lot of pain. The more loving vibrations he receives from his family, the easier it will be for him to heal the pain.

SO: I do not understand this.
SS: Look at a small child – he sometimes smiles in his sleep, sometimes cries. This is because he has memories of the past life. The other factor is that he is receiving the vibrations of pain from his past family – those souls who are in pain because of his departure. They have not yet been able to overcome the separation. Suppose a young child leaves his body; his parents will not be able to get over the trauma for years.
So we have to remember that a soul taking birth in our house is in pain, and should now receive so much love and power that it gets healed. But if it experiences stress even in its current surroundings, how will it feel?
So, let's not get picky about issues like diet and cleanliness. These factors are important for the health and hygiene of the child, but not at the cost of receiving negative vibrations of conflict, anger and hurt. We have to radiate pure and powerful vibrations to the child. This is our responsibility towards him. These days, while feeding the child, we switch on the TV or give him a phone or an iPad. These things are damaging for him.

SO: Parents say children do not eat unless they are distracted by these things.

SS: But we never had these gadgets when we were growing up. Even today, many homes don't have these things. Don't children eat food there?

Scientific research has shown that a child must not be exposed to gadgets too early in his life. The more we expose him to technology, the more he will be distanced from his innate abilities. We elders have forgotten our intuitive power and innate capacity because of being exposed to technology and gadgets. The child is still young and in his formative years. If the parents feed him in such a manner, it will become a habit with him and they will have to continue doing so for years.

The elders too must not watch TV while eating. Food, the mind and the body are connected. So we must check what we are consuming along with the food.

It is because parents do not have the patience to feed the child slowly, that they distract him with TV while he's eating. Distracting him with gadgets will only harm the child. It is not good to expose him to screens and their rays, and to make him addicted to gadgets. In fact, when the child is young, parents should keep gadgets out of his reach. The later they expose the child to gadgets, the better it will be for his development and intuition.

These days parents take pride in stating that their child uses a phone or an iPad comfortably. Actually, it's nothing to be proud of. Children today are losing their innocence early because they are connecting with gadgets at a young age. Let their purity develop. Expose them to gadgets much later.

SO: Children also lose out on physical activity when they start using gadgets. They should be playing games outdoors instead of video games.

SS: Children are not getting empowered emotionally and spiritually. We think that by being tech-savvy, children are becoming intelligent. But emotional and spiritual development, which is the most important of all, is missing. It's being neglected. Our emotional and spiritual strength is the foundation of our development.

SO: That's a nice thought. Let's meditate on it.

MEDITATION AND REFLECTIONS

Let me look at myself ... the four aspects of my life – physical, intellectual, social and spiritual ... for a balanced life, I pay equal attention on all four aspects – physical health, intellectual development, social connection and spiritual wisdom ... I give a balanced, holistic, happy and healthy life to myself and my family ... I invest equally in all the four aspects from today ... emotional health impacts all other aspects of my life ... because my mind has an effect on my body ... on my relationships ... let me take care of how I think and how I feel ... I create balance in my life and family ... Om Shanti.

MANTRAS FOR BEING LOVE

- The wisdom we get from our elders is according to our rich culture and environment. Science tells us what is right for our body while spirituality tells us what is right for our mind.

- The staff that takes care of our children is doing it as a job. They are perfect in what they do but they cannot give the vibrations of love, power and blessings which grandparents, parents and others in the family can.

- Even if a mother of the child does not get along with her in-laws, she will need to accept that her child has a special karmic connection with the grandparent souls.

- There will be differences of opinion about the upbringing of a child, but we cannot afford to let it escalate into a conflict. Our priority is to create the energy of harmony for the happiness and health of the child.

A Child is an Old Soul
in a New Costume

Suresh Oberoi: We were talking about how deeply parents influence their children, and that they should take care of themselves right from the time the child is in the mother's womb, as the soul has very high catching power then.

Sister Shivani: While talking to a child we should always remember that we are talking to a soul. We must understand that it is the body of the child that needs to develop physically, not the soul. Let's say, before taking the costume of a child's body, that soul was in an 80-year-old costume in its previous life. The soul is like a CD. It was playing in another CD Player earlier. The current player (body) is not fully ready yet. But the CD is well-recorded so the soul understands everything.

Just as when a person is in coma, he can't hear or talk, he may not even be able to comprehend things, but the soul is catching everything. The soul is only unable to connect to the body or brain, and the brain is unable to send signals to the body. The physical body is not fully functional, but the soul is 'listening' and feeling, though it may not be able to express itself.

The soul is like an operator, the brain like a computer, and the body like a machine attached to the computer. The operator, that is 'I', gives an instruction to the computer. The computer, that is the brain, processes it. Then it sends a signal to the machine, that is the body, which works accordingly and performs actions like eating, talking etc. So all the power lies with the operator. When someone is in coma, the operator is fine but the computer is unable to process information.

Similar is the case with a child – the body [machine] is still developing, so the child can't walk or talk properly. The brain [computer] is still developing, so he is yet to learn to reason. It is not the soul [operator] but the bodily machine that is one year old.

SO: My daughter had to go somewhere once. She sneaked out while her son was playing with me. Later, he started looking for her and cried a lot. So I told her that she should inform the child before going out. The next time, she told my grandson that she was heading out, and that he should stay with me until she returned. The child understood everything though he was only ten months old.

SS: Who understood everything?

SO: The soul.

SS: Yes, because the soul comes with all its sanskars, so it understands everything. We must realise that the child is an old soul in a new body, so we must communicate properly, with maturity and understanding with him. We do not need to talk to him like a child. The child is listening to and understanding everything, though he may not be capable of responding well.

SO: We've tried talking to our grandson with maturity, and it works each time. When he was to be vaccinated, we prepared him by saying that it would hurt him slightly. He understood it and was able to bear it.

SS: The soul has experienced things before, so all we need to do is to give it information. We need to experiment with these things and see the result. We have to talk to the soul with respect and dignity. Parents scold and even abuse the child at times, believing he is young and they are allowed to treat him this way.

SO: We think we are disciplining the child.

SS: If someone raises his hand against another person – a husband hits his wife, or a boss slaps a junior – it may not hurt much physically, but who is deeply hurt? What will I feel if it happens to me?

SO: I will feel embarrassed, disrespected and low.

SS: Yes, disrespected.

Parents give themselves the permission to hit the child when he is young and in their control.

SO: I've seen that things change when the wife says 'it's enough' or if the child warns that he will hit back.

I was once rude to our pet dog. He went under the bed and did not respond to our calls for hours. He did not eat his food, even though I tried to make up with him. So even animals feel hurt.

SS: When elders hit a child, they crush his self-esteem which is still developing. His dignity is hurt. Look at it another way. The same soul, a year ago, when it was in an old body, could have been the head of a family.

170

SO: And it must have been used to getting respect.

SS: Suppose we are used to getting respect from everyone. Then we go to another place where we get completely opposite vibrations. How would we feel inside? So when that soul was in the body of an elderly person, people probably listened to him and sought his opinion and blessings. Now, after a change of body, that soul gets scolded and even slapped, because he is in the costume of a child. What impact would it have on the soul?

SO: It happens even in one lifetime. A father is first listened to and respected. Later, the son rejects his views as old-fashioned.

SS: But when it happens in our lifetime and we are old enough to understand, we can comprehend the situation. Most importantly, we can also talk to someone about it.

SO: With time, one also accepts things.

SS: Yes. But a child can't express himself. He can't even say I get hurt.

At a public programme, we invited children below ten years of age in the audience to come up on stage. We asked them what was the biggest cause of pain in their life. The most common answer was that they were extremely pained when parents scolded them or punished them. On hearing this, many parents had tears, realising that their actions had hurt their child. Parents think they scold their child for his own good. Their intention is pure, but what is the energy that the child receives?

SO: I've raised my hand against my children even in front of their friends.

SS: All we need to do is put ourselves in their shoes. If we are with our friends and the authority figure in our life treats us in such a way, how would we feel?

SO: Such wounds take long to heal.

SS: It is very difficult for such wounds to heal. Even after one grows up, one may be unable to forget the hurt. This is because the wound was inflicted by none other than the parent, at a time when the child was most impressionable.

For a child, the parent is the most important person, an ideal and God-like figure in his life, at least till he grows up. It may not matter as much if his neighbours or teachers at school scold him. But whatever a parent says is the truth for the child. So if the parent says 'you can't do it' or 'you are no good', then this becomes the child's reality. Who is speaking to whom is important in this case.

SO: I once told my guru not to send my son for some work at a bank because he could be careless and lose the money. The guru said my attitude was negative and gave bad vibrations to my son. It was like cursing my own child.

SS: Yes, that's true. What is a blessing or a curse? A blessing means pure, powerful, empowering energy.

SO: We often compare children and say that one can do it but the other can't.

SS: This is like writing the destiny of the child. If you ask a parent 'why did you say that', they will respond 'because it's the truth – the child has not been able to do it'. Since it is coming from a parent, the child believes it to be true and creates his self-image accordingly. A child gets his introduction from his parents till the time he grows up to understand himself. The opinions of the parents and elders are the colours the child uses to create the image of himself.

SO: What a beautiful phrase – a child gets his introduction from his parents. Their words seep into his vocabulary. He says 'I am weak and can't do it', just because his parents told him so.

SS: The child internalises the belief. When he grows up, he does not realise that the belief was formed in childhood. He has taken it to be the truth about himself. He continues to think 'I can't do it, I am clumsy, I am slow'. When was all this programming done? It was done when the operator [the child] had given the parents the power to programme his computer. The system is now functioning according to the instructions fed into it by the parents years ago. If the parents say 'you're wonderful, you're good, you're wise and beautiful', then the child will create a self-image accordingly.

SO: When the elephant is oblivious of its own power, it does not realise that it can break free from the chain that binds it. Even if it is tied to a small plant with a mere thread, it does not attempt to free itself because it has seen itself tied up from the beginning.

SS: This is conditioning. When it was young, it had tried to break free but could not. At that time it did not have enough power.

SO: This is because when it was young, it was tied with a heavy chain to a tree. So it accepted that it could not be free ever.

SS: Yes, 'I can't do it' became its belief. It carried this belief throughout its lifetime.

SO: Even such a powerful animal lives all its life according to what was fed into its belief system when it was young. This means we can really mess up the programming of a child.

SS: We also have the power to create a very positive programming in the child's mind.

Sometimes parents use abusive language with their children. They have to remember that their every word is introducing the child to himself, and he is forming his self-image based on that. They dont't need to create his image based on falsehood, by telling him 'you are the best'. But they must check the words they use to teach and discipline him.

SO: Is it possible for the parents to improve the self-image of the child, which they have distorted?

SS: Yes, they can do it, but the child will also have to do it with them. When the child grows up, he has to choose new colours to form his image. Even if the parents had criticised him, he should now choose new colours for his painting. He should tell himself that even though he believed 'I can't do it', that is no longer true because he has achieved so much in life. The individual must now act as a parent to his own mind and condition it differently.

SO: But if I have been instrumental in my child creating a negative self-image, can't I make amends now?

SS: You can change the vocabulary you use with him. Vocabulary here means not just words, but also every thought you create for him. Every thought and word of yours must be a blessing for your child, not the opposite. It should be so, even when the child commits a big mistake, because you have to give him the energy to rise again.

Whatever phase of our life we are in today, we can bring about any change. With children, we have to understand that his destiny is shaped by his thoughts, which are created according to the information we give him. So we must be very careful about how we programme his mind.

If the child has already grown up, we can now change our sanskar of criticism. We can choose to create powerful words and thoughts for him. Most importantly, let's decide never to raise our hand against anyone, whatever their age, because we don't have any right to disrespect anyone. When we hit our child, we disrespect him and still expect him to cultivate self-respect. We thus defeat our purpose.

MANTRAS FOR BEING LOVE

- When we communicate with a child, we need to remember we are talking to a soul. The child may not be able to communicate because the brain and other organs need to develop, but the soul can understand everything.

- By physically hitting a child, we disrespect the soul, and attack its self-respect. Treat the soul with respect and dignity even if the body is young.

- Parents' energy of criticism and anger towards the child created in the name of disciplining him, causes emotional pain to the child. The child carries wounds which can stay for a lifetime.

- Whatever a parent thinks and speaks about the child, becomes the opinion used by the child to create an image of the self.

Empower, Do Not Criticise

Suresh Oberoi: Respect is the basis of human relationships. Comparison and criticism have grown so much today that there is no room for respect. We are rude while correcting others, and exaggerate small things.
Sister Shivani: We must give our feedback and opinion to others, but criticising them is an altogetherly different thing.

SO: We tell others 'you always do this'.
SS: When we say 'you always do this, it is not the first time', we attack the person involved, instead of the act. Even if someone makes a mistake, for example, a person drops and breaks something, what should our feedback be about?

SO: It is a very good point – we do not attack the act but the self-respect of that person.
SS: Right. So, if I make that mistake and you are in a position of authority, you should tell me 'you did not hold it properly'. Most importantly, tell me how to do it right the next time

so that I do not drop it again. It is your role as a friend, parent or authority figure to give your feedback. However, feedback must not be confused with criticism. There is a lot of difference in both the responses. The language of criticism is 'I have taught you so many times but you will ever learn' or 'you always do this'.

SO: We also say 'you have been doing this job for many years, but you have hardly learnt anything'.
SS: Suppose you are angry, and you are criticising me. Anyone witnessing the scene will feel sorry for me, because I will look like a victim. After receiving negative energy and harsh words from you, I will create hurt. But if you compare both the sides – one that is receiving criticism and the one that is criticising – whose loss is greater?

SO: I do not think that a person who criticises others, experiences more pain.
SS: The one who is criticised feels hurt as he receives the negative energy that crushes his self-respect. The other person criticises. How would he feel while constantly creating anger within?
We experience both these roles, so we must try to understand them and heal ourselves. Criticism is violence. One form of violence is physical, the other is through words, thoughts and energy. It is still easier to forget a physical injury, but the hurt caused by negative words and vibrations can be hard to let go of. It could take very long to recover from it.

SO: It could even stay for a lifetime.

SS: If I am criticised, I will experience hurt in that interaction. But the one who criticises me will carry the sanskar in all his interactions. It will become his way of talking in general. It will not be limited just to his words and interactions. Even when alone, he might keep creating thoughts of criticism such as 'he should not have done that' or 'they do not know how to do it' and so on.

SO: Even if he does not criticise people, he will criticise maybe the government, infrastructure, the state of world or even God.

SS: If someone criticises us, we cannot change him because that person is not in our control. But the choice to remain stable in such a situation or to get affected, is ours.

A person who criticises has a subtle fear in his mind – of whether others will obey him or not. This is because criticism is accompanied by an energy of control. Constantly living in anger and fear, there is great pain, so his spiritual battery keeps depleting. Thus, both criticising and receiving criticism deplete our energy.

SO: One may even criticise to cover up one's mistake.

SS: Right.

Parents feel they have to teach their children. Do give them feedback, but first separate the person [child] from his act. Then talk about the action. The more we attack the person, the more his energy depletes. This causes him to repeat his mistake. So, instead of saying 'you do it wrong every time', our intention must be to correct the mistake and avoid it in future. Also, we need not bring references from the past into our conversation because that is no longer in our control.

SO: If I have a habit of criticising, it will create turmoil within. As thoughts affect every cell of the body, my health will go down. I will also receive negative energy from others.

SS: When you criticise me, you experience that negative energy inside you first. When I get hurt by what you say, I will hold you responsible for that feeling. Even in the most beautiful relationship – where no one consciously creates negative thoughts for the other – if someone gets hurt, that negative energy is automatically reflected back to the person who became the stimulus for causing that hurt. So the longer I feel hurt, the longer my negative vibrations will keep flowing back to you. This two-way leakage makes criticism an easy way to discharge soul power.

Though we know that a soul creates its own hurt, but if we become the stimulus for triggering that pain, we will be affected too. So we must pay attention to this fact and make up quickly. Instead of finding fault with the other person and thinking 'I was right, it is the other person's problem that he gets hurt so easily', we must try to resolve things quickly.

Till the time someone stays hurt because of us, our own battery is discharged. This is because if a discharged battery is connected to us, our power goes down too.

SO: If I am convinced that I did the right thing by criticising you, why will my energy be depleted?

SS: Yes, since I am creating hurt inside, and those vibrations are being directed at you.

SO: But I will not receive those vibrations if I believe myself to be right.

SS: You cannot block the vibrations coming from others. You can now choose to respond with positive energy. Otherwise, the more time I take to normalise, the more I will think negatively of you.

SO: The person being criticised must feel depleted. Why should the other person's energy go down?

SS: What happens when someone blesses us?

SO: We feel happy.

SS: Yes. Similarly, if someone sends us energy that is the opposite of blessings, that too will reach us, but it will be a subtle experience.

SO: So a karmic account is created.

SS: Yes, and it is continuous.

Many times we feel if someone is hurt, it is his problem because he has a tendency to feel hurt at the slightest comment. Instead, we can take responsibility of healing him. Otherwise what are relationships meant for? A relationship means understanding each other's sanskars and to be there for each other.

SO: This is being love.

SS: Yes, the moment we radiate love towards the family member who is hurt, it becomes easier for him to come out of pain.

SO: But for that, I must realise that I need to radiate love at that moment.

SS: We can easily make out when the other person is hurt. So why not create a thought or express a gesture so that he gets rid of his pain faster? Otherwise he may take hours, even days, to recover. And for that duration, the negative vibrations coming from that side will continue to reach us.

We need to remember that all of us souls are connected to each other, like one battery is connected to another. So, if the other battery is discharged – which means anyone around us in the family is disturbed – we will feel it too.

SO: A saint had a few disciples, who used to carry pots of water for their morning rituals. The saint had told them that all the pots could be used, except one. One of the disciples got curious, and the next morning filled that particular pot to see what was so special about it. The pot broke. Crying, he confessed his deed to the saint. The saint lovingly explained that the pot was very old, that is why he had asked them not to use it. He said since it was anyway going to break soon, the disciple did not need to bother about it.

I used the same lesson in my life. Once, my daughter broke my favourite cup. Since I had heard this story, I told her that just like human life, everything is bound by its expiry date. She was relieved to hear that. Had I scolded her, she would have gone into a cycle of self-doubt.

SS: What did you do at that moment?

SO: I empowered her.

SS: Now you have to do the same with everyone.

SO: But I did that out of love for my daughter. How can I do it for others?

SS: Remember 'being love'. It means we do not have to make

an effort to love others because love is our original quality that radiates naturally from us to all souls. The energy of love gets blocked when we criticise others. Only one of these two energies can flow at any given moment.

No matter how big the loss, an object is after all just an object. A soul is definitely more important than the mistake it makes. Even if a soul has committed a big sin, the most essential aspect is its empowerment. Once empowered, a soul will not commit the same mistake again.

SO: Even doctors can commit mistakes, sometimes fatal ones.
SS: Yes, it is possible. At that moment, if that doctor is further criticised, his work efficiency will go down drastically. So, however grave the mistake, let us focus on the act and not attack the person. We should tell that person that is not the right way to go about the task. Most importantly, we should tell him how to do it right the next time.

Even in a parent-child relationship, parents usually do not focus on what must be done the next time, but they mostly talk about the past. Never should the conversation focus on something which is over, because that depletes our power. Our conversation should be centred on solution, improvement and empowerment. We should not use punishment, criticism, anger or insult because they make the other person lose his self-esteem. If we take care of these small things, being love will become an enjoyable journey.

SO: When I criticise my wife, do I not I love her?
SS: Every soul radiates love naturally, but the moment it creates criticism, the energy of love is blocked. You cannot

simultaneously love someone and criticise him too. It is like saying 'good morning' when you actually wake up feeling low. Love is the natural energy of the soul. So it does not have to make any effort to radiate it.

SO: This is a great thought. Let us have a meditation on it.

MEDITATION AND REFLECTIONS

The power running this body – beautiful, loving energy – is 'I', the soul that thinks and feels ... love is my natural sanskar ... when I am in the awareness of this original sanskar, love radiates from me to other souls ... it's my perfume of love ... today I pay attention that if someone makes a mistake, I give my opinion or feedback ... I give advice for tomorrow ... but my flow of love remains uninterrupted ... being love and giving feedback ... attention – I am a loveful soul talking to another soul ... Om Shanti.

MANTRAS FOR BEING LOVE

- Giving feedback and opinion is different from criticising. Feedback talks about the deed, criticism attacks the doer.

- When someone makes a mistake, we can explain the mistake and focus on how he can do it better next time. Criticism attacks how he did it wrong in the past also.

- Criticism depletes the energy of the one being criticised and also of the one criticising. The criticiser creates emotions of rejection and anger, and fears 'what if they don't listen to me'.

- If we become the stimulus for others to create hurt, their vibrations will deplete them and us. We need to resolve it immediately so that they get healed and we are protected.

A Child Carries Forward
Past Sanskars

Suresh Oberoi: We have discussed about criticism. Another aspect is comparison. Parents often rate one of their children as superior to the others, and insist that they all match up.
Sister Shivani: We criticise because we do not agree with a particular sanskar of another person. For example, there are two children in a family. One is shy and introverted, the other is outgoing and extroverted. There is likely to be comparison between the two, and the first one could be criticised for being timid. Parents may say 'he is so meek, how will he manage in life ... he cannot even speak confidently to people'.

SO: Is comparison as bad as criticism?
SS: Parents mistake their child to be a clean, fresh slate on which they can write whatever they feel like. They think 'he is MY child so he must have my sanskars'.
Soul consciousness or simply having knowledge about the soul

is the key to resolving many problems. Just remembering that 'my child' is actually a soul who has been on a long journey before being born into the present role, and that he has carried forward several past sanskars, can clear many things.

Even in a single lifetime, a soul has many experiences, faces many situations and acquires several sanskars. Then it leaves that bodily costume, and in the next life it forms new relations, goes through new situations and acquires more sanskars. Thus, a child is a soul that had donned several bodily costumes in its past lives, and has carried forward so many sanskars. But we very easily decide 'MY child should be like me'. We so easily say 'my two children should have similar sanskars'. We forget that they are actually two souls with different backgrounds.

In a past life, a person may have experienced tragedy or betrayal. Suppose there was a natural calamity, such as a flood, due to which a family got scattered, and someone from among them left his mortal coil. In the last scene of life, that soul saw itself losing everything it had – family, achievements and possessions. The last state of that soul was one of pain, fear and loss.

Now, that soul is reborn into another family. In the present life, fear will be that child's predominant sanskar because it has been carried forward. He will cling tightly to his parents, be afraid of being abandoned, and of going out into the dark. He may even be scared of water bodies. The parents will wonder why their child is so timid.

SO: They might even joke 'he is not our child, must have got exchanged with someone else's in the hospital'.

SS: This is because the parents can see so much difference in their sanskars and the child's. If they continue to criticise and ridicule him, the existing sanskars of fear and pain will deepen. On the other hand, if they are spiritually awakened, they will understand that their child is actually a soul whose past is unknown to them.

I once met a mother who said that her child was super intelligent. He had already learnt many languages, his memory power was very high and that he could grasp things quickly. But, she said, she wondered how it was possible, as no one else in her family was so sharp. I told her that the soul had carried forward its past sanskars.

But there was one persistent problem, she said, which was that the child was so afraid of water that he refused to go anywhere near a swimming pool. Nothing could motivate him to take the plunge. One day, she scolded her son rather harshly when he again refused to enter the pool.

When we can accept a soul's outstanding quality, which is different from ours, why do we compare it with others the moment we see its weak sanskars? We must accept its sanskars as a carry forward from its past. The parents' role should be to shower that soul with so much love that it heals its past sanskar of fear. They can protect that soul by not comparing it with others.

When we compare two souls, we forget that each has come from a different past. Suppose, in its previous life, one soul had lived in a metropolis, while the other had lived in a small village. The upbringing, culture and personality of both the souls must have been drastically different. If in their present lives, these two souls are born into the same family, we will wonder how two siblings can be so different from each other.

We need to motivate and empower siblings individually, without comparisons. Otherwise, comparison will become such a deep-rooted sanskar that they will continue to compete and compare themselves with others when they grow up.

SO: I have observed that if siblings are compared frequently, they tend to develop animosity towards each other.

SS: The firstborn receives the attention of the entire family. When he turns a bit older and another child is born into the family, it gets difficult for him to accept if nobody explains anything to him. The only thing he can understand is that his parents' love and attention – which used to be exclusively for him – are now divided. Therefore initially, at least till he develops a better understanding of things, he may not really like his sibling. So sibling rivalry sets in at a very early age. It is the responsibility of the parents to introduce the younger child to the older one in a manner that strikes a balance and creates harmony.

If, however, the two children are frequently compared to each other, then the message that parents unknowingly send across is 'your brother/sister is better than you'. The child receives this message and perceives that his parents love his sibling more than they love him. Comparison becomes painful for the child because of these underlying messages.

SO: Some children complain that their parents do not love them as much as they love their siblings.

SS: A child feels so when his sibling is appreciated, while he is told 'you are not as good as him'. If, later in life, when the child has grown up, parents try to convince him that they love both him and his sibling equally, he may not believe them. This is because by that time, the feeling of having been discriminated against would be deeply ingrained in him.

Comparison is not good for either of the children because it leads one to develop an inferiority complex, while the other gets a superiority complex. So it is important that we recognise the two children as separate individuals.

SO: Comparison is made even with neighbours and relatives.
SS: Yes.

If we want to change a sanskar in a child, or anybody for that matter, we must look at him as an individual. If we want to talk to someone about his weaknesses, it is of utmost importance that we first talk about his good qualities. Otherwise sanskar transformation becomes difficult. This is true for any scenario.

If we tell someone his negative points only, he will feel emotionally low. After that it will get difficult for him to bring about a change in his sanskars. So, first talk about the good qualities of that person. This will boost his self-confidence. As he becomes empowered, he will be ready to make the required changes in himself. If we want to inspire someone to transform his habits, we must set a foundation for it first. But we hardly focus on good qualities. We do not appreciate specialities and take them for granted.

SO: We have got used to criticising, comparing and ridiculing others.
SS: We must change our habits. We should check every day – 'Did I appreciate my staff and family today for any of their special qualities?'

SO: Before that, we must learn to pat our own back.
SS: Appreciation is fuel for transformation. Unless we appreciate, the 'motor' will not be fuelled. Then how will it run? Every soul has specialities. The more we highlight those, the more empowered that soul will be. The more we highlight its negative qualities, the weaker that soul will become.

Usually, when we highlight a person's qualities, we state them in a single sentence. But when we speak about his negatives, we talk in great detail. Let us do it the other way round, as every soul is already familiar with its own weaknesses.

SO: Many a times, grown up children accuse their aged parents of not treating them fairly. Even if parents made a few mistakes, can the children not forgive them?
SS: Without realisation and understanding, the wounds of the past may not be healed.

SO: And what about the good things that their parents have done for them?
SS: Parents do a lot for us, but what are the things we remember?

SO: We mostly remember the instances when we were hurt.
SS: Sometimes, we may acknowledge and appreciate what others have done for us, but if they also criticised or hurt us in the past, the wounds of those bitter experiences may not have healed.
Let us say you gave me many gifts. I am grateful to you for them. But once, you also hit me hard and I was wounded. I did not recover from it, nor did anyone help me to do so. The wound never healed. You may say to me 'why don't you remember the gifts I gave you'. The truth is that the gifts are still there with me, but it is the wound that hurts.

SO: Sometimes we even take the gifts for granted.
SS: Even if that is not the case, the wounds of the past will continue to hurt unless they are healed.
Many adults are stuck in the past. Their body has matured over the years, but the soul within is still that same child. The wounds of childhood or the past will not heal just because the bodily

costume has grown older. They can be healed neither through intelligence nor education, but only through spiritual wisdom. Even successful senoir professionals complain about their past because the wounds of the soul have no connection with how many degrees one earns or one's physical age. So we must be careful with the way we talk and behave with others, as they may carry the hurt for long.

Also, let us check within. If I have wounds inside, let me heal them today because they will not heal on their own, and the pain might become chronic. For healing the self, I must remind myself 'even if my parents did not treat me well, their intention for me was not bad ... they did not harm me intentionally ... I got hurt then because I did not understand many things, but today I do'. This is me talking to myself and healing my own wounds.

SO: If the parents' intention was good, why did they criticise or hurt the child?

SS: Their intention was good but their approach was not. It is like you gifted me something but handed it over to me rudely. As a result, I felt hurt. When I look back today, I can tell myself 'whatever be the case, the gift was good'. This is healing the self to finish the hurt that I have been holding on to for years. There is another way to heal the self. It is to realise the fact that, though ideally a parent soul should have an equal relationship with all the children, but that may not be the case in reality.

SO: Because all the children souls have a different past karmic account with that parent soul. One may have been born to seek revenge, the other one may have come to shower love.

192

SS: Yes, that is it. On surface, it is a parent-child relationship. But actually the parent souls have a different karmic account with each of the souls who have come into their life as children. So the parents' interaction with all their children will be different. This is a very important aspect that can help us to heal ourselves. With this knowledge we will no longer complain about our parents being partial.

SO: It is difficult to imagine that somebody in my family did something to me because of our past karmic account.
SS: I know of a person whose parents stay with him. He does everything for them and with a lot of love. However, it is his brother who gets all the appreciation from the parents, and this has been happening for years.

SO: One is serving, the other is being rewarded for it!
SS: The one serving the parents will have to remember the following – 'I have a karmic account [give and take of energy] from past lives with my parent souls ... if I am not given any credit for my efforts, that is also part of that ongoing karmic account ... and, if my brother is getting credit for it despite putting in little effort, that is also part of his karmic account with my parent souls'. When we understand the knowledge about the soul and karma, several questions on our mind are resolved. It becomes easier to heal ourselves and accept reality.

SO: All this is very interesting. If we understand this knowledge, being love will become so much easier for us.
SS: Yes. When we understand spiritual truths, our energy of love

is no longer blocked by questions such as 'why is this happening to me' or 'why does he behave like this despite being family'. We now know that any relationship is actually a connection between souls.

SO: Things have become a lot clearer now.

MEDITATION AND REFLECTIONS

I, the soul, am on a long journey ... I have taken several costumes, faced many situations and formed several sanskars ... today I am in this bodily costume ... whatever relationships I have, I have met all of these souls before ... parent, child, brother, sister – I have a past karmic account with everyone ... it is becoming easier to understand my relationships, their energy and others' behaviour towards me ... because now I understand that these are not just roles but souls whom I had met before ... the exchange of energy had started before, the same karmic account is being continued ... I have started getting the answers to my questions ... my pain has healed ... the energy of love, which was previously blocked, now flows naturally ... Om Shanti.

MANTRAS FOR BEING LOVE

- In each birth the soul has had different parents, environment and situations and so different sanskars.

- The soul carrying sanskars of many births is born as a child and we expect the child to be like the parents. Sanskars of the family do influence the child, but most of his sanskars will be what he carried forward from previous lives.

- Comparison causes the child to feel that the parents love his sibling more than him. This causes low self-esteem and sibling rivalry.

- When we want others to change their sanskars, we need to empower them. Empowerment comes from appreciating and highlighting their beautiful sanskars.

Respecting Our Choices

Suresh Oberoi: Someone sent me a beautiful message. It says, 'The attitude you have as a parent is what your kids will learn. They do not remember what you teach, they remember what you are.'
Sister Shivani: Very beautiful.

SO: I will share another one – 'Do not worry that your children never listen to you, worry that they are always watching you.'
SS: These two sayings bring out the essence of whatever we have discussed till now.

People may not remember what we tell them. This is especially true for children whom we start training about right and wrong from a very young age, when they are most vulnerable and receptive. The message says – Do not worry that they are not listening to you, worry that they are watching you. Let us add another sentence to the quote – 'The most important thing is they are always around you.' Even if you are doing something they cannot see, they are definitely absorbing your vibrations.

SO: How is that?

SS: Whatever we think and believe is part of our vibrations. We may not say it, they may not hear us or see what we are doing or thinking. But we must be careful as they are around us and consuming our vibrations.

SO: One of my relatives consulted a specialist to see what he could do to make things better for his child, who had of late become irritable, fearful and had lost appetite. The doctor said, 'You will have to change yourself because you and your child are one.' I now understand what he meant.

SS: Yes, remember that a child catches and consumes the parents' thoughts and beliefs and makes them his own. He may not obey them, and may even forget the things told by them. But he definitely catches their attitude. It is important to realise this aspect because many times what parents believe, what they think, and what say do not match with each other. They may mistakenly think that others can only hear what they speak, and their thoughts remain hidden.

Sometimes parents teach their child 'do not lie, honesty is the best policy', while their personal belief system is 'in today's times, one cannot survive without lying at times'. The parents' belief system is carried into their attitude and energy field. That is what the child catches, even if he forgets what the parents have taught him.

SO: If we tell someone that his clothes do not suit him, he may feel hurt. Must honesty be spoken with a certain tact?

SS: The most important and desired aspect in our relationships is integrity. Integrity means that we speak the truth with each other. But before that we must speak the truth with ourselves. Check – are my thoughts, words and actions in harmony with each other? If not, there will be conflict inside me because of disharmony between these three energy fields. Then it will not be possible for me to create harmony outside, and the qualities of trust, honesty and loyalty will be missing in my relationships. How can I be honest with you if I am not honest with myself? This is just like I cannot respect someone if I do not respect myself, or I cannot love another person if I do not love myself. So integrity is important.

Now let us take your example. If we tell someone that his dress is not suiting him, he may feel bad. This is because others have become dependent on our opinion for their happiness. They wait for our approval and appreciation. This applies to even bigger decisions in life.

SO: My grandchild does that. Even if just jumps, he wants us to appreciate him.
SS: We learnt it all back then in childhood. That's why the message is so important.

Let us take the same example again. We buy a new dress, wear it to a function, and then wait for others to appreciate it. If someone does not say anything about our dress, we ourselves intentionally bring up that topic for conversation. We literally stand there waiting for others' appreciation, because without that we are not sure of our own choice. We feel validated only when people make us feel so. If others appreciate us, our happiness index shoots up, irrespective of whether they mean it or not. This means our happiness is dependent upon public opinion.

SO: We actors get used to hearing words like 'excellent shot' from our directors after we enact a scene. But, sometimes, if a director is not that expressive and just says 'okay' after each shot, we begin to feel unsure of ourselves. We think maybe we have not performed well.

SS: This means when others do not appreciate us, we start to doubt ourselves. Whether it is a film scene or life, we should have faith in ourselves. We should be able to judge our own performance, irrespective others applauding it.

SO: Even when applauded, I sometimes ask for a retake if I am not satisfied with my performance.

SS: In this case you are appreciated but you feel you could still do better. This is easier. The other situation is difficult – when you do not receive appreciation for your work. Then you have to keep the faith that your performance was the best you could have given at that time. This can be applied to any situation in life. Let us get back to the previous example. Your question was whether we should speak the truth or not while giving an opinion. Usually people lie and say 'you are looking very beautiful' even when they feel otherwise because they do not want to hurt the other person. If a person says 'this dress is not looking good on you', what will happen to the receiver's happiness index?

SO: It will go down.

SS: This is because the happiness index became high or low on the basis of others' opinion. If something is dependent on others' opinion, it will rise when the opinion is positive and fall when the opinion is not so positive. This is because our remote control of emotions is in someone else's hands.

Is it necessary that the dress one chooses will be liked by everyone?

SO: No, it is neither necessary nor possible.
SS: Why so?

SO: Because everyone's choice is unique.
SS: Yes, this is it. We must always hold on to this truth that everyone's thinking, choice and understanding of right and wrong is different. And that is why everyone's opinion will be different. When someone disapproves of our dress, what should our state of mind be at that time?

SO: We should still like it because we bought it ourselves, with our own choice.
SS: We will be able to face criticism with a stable mind, only if we have a habit of being stable when we are appreciated. If appreciation gives us an ego boost, we are sure to experience a low when faced with criticism. Spirituality teaches us to stay stable in both scenarios.

SO: Is it possible?
SS: It is possible.
Let us say you bought a dress according to your choice and as per your definition of 'nice'. If someone does not like your dress, you should respect his choice. Understand that his choice is different from yours, and that it is perfectly okay to have a difference of opinion. However, the problem occurs when we do not remember all of this upon coming face to face with such a situation, and we start doubting ourselves immediately.

SO: Maybe when I bought that dress, I was not too sure about it myself. Now even others are adding to that doubt.

SS: See, we start drifting into doubt so soon. The moment we receive criticism, we start needing affirmation. So we will ask two more people 'how do you like this dress'. If they say 'it looks really nice, why do you think it is not suiting you' we start blaming those who had criticised our choice. We disrespect them because we did not respect our own choice in the first place. When we disrespect our own choice because of others' opinion, it is not possible to respect others.

Let us go back into our field of action understanding that everybody's choice and opinion are different. If choices of food and dress vary, will our ways of thinking not be different?

SO: Surely they will be different.

SS: This is because our choices and thinking are based on our sanskars, which are different.

Everyone is entitled to his opinion. Even if others do not approve of our choice, we should stand by it. Otherwise we give others a subtle message that they should lie to us and give a favourable opinion about our choice, because we do not have the power to listen to the truth. We accept those lies in order to please ourselves. We are thus basing our self-respect on lies – that is deep much our feeling good about ourselves has become dependent on other people.

SO: Does it mean we do not know ourselves?

SS: We simply do not trust ourselves. To know ourselves is still a deeper subject. But today we do not even stand by our basic choices.

SO: But what is wrong in taking others' opinion? For example, I might take my driver's opinion while buying a car.

SS: There you are seeking an advice, and we do it all the time. But here we are talking about a decision we have already taken.

Suppose you took a decision in life which was not approved by anybody else.

SO: But I must have a reason for making that choice.
SS: Yes. If you are comfortable with the decision and liking it, and if you are not hurting others, then you are entitled to it.

SO: When any of my family or friends go out in the cold, I ask them to be well-covered. Sometimes they refuse to do so, saying it would affect their fashion quotient. They are ready to compromise on their health.
SS: We are not thinking of our own comfort.

SO: It means we have become so weak that we are literally begging for appreciation. We complain when nobody appreciates the expensive jewellery we wear to a function.
SS: In fact, we may no longer like that jewellery worth lakhs, simply because no one else appreciated. This is a weakness. Clothes and accessories are small things. But when we take bigger decisions in life and do not trust ourselves enough, or if we, do not have integrity, we become dependent on others' opinion. Remember, people's opinions are bound to vary.

SO: Sometimes, people tell their friends 'why did you get married to this person – you are so good looking and your spouse is no match for you'. That opinion may adversely affect that person permanently.
SS: So always remember – my choice, my decision.
For example, when I decided to join the Brahma Kumaris, none

of my close friends supported me. In fact, they criticised me and tried to convince me out of it. They also thought something was wrong. At such times, it is important that we are convinced about the correctness of our own decision.

It is possible that tomorrow one of our decisions may go wrong, but it's fine. All our decisions cannot always be right. But they are our decisions, and we took them because we were convinced about them. We are responsible for their consequences and should be ready to face them. If we do not take our own decisions, we will not be able to develop our decision-making power.

MEDITATION AND REFLECTIONS

Let me look at myself ... I – the soul – the sentient energy, beautiful being ... all my thoughts and sanskars are according to my perspectives ... situations in my life are based on my past karmic account ... my thoughts and decisions today are my present karma ... I can take others' advice, but after that the decisions is my own ... I respect and trust my decision ... I respect my choice ... my choice is not dependent on others' opinion ... my happiness is not dependent on others' appreciation ... I live in self-respect ... respecting my own choices and decisions in life ... I am ready to create a change ... Om Shanti.

MANTRAS FOR BEING LOVE

- Children may not listen to what we say to them but they will always be influenced by our belief systems and attitude, because that creates our vibrations.

- To have integrity in our relationships, we need to have integrity within ourselves. Integrity means our thoughts, words and actions are in harmony.

- When we depend on people's appreciation for our performance, choices and decisions, our self-respect becomes dependent on their approval.

- Different people have different perspectives and therefore different choices. So people will have different definitions of right and wrong, good and bad, like and dislike. We cannot expect them to always approve of our choices and decisions.

Transformation From Inside Out

Suresh Oberoi: Love is our innate quality. Yet, interestingly, through this series, we are trying to explore ways to revive it. I sometimes struggle so much to be my true self that I feel unsure about love being my original nature.

Sister Shivani: This is because we have been acting against our original quality of love for a long time now. Let us look at it in this way – health is natural to us but we catch diseases if we do not take care of ourselves. Then, over time, we start to believe that perfect health is unachievable. Similar is the case with being love. Today we have become so dependent on others' appreciation for feeling our original quality that we feel sure only when they approve of our choices.

SO: You have always insisted that irrespective of how others behave with us, we must protect ourselves through the choices we make on the journey of life. After all, an expert driver not only drives smoothly but also saves himself from rash drivers on the road.

SS: Yes. And it is most important not to get stuck with every person coming our way. Instead of keeping attention on ourselves while driving, we start commenting on others' driving style, we are bound to meet with accidents. We should apply the same wisdom to our life.

SO: Love is natural to us, but instead of staying in this awareness, we get influenced by almost everyone around us. Why does this happen?

SS: Because we have handed over the remote control of our lives to others. It all started from childhood.

When people have visitors at home, they tell their child to perform in front of them – dance, recite a poem, or show what he's achieved at school. After the performance, everyone appreciates the child. It is good to appreciate, but what is being appreciated – the performance.

Let us say, we tell the child 'you danced very well'. But we actually say 'very good boy'. The child processes this information as – 'when I perform well, I am appreciated, and that is when everyone feels that I am a good person'. This becomes his belief system. Had we said 'you are a good artiste', it would have been a different thing.

Similarly, when a child does something that elders do not approve of, instead of disagreeing with the act, they say 'you are a bad boy/girl'.

SO: When someone serves a nicely-cooked dish, instead of praising the food, family members say 'what a nice person'. They do not say 'the dish is tasty'.

SS: Yes. These things may seem to be small but they carry significant messages. Appreciation creates a form of emotional programming for the person receiving it. He tends to believe that he is a good person only when he performs well and is appreciated for it.

SO: And when he does not perform well, he considers himself not good enough.
SS: Yes, because people never say 'bad performance', they instead label him as 'bad person'. Bad performance is not an issue, because there will be ups and downs everywhere. The problem is to attach the self-respect of a person with the quality of his performance, or to look at the performance as a measure for his goodness.

SO: We do not separate the talent from the person.
SS: The risk of not separating the person and his act is that it makes people dependent on others' appreciation in order to feel good about themselves. This is true especially for children. We have discussed that the parents' opinion becomes the child's introduction to himself. When parents say 'you are a very good child', the child programmes his mind in this way: 'When I do something that makes my parents happy, they tell me I am a good child ... so to become a good child, I have to perform well ... that is when I will be appreciated ... when they don't appreciate me, it means I am not a good person.' This conditioning stays with the child from a very young age and it is very risky.

SO: When our dog would not obey a command, we would say 'bad boy'. But our dog trainer said, "Do not be angry with your pet. Instead, just say 'bad habit' because this gives him the message 'that the habit is bad, not him'."

SS: This is so beautiful – bad habit, not bad boy. There is so much difference in the message.

SO: That pet led a happy life with us. In fact, he lived five years longer than was expected.

SS: This means that a good boy with bad habit is fine. Now we have to use the same wisdom with everyone around us. If it can impact a pet so deeply, then just imagine how much human souls would be affected by it.

If parents try and change their own conditioning, their family's conditioning will change automatically. It is important that parents communicate to their children that even if they make mistakes, they are still good individuals. This is because any soul is originally beautiful.

When a child is born, he is completely innocent. But by putting labels like 'bad child' on him, elders lower his self-respect. That is why he continues to look for others' appreciation even when he grows up. This is the reason people are so dependent on public opinion. This is also why people lie to please each other.

When we lie to please each other, we add lie, cheating and manipulation to the foundation of our relationship. And because truth is absent in the roots of our relationships today, they are weak and break down easily. If I know what I need to say in order to please you, and what I can say to disturb you, then your remote control is in my hands. I can manipulate you the way I want. People are manipulating each other's emotions so much today.

SO: On my birthday I received many gifts and cards. But the

one that touched me the most was a two-line note from my mother. There was so much purity and truth in those simple words, while many of the other messages were not even in the sender's own handwriting.

SS: Why are people doing all this? Just to please each other. Why is it important to please each other? To get appreciation in return. Why is it important to be appreciated? Since they believe that it makes them a good person.

This means that everyone is constantly wanting appreciation from each other. Now, we need to revisit this emotional programming because. We may be happy receiving appreciation, but we might get acutely disturbed on receiving a different response from others. We have to be firm on one point – that everyone has his own opinion and way of thinking, because everyone's sanskars are different. So, if another person expresses an opinion which does not match with ours, we should not get disturbed. We should respect him and his opinion, even if our view points are completely opposite to each other. It is not necessary that his opinion matches with our definition of right. When we remain so stable in our mind, people will start speaking the truth to us.

We also have to be firm on another aspect. We must speak only what we think. There is no need to please others with lies. If we lie to others, it will have a negative effect on our relationship with ourselves.

SO: If my daughter bakes a cake for the first time and asks for my opinion, is it a lie if I appreciate her although it is not good?

SS: It is a lie when you think one thing and say another.

SO: My reason behind appreciating her is to encourage her, otherwise she may feel disheartened.

SS: Perfect. We must encourage others, motivate and appreciate them, but we must also maintain the integrity of our thoughts and words.

For example, if we don't like someone's dress, we can create the thought 'it may not go with my taste but it may be to the liking of that person'. Then we can appreciate honestly in words 'as per your liking, this dress is fine for you'. This way we can maintain harmony between our thoughts and words. But if we are thinking 'what a bad choice' and saying 'you have a great taste', it is risky because our words are contradicting our thoughts. We are sending across two messages to the other side.

SO: Is this the reason we are moving away from our original nature of love?

SS: If there is no integrity between our thoughts and words, there cannot be harmony between our energies, as we are not being true to ourselves. So even if we want to convert something – i.e. convey a truth but not be rude – then we must choose the right way of doing it. While giving our feedback, it is important to state that the opinion is 'according to me'.

Suppose you wear a white dress to a dinner party. Someone comes and says to you 'in my opinion, one should not wear white to a dinner; black is a better option'. That is his choice. Now the ball is in your court. You can say 'black may be a good colour to wear to dinner, but I like white'. This is respecting each other's opinion. This way our energies will be in harmony – both within and while interacting with others.

Let us start with ourselves. Let us speak only what we think.

If something is not appropriate for speaking, it is not worth thinking either. Underline this. If we do not say something because we do not want to hurt others, we must avoid thinking it too, because the vibrations of our thoughts reach them. Also, those thoughts create negative energy inside us.

If we have a habit of thinking one thing and saying another in order to cover it up, a lot will pile up inside us. Then one day there will surely come some stimulus which will break open that inner cupboard. If that happens, others will be shocked to hear us speak. We ourselves may not be able to believe our own ears. So there is no point hoarding everything inside as that will create disharmony within us and in our relationships. Even if our inner cupboard remains closed and hidden from others, its vibrations definitely reach them.

SO: If someone has hurt me and I find him really horrible, how should I deal with it?

SS: If you hold on to the thought 'he is a horrible person', you will be the first one to feel the pain because you are the creator of that negative thought. Now change your thought and think: 'He did whatever he thought was right, even if it was totally wrong according to me ... I may not approve of it ever, but he acted according to his sanskars and perspective ... that episode is over now, I need not cling to that pain any longer.'

In our close relationships, we can even communicate to the other person 'your ACTION is hurting me' and not 'you are hurting me'. We can tell him 'if you change, it will be comfortable for me'. In case he does not change his act, we will have to learn to accept it because we cannot keep holding on to pain.

We must never send two conflicting messages to the other person–

one as thought, another one through words. If I text you two different messages on your phone – one saying 'horrible person', the other one, which reaches you just a second later, saying 'wonderful person', how will you feel? In many relationships, people talk very sweetly to us but we do not receive good vibrations from them. Those relationships cannot be strong.

We know how to convert but we are converting at the level of words while still holding on to the negativity inside. If we really have to convert, let us do it at the level of thoughts because if we keep our mind clean, there will be harmony between our thoughts, words and actions. This will make our relationships harmonious. If our thoughts are clean and pure, there will be no risk of our inner cupboard suddenly breaking open one day and a lot of clutter (unpleasant thoughts and words) spilling out. Life will become relaxed, easy and uncomplicated if we stay honest.

If we do not hold on to any negative thoughts, our vibrations will be clear. As a result, we will not need to make any extra effort to speak sweetly and softly. The change will be automatic because we would have already worked on our thoughts. What is within flows out naturally. If we are clean inside, even our criticism does not hurt others. This is because the vibrations reaching them are pure and powerful.

MANTRAS FOR BEING LOVE

- When a child performs or shows his achievements, everyone appreciates him and calls him a good child. At that age, he develops the belief that when he performs and people appreciate him, then he is a good person.

- As a child, whenever we made a mistake, people criticised us, the doer, and not the deed. Our self-esteem became dependent on public opinion. We started to believe that if people appreciate us, we are a good person, and if people criticise us, we are a bad person.

- Even if habits are wrong, even if the present sanskars are negative, originally each soul is pure and beautiful. Separate the person from his habits. This will empower the soul to emerge its purity and that will help it to change its habits.

- When we give our opinion to others, our thoughts and words should be in harmony. If we create negative thoughts but speak sweet words, it is conflicting energy. Convert at the level of thoughts, not words. This is integrity.

Act According to Your Capacity

Suresh Oberoi: One of our biggest challenges today is the thought – 'what will people say'. We worry about what others might think about the size of our car, the clothes we wear or the cutlery we use. If we pay as much attention to being love, it will bring great benefit to us.

Sister Shivani: Since childhood we have programmed our mind to worry about people's responses. If we feel good about ourselves only when others appreciate us, then not just our work but our self-esteem becomes dependent on them. Then public opinion starts to matter a lot to us. If we check thoroughly, we will find that we are constantly looking for others' approval from the beginning of the day – right from the time we select what to wear for the day.

SO: We all want to look perfect when we leave home in the morning, but we have never really given a thought to what people might say if we go out without a smile on our face or love in our heart.

SS: We think people love, respect and accept us on the basis of what we wear, how we talk, what we do and our social status. So our focus is always on the external dimensions.

Worrying about people's opinion has become such a deep-rooted sanskar that we take even crucial decisions of our life based on it. The general feeling is that since we live in a society, social approval is a must. We must take care not to hurt others. But beyond that it is fine to base our decisions on our comfort level and the comfort of our family.

Being love is blocked when our mind is not at peace. It is difficult to be peaceful if our mental state is dependent on others' responses as opinions are bound to vary. Even if we try our best, some will appreciate our decisions, others will criticise them.

SO: There is a popular fable about a father and son who were travelling with their donkey. On seeing them, some passers-by commented that it was shameful that the young boy was riding the donkey while his old father had to trudge along on foot. Upon hearing this, the father and son switched positions. Sometime later, others on the way said that it was cruel of the father to make his son walk while he himself rode comfortably. This time, both father and son got on to the donkey's back. But people still found fault with them, saying it was wrong that they were burdening the poor beast so much!

SS: We have all read and enjoyed the story. Its powerful message is that after trying all the possible combinations between the father, son and the donkey, there was always someone who found fault with them. This means that the characters in the story should have acted according to their own comfort level rather than that of others. This is applicable to our lives too. Each one gives an opinion through the filter of his own sanskars, so that opinion is right according to his perspective.

Let us take your example. If you travel in a small car rather than the big, expensive one you have, one person may frown upon it and say, 'Such a renowned family travelling in such a small car!' At the same time, someone else may appreciate your modesty. Remember that both of them are giving opinions based on their own sanskars.

SO: Another person may think of us as misers who keep their expensive car safe at home.

SS: Right. As there are different people – i.e. different souls with different sanskars – so there are different opinions. If we take into consideration everyone's opinion to run our lives, we cannot be at peace.

Suppose someone tells you 'white does not suit you, you should wear blue instead'. You listen to him and change. Then someone else says 'black would look much better on you' and you promptly follow his advice too. Then a third person says 'black is a bit too dark, maybe you should tone it down to grey'. If you keep changing according to others' opinions, what would happen to your personal choice? It is okay to seek others' advice, but it is certainly not okay to run our life according to their opinions in order to please them.

When our sense of satisfaction is founded on satisfying others, it becomes impossible to attain it. There is great liberation for us if we change this sanskar. It does not mean we should not live with others. We should live with them and do the best we can for them. But for the sake of personal stability, we should run our lives according to our own rights, wrongs, comfort level and capacity.

SO: If we are so individualistic in our approach, will we not become egoistic and rigid? If, for example, I tell you that your capacity is much beyond what you think, what is wrong with that?

SS: That is an advice; it is a separate thing. It is okay to seek advice and feedback but after that I should take my own decision and act upon it.

Let us take the example you mentioned initially. Your decision to use simple cutlery or silverware should be taken according to your capacity. It should not be taken in anticipation of the opinion that others will form about you, on the basis of your presentation. Sometimes we do things that are beyond our capacity.

SO: Yes, sometimes people borrow things from neighbours in order to impress their guests.

SS: We do more than our capacity because we are hungry for others' appreciation. Our mind will not be at peace while seeking such appreciation or even after that. And when the mind is not stable, our original energy of love will be blocked. So we should act according to what we feel is right intuitively, naturally, and according to our own wisdom.

SO: The world has become a place which does not let you change, even if you want to. When I take small steps to let go of my ego, such as when I fly economy class, the airline staff asks me if I want to change my seat.

SS: It is okay. We know that this old sanskar of 'what people will say' is very powerful in people around us.

SO: Once, when my flight landed, I carried my own luggage. A co-passenger asked me why I did that. I told him that I was trying to change and win over my mind. He said I would have to undo a lot within me and that would take a lot of effort.
SS: If you try to change any of your sanskars, your mind will resist it initially. In the given situation, it will think 'what will people say if I travel economy class'. But it is not really so difficult to change ourselves.

We, however, do not need to make such adjustments with our comfort level deliberately and travel by economy class purposely. The point is that we should act according to the situation and our capacity at any given time.

SO: Yes, it does not make sense to discard the comforts we have. This was just a personal exercise, a sort of 'spiritual homework' that I was trying to do.
I know a lot of renowned people who live humbly. Their work speaks for them.
SS: More than their work, people are respected for their values and principles in life.

If we achieve great success in our career but our values and principles are of another quality, then we will not win others' respect. People may still offer us a seat, even salute us, but the respect that is evoked naturally, will be missing. The salute that comes from within is not meant for our possessions, position or success. We earn that for our qualities.

SO: When we go to a hotel, the doorman actually salutes our car and not us. If we want to be truly respected, we have to rise above all this.

SS: Yes, and the more we rise above all these things, the more we will conquer our ego and break the barriers that we have created for ourselves. Whenever we notice a positive shift in ourselves, we should pat our back. We must tell ourselves that it is not so difficult to change or to break out of self-made boxes of limited thinking.

SO: I have lived in too small a box of limited thinking, myself. Earlier, I used to wait for the porter to come all the way to the plane just to carry my handbag.

SS: While doing all that, what was your mental antenna catching? You were thinking 'people are watching me'. In the confines of your home, you will lift even heavy luggage without any hesitation, because you know that no one is looking.

SO: I had developed a liking to be treated royally. I picked up the habit from some of my seniors.

SS: In your mind you defined a 'movie star' as someone who did not do a particular set of things, such as carry his own luggage. You programmed your mind with the thought 'when people behave in this manner, they receive others' respect and appreciation. If they do not do certain things, they are not considered elite'. All the conflict lies with this mental programming.

SO: Now I travel by economy class deliberately.

SS: Simplicity is the easiest way to keep our mind at peace.

We need to eat well, wear neat clothes but stay simple. Most importantly, we should think simple. If we are mentally entangled all the time and base our self-respect on others' opinions, it becomes difficult to sustain our peace of mind.

Today, many of us are taking major decisions in life, such as those about career or relationships, according to others' opinions. Many times these decisions go wrong. Let us take the example of a student choosing his career path. He will choose it on the basis of two main factors – his sanskars and karmic account. He will intuitively get pulled towards that side. People around him will give their opinion on the basis of their own sanskars. Even if all of them are right, it is the student who has to ultimately adopt the profession. So the decision must be taken on the basis of his choice and capacity.

After taking any decision, we will receive both positive and negative responses from others, so it is best that we take the final call based on our own comfort and the comfort of our family. This approach will make our lives very simple and easy.

SO: Yes, today my life is simple. In the 1970s, most of my family and friends told me not to make a career in films. They said the industry was not suitable for a person belonging to a business household.

SS: If you had accepted their opinions, your life would have been very different from what it is today.

SO: I would have been very unhappy. Watching other actors perform in films, I would have felt miserable about myself.

SS: Because you would have suppressed your intuition for the sake of public opinion.

Today we are performing so many rituals, following traditions, and even organising prayer services just based on the thinking 'if I don't do it, what will others say'. Some people find it hard to fast for nine days during Navratras due to health reasons. They still do it because they want a favourable public opinion. If we do even such pious things out of social compulsion, we will not be able to sustain the pure intention behind them. Our intention will be adulterated.

SO: I like the word intention.

SS: It is the intention behind the karma. If we are organising a *jaagran, kirtan* or prayer service in our house, we should do it out of love for God and because of our relationship with Him. We should feel like doing it.

SO: Sometimes people brag about the elite guests who visited their home during a *puja* or about how lavish their arrangement was.

SS: In such a case, a person would feel nice about organising a prayer service, but that would only be a 'feel good factor'. He may not experience the soul empowerment that the act was meant to give.

We are going away from our originality today because we are not checking the intention behind our actions. That is why people say there is so much show-off in the world today. Everyone is trying to make things perfect on the outside, doing things beyond their capacity. We are hardly checking the intention behind the actions. If our intention is to get people's appreciation, or if fear of what others might say drives us, we will not be able to stay happy. Then we will not be able to radiate our originality.

Let us work on this sanskar today. It's a big blockage for being love and is relatively easier to change. Whatever we do in our lives – from the small things to the bigger decisions we make – we must act according to what we feel is right for us and our family. We can start with it as a one-month experiment. Then life will become very simple and beautiful.

MANTRAS FOR BEING LOVE

- If we become dependent on people's approval for taking decisions in life, we may end up with decisions that are not right for us.

- Different souls, because of different past and present sanskars, will always have different opinions in the same situation. It is not possible to get everyone's approval on any choice we make.

- If needed, take advice and opinion from family and friends before taking a decision. But do not make choices to please people or get their appreciation.

- The original qualities of the soul radiate when we are calm and stable. When we keep getting affected by others' opinions, we will remain disturbed. This blocks our energy of love.

Everyone Has a Unique Journey

Suresh Oberoi: I find the discussion on parent-child relationship very interesting. Ever since I became a grandfather, I have had many new experiences. At home, there is a sweet competition between us grandparents about who is loved more by our grandchildren. It is possible that the sense of competition is instilled in children by parents and family members.
Sister Shivani: There is no such thing as 'sweet competition'.

SO: But parents often ask their children, 'Who do you love more – mummy or daddy?'
SS: This is very damaging. There is really nothing sweet about it as we are teaching a child the concept of loving more, loving less. The child is otherwise totally ignorant about it.

SO: That is bad. I never realised that.
SS: Things said in a lighter vein may actually become the child's reality. When parents ask the child to choose his favourite, who is the competition actually between?

SO: Husband and wife.

SS: Yes. This competition can be between a daughter-in-law and mother-in-law too.

SO: It could be between grandparents or even among the staff.

SS: Yes, the sanskar of competition is very subtle. We think it is present only at workplace, in the professional and business world, or that it dwells in the desire to have a greater social status than others. But there can be competition at a subtle level even at home. Just as you mentioned, it can be over who the child listens to more, or who takes better care of the house. When we think we can do things better than others, at that moment we do not create the right energy. We subtly block the energy of love for ourselves and others.

A lady once told me that her entire day was spent in taking care of her child, but her husband never valued her efforts. When, one day, her husband offered to take care of the child for some time, she thought to herself, 'Now let us see how he manages everything.' This means she had already created a subtle thought that he should not succeed, as this would make him realise her worth. What kind of energy did she create for her husband and child? This is a sort of competition that family members indulge in, unconsciously.

SO: What if the husband was able to look after the child properly?

SS: Perhaps, then she would not be happy about it. Sometimes we are confident that no one can do a particular job better than us. If someone even from among our family members does that job well, we are not able to accept or appreciate it. We should be aware of our own thoughts, and check if we feel as good about others doing well in life, as we feel about ourselves. This is how we can create the energy of love for all, including our family members.

So, competition can never be nice.

SO: It all starts right from school when students compete for different activities.

SS: That is a different thing because there we compete intentionally as we are aware of it. It gets risky when competition becomes our sanskar and goes into an automatic mode where we lose awareness of operating through it. After that, we do not realise who we are competing against. Even a parent and child can get caught in competition.

Let us take an example. A father sets up a successful business empire after years of toil. Later, say after 25 years, his son comes to lead the organisation. If the son is able to make a positive difference to the set-up using his new skills and is appreciated for it, or even if he is liked more by the staff, then the father may not subtly like it. At that moment, the father is in competition with his own son!

If the staff at home obeys the wife more and the husband does not like that, it means there is a subtle competition between the couple. Competition means we are not happy about others doing better than us. It is the easiest way to block love.

SO: What does being love teach us?

SS: Being love teaches us that if someone's relations with others are better in comparison to us, it is very good. For example, if others are able to take care of your grandchild better than you, that is very sweet and nice of them.

SO: If a daughter-in-law feels that her child is loved more by her mother-in-law, she should be happy. After all, it is her own child who is receiving the benefit.

SS: Yes sure, but due to the sanskar of competition she ends up thinking 'why did I not do it'. The language of competition is 'who is better, who is number one'.

SO: I was a child when my sister-in-law passed away. It was my very first experience of losing someone close, so I was in great pain. For some reason, the funeral pyre did not light up at first when the last rites were being performed. The family pundit then intervened and rearranged the wood, after which it instantly caught fire. The pundit then started bragging about how he was better than others.

SS: When competition becomes our sanskar, it operates on automatic mode. Then we are no longer able to judge if our actions are suitable for the place, relations or occasion, or if they are affecting our own family. We must take utmost care of our sanskars as they get passed on to the younger generation. A child has no sense of competition and he learns it from his surroundings.

SO: If I do not teach my children to compete, they may lag behind in the race of life.

SS: We really need to rethink the concept of competition.

Parents must encourage children to do their best and then evaluate their performance. If children are unable to perform up to their capacity, they can be encouraged to work harder the next time. But that's not what parents usually do. For example, when a child comes home after taking an exam, his parents' first question is 'how did it go'. The child answers 'it went well'. Their second question is 'how did others perform'. It is an irrelevant question but they ask it. If the child answers 'others performed quite well, too', then parents worry that their son or daughter might lag behind the rest of the class.

If the child says 'others did not perform so well', then the parents are more relaxed. This means that parents are not focusing on the child's individual capacity. It is they who instil in him the feeling that he must outperform others.

Every child has his own capacity and level of intelligence. Be it studies, sports or other fields, the parents' role should be to harness his potential and enhance it. But when they compare him with others, there could be two losses. They could either fall short of utilising his full potential or they try to stretch him way beyond his capacity. Most importantly, they will end up ingraining in him the sanskar that his aim is – to be better than others, rather than to be his best. This will only bring dissatisfaction.

SO: But if we do not outdo others, we could fail in life.

SS: Can we not focus on our own capacity, instead? We can take inspiration from others' performance and use that to enhance our own. But if we always strive to overtake them, where will we end up? If we overtake one, there will still be someone else ahead of us. We will then want to surpass him, and then the next one and so on. As a result we will never be happy or satisfied.

Even in sports or in an actual race, where we are competing consciously, we are told to focus only on our own performance. What will happen if we keep looking here and there?

SO: The lack of concentration will slacken our pace.

SS: Also, emotions such as fear and anxiety will be created, so our efficiency will go down. On the other hand, if we concentrate on our game, we will perform to the best of our capacity.

SO: In a race, if we lose focus even for a second, it's all over for us.

SS: If even a second's distraction can make us lose a race, imagine what we would be doing to ourselves if we kept looking here and there throughout our lives to see who is outpacing us.

Now let us look at it spiritually. Spirituality teaches us that all souls have their individual karmic accounts. Even if two souls put in the same amount of effort in the present birth, their results will not be the same. This is because they carry different sanskars and past karmas, and both these aspects influence their destiny. If the input factors that determine success are different for all souls, then how fair is it to consider life a race?

Some children work really hard but still do not get good results; others do not slog that much but pass with flying colours. Similar is the case in business.

SO: When I was studying at film school, everyone used to say that while my batchmates would get jobs easily, it would be hard for me. But in fact, I was amongst the first to be selected from our batch.

SS: When we judge someone, we do so according to their current parameters – be it performance, skills, looks. We decide on that basis what that person will be able to do or not do. You said what happened in your case was exactly opposite to what people had expected. If the present logical parameters were so clear, how was the result so different from what was expected? And yours is not an isolated case, there are so many similar ones.

Let us take a hypothetical case of two people with identical present parameters. Let us say they are identical twins, so their time of birth, parents, living conditions are the same. Let us say their current talents, skills, education, intelligence are also similar. If they happen to set up the same business, will the result be the same for both?

SO: Not necessarily.
SS: The result will not be the same. When all inputs are the same, the output should be identical. But that does not happen because there is one very big factor that is different for both of them – their past karmic account.

Let us suppose that one of them accumulated a lot of positive karma in his past lives. He might have cooperated with others and many people benefitted because of him. That past account, which has been carried forward, will bring him greater success in this birth.

Suppose his sibling's past karmic account is that he had tried to obstruct others' success path. That past account will weigh down his present. Even if he will makes extra effort now, he gets lesser results. When the past karmic accounts are not the same, where is the scope for a fair competition in the present? Always remember that no two souls can be in a race with each other in life, because their input parameters are never the same.

It is surprising when we sometimes hear that a student who had slogged all day long failed his exam, while another one, who was completely relaxed and had even watched movies the day before the exam, passed with flying colours. The reason is that the first student had opend his text books only a day before his test, while the second one had been preparing for it round the year. So, we need to look at the complete picture.

Similarly, when we judge ourselves and others, we only look at our current lifetime. We often wonder why we did not make it to our goal when we had worked really hard, and had everything it takes to succeed. We may have made great effort recently but probably did not work as hard in our previous lives. If another person's karmic account from his previous births is much better than ours, how can we compete with him?

SO: As a young boy, I used to pay full attention in class, and my lessons would get etched in my memory. I never had to do any last-minute preparations before exams.
SS: But not everyone is able to register classroom lessons so well. Each one of us has a different grasping ability and memory.

SO: Is this also a carry forward of past sanskars?
SS: Yes, our present intelligence level is because of our past karmic account and past sanskars.
Let's remember that everyone's journey is different. We have a choice to surge forward, but if we keep looking here and there, we will miss our chance.

MANTRAS FOR BEING LOVE

- Comparison and competition come from the feeling of being and doing better than others. When we feel we are better than others, it increases our self-worth.

- Feelings of competition created in professional life become our sanskar. Our sanskar makes us compete with family and friends and blocks our energy of love.

- When others in the family are able to do something better than us or have better relationships, we should appreciate their qualities. If we create jealousy or feel inferior, we are sending them negative energy.

- Our intention should be TO BE and DO the best of our capacity. Let's focus on our qualities and skills and keep doing better in reference to our own capacity, not in reference to other people. The purpose of life is to be OUR BEST, not BETTER THAN OTHERS.

- Wanting to be better than others is a never-ending race. We will not be happy because there will always be someone ahead of us. Fear, stress, anger, insecurity and jealousy will be created with feelings of competition.

- Professional success, health relationships and other aspects of each soul will be affected by their past karmic accounts. So they cannot be judged on the basis of their present life karmas alone.

- Even if all the present parameters of two souls are the same, comparison or competition between them is unfair. This is because the past karmas of the two souls are different.

Karma and Relationships

Suresh Oberoi: Does our karmic account begin soon after we are born, or are we born into a family because of it?
Sister Shivani: We form a karmic account with souls with whom we have had an energy exchange in the past. We look at our parents, spouse, children, family and friends through the label of roles that they are currently in. If we remove the labels, what remains is the energy exchange that I, the soul, have had with these souls. The nature of exchange with some souls is harmonious, with others there could be a slight undercurrent of disharmony, and with some there could be conflict. Sometimes we feel that we do a lot for a particular person but there is never a similar response from his side.

SO: If I have done a lot for someone but that person is not responding in the same way, does it mean that I have a pending account with him?
SS: Yes.

SO: My astrologer told me 'you will do a lot for others, but they will not give back'. I would feel very sad after hearing that and think that life is so unfair. I would blame God and the universe for it.

SS: Energy exchange means give and take. Some of us can be in debt. Suppose you did a lot for me. I received your positive vibrations at the subtle level, and your cooperation, assistance at the external level. So there was exchange of energy between us. Then comes a time when we both change our bodily costumes – in other words, we take rebirth. In the new lifetime, or maybe yet another one, we are bound to come in contact with each other again through the label of any relationship for that debt to be cleared.

SO: We could meet as friends, siblings or relatives.

SS: Yes, anything. I could even become your child.

SO: The astrologer should have added a sentence while telling my future: 'You have to give to others because in the previous lifetime you received a lot from them. You are clearing your own debt, so you should be happy.'

SS: Let us change it to another sentence: 'It is your sanskar to give to others, so keep doing good for them without calculating what you get in return.'

SO: We have a watchdog in our house. The moment anyone is at the door, he is the first one to alert us. He does not wait for the staff to do so. We can learn the art of giving unconditionally even from animals.

SS: Your pet acts according to his sanskar.

SO: It is his duty to do so.

SS: No, there is a lot of difference between 'sanskar' and 'duty'. Let us say it is the children's responsibility to take care of old parents. But each child responds to this duty as per his sanskar. While one child may take good care of them, another one may be casual about it, and the third one may not be bothered at all. Some even tell their sick parents 'you get yourself treated by a good doctor and I will just pay the bills'.

SO: Another one may even refuse to pay the bills. He may ask his parents to get the finances from his brother.

SS: Yes, this too could happen. There could be different responses and energies. Many choose to term it as luck. But the fact is that destiny is decided on the basis of the past karmic account between souls – in this case, the previous energy exchange between parent souls and children souls.

If we are bound to give others due to our karmic account with them, we will either feel like doing it or end up doing it somehow. Even if we are logically convinced that we should not help others next time because we get nothing in return for it, when the situation comes, we will end up helping them again. This is because our sanskar of giving and our pending karmic account will play automatically.

SO: Yes, I have seen this. I know a family of eight siblings that was fighting a court case against someone. One of the brothers used to take care of all the legal matters all by himself. There came a point when he said he could not do it single-handedly anymore. But as the date of the hearing drew closer, he again found himself handling everything, while the rest of the family remained carefree as usual.

SS: This is bound to happen because his destiny is based on his previous energy exchange with those souls. It is pre-decided by his own karma that in this lifetime, the souls in his connection will rest, while he will toil. No one can avert it.

SO: When I go through similar situations, I get negative thoughts for others, such as 'they are not bothered about my efforts and on top of that they are questioning me'. Even when that episode gets over, the negative thoughts linger on.
SS: We have to understand that whatever good we do, we do it according to our positive sanskars and our past karmic account with other souls. If others criticise us, they do so on the basis of their sanskars and karmic account. But how we choose to deal with any such situation in the present moment is also our karma. This realisation is the way to convert it into positive.

SO: I sometimes think that I too should be stubborn and not do anything for others. But when it is time to act, I give in again.
SS: You will not be able to take a strict stand because you are bound by your karmic account.
Your karmic account will draw you towards certain situations, relationships or a particular career. Even if the whole world tries to stop you or you try to stop yourself, you will still go there because you are being pulled in that direction.
If I take a loan but refuse to repay it, the people or the credit card company who I owe the money to, will not let me get away with it. They will use all means in their power to draw the money from me.

SO: True.

SS: Similarly, the souls with whom I have a karmic account will come into my life to settle the account and so my thoughts will automatically be drawn in that direction. The only thing I need to check here is whether the quality of my present karma, which I may feel compelled to do as per my karmic account, is right.

Suppose I do not want to help someone but I am being pushed in that direction. I should still know that it is good karma. On the other hand, I must resist myself if I am being pushed into doing negative karma. At that point, I have to use my willpower to make my present positive karma overweigh that past karmic account.

SO: What if I do a good karma but get a negative return? For instance, I helped a friend to choose his life partner but the couple remained in conflict with each other. I felt guilty.
SS: The intention behind your karma was good. You wanted to help him. Whatever happened later was the consequence of the couple's decisions.

SO: I had convinced and encouraged them to come together. Later, they got divorced. So I also got entangled in that karmic account. Sometimes, when we try to help others, it could go wrong.
SS: One thing is certain that those two souls – who got married and later divorced – had a karmic account to settle. So it was bound to happen. But the learning you could take from here is – never take a decision for anyone else, not even for a child. A standard assumption by most parents is that they know what is right for their child. Their intention may be very nice, but it seems 'right' to them through the lens of their own capacity and sanskars i.e. from their point of view.

SO: Naturally, parents will decide according to their wisdom and see things through the lens they are wearing.

SS: Perfect. So that decision is right according to the parents' definition of right. But it may not necessarily match with the child's definition of right. It would be right for both of them if the sanskars and capacity of both the parties are the same. This is possible in some cases, not all.

When parents tell their child 'do it because we say so', this is where the situation gets messy. The child may not use his own intellect and obey the parents out of fear, love, respect or duty.

SO: In many families, people are asked to act according to the advice of their elders.

SS: What the elders say is definitely right, but it is right according to their capacity. Suppose you advise someone to go for a 2-km morning walk daily because it is good for health. You thoroughly explain to him the benefits of walking, and of breathing in fresh air. Everything you say is right.

SO: But he may collapse after walking half the distance.

SS: Why would that happen when your advice was right? Because for you, walking the said distance would be no big deal as perhaps, it is your routine. But while suggesting the same to another person, you did not evaluate his capacity.

SO: Why didn't the listener evaluate the advice given to him before following it?

SS: You just gave the example that many people obey elders out of fear, respect or responsibility, so there may not be enough room to evaluate their advice. Some parents even emotionally manipulate their children or threaten about consequences if they don't obey.

SO: They threaten to snap all ties with the child.
SS: Yes, a lot of such things are said.
Getting back to that example, if that person implements your advice of walking 2 kms, he may collapse midway. When he falls down, in that moment, the karma which is created includes you too because you were instrumental for it. This is because you did not just give him advice but also enforced it on him.

SO: But it must be mentioned in his karmic account that he would fall at that moment.
SS: But how did it come about? You were instrumental. Let us take a learning from here, that we will not become instrumental for such karma.

SO: As the head of the family, I got two couples married and both the marriages failed. I felt guilty for years. When my children grew up, I changed my approach. When a proposal came into our family for an arranged marriage, I let the boy and girl meet and decide for themselves. I am very happy with my decision.
SS: This approach should be applied in all aspects of life, even smaller situations. We should not take a decision for another person. We must give advice and then leave it to him to decide. When someone comes to seek our advice, our language should be – 'according to me, this is the right thing to do' or 'if I were you, I would do this'. Do let him know that he must decide what is comfortable for him. Underline it.

SO: Some parents tell their children to make the same choices that they did in their married life. But things could be different for both of them.

SS: Yes, the parent and child will have different sanskars and karmic accounts. So, one should not take a decision for the other. When someone comes to us for advice, it gives us a sense of power. We feel good and do not take much time before giving our verdict on the matter. The person seeking advice is in a weak state of mind. He does not want to take a decision for himself, that is why he is looking for someone else to do it for him. The most important thing is that he does not want to take responsibility for the decision. So we really have to be very careful.

When we leave that person to take his own call, he will try to explore the solution. His karmic account and sanskars will ultimately bring out the right decision for him.

SO: The universe also helps.

SS: The universe is nothing but the thoughts and energy we receive from others. We can use our intuition to catch the right decision. Just like love is our original quality, wisdom is another innate quality of every soul. However, we have acquired several layers over our original wisdom.

SO: We often underestimate ourselves by thinking that others are wiser than us; we feel it is better to consult them. By doing so, we give away our power to them.

SS: Even if we go to mahatmas and saints, we can seek their blessings and advice, but not our decision. This is because they will suggest a decision according to their wisdom, sanskars and capacity. Even if they decide for us on the basis of our capacity, it is we who will finally implement it. So even after listening to their advice it is not necessary to implement it immediately. It would be better if we take home their advice and sit with it for a few days. We should try it on ourselves, see if it works for us, and check if we have the capacity to implement it. That is when that karma will be ours, the responsibility of that decision will be ours, and so will be its consequences. Then whatever be the result, we will face it well because the decision was ours. On the other hand, if someone else takes the decision for us and it does not go well, we will have a tendency to blame that person. The moment we indulge in blame game, our spiritual energy goes down.

MEDITATION AND REFLECTIONS

Let us sit back comfortably ... I, the soul, have come into this bodily costume to play my part with other souls ... all souls that have come into different relationships with me, I have met them before ... when we met last time, an account was started ... even though we changed our bodily costumes, that account continues ... all those souls are around me once again in different roles and relationships ... everything that is happening is absolutely fair and accurate ... never does my mind say 'this is not fair' ... it is fair according to the account that was shared between me and the other souls ... that account is continued ... now my attention is only towards my present karma ... however the past was, it is no longer in my control ... but my present karma – i.e. my thoughts, words and actions – is deciding my future ... I take care ... irrespective of what others do, my karma is clean, pure and beautiful ... Om Shanti.

MANTRAS FOR BEING LOVE

- Karmic account means a connection with any soul with whom we have had an energy exchange earlier.

- All our family and friends today are souls whom we have met in earlier lives. When we met before, there was a relationship experience and an energy exchange. In the present life our relationship will be largely influenced by our past experiences.

- There will be some souls who will do a lot for us while we do nothing much for them. There will be some for whom we do a lot and get nothing in return. There will be some who will create obstacles in our life. All these present experiences are a carry forward of the past energy exchange with them.

- Never take a decision for others. We take the decision according to our sanskar and capacity but it has to be implemented by them according to their capacity. Give advice and empower them to take their own decisions.

Detached Intervention

Suresh Oberoi: We have discussed about karma. It feels as though we cannot do anything as the slightest act entangles us in a karmic account.
Sister Shivani: Keep doing good karma. Do not focus on what others are doing.

SO: But how would I know my capacity?
SS: All of us have wisdom and decision-making power. These are innate qualities of every soul, just like love, peace, happiness, purity and will power.

SO: If all these qualities exist in the soul, why are we looking for answers outside?
SS: Because too many layers have accumulated over our original qualities. Suppose both of us wear white. Over time, your dress acquires two layers of dust and mine gets ten layers over it. So your original white colour is still visible, mine cannot be seen at all.

Similarly, if I sense that your originality is still intact, I will feel that you are wiser than me. So I will come to you with my small problems. But if you keep taking decisions for me, my original qualities will never emerge.

You can help me remove those acquired layers so that my originality emerges. This means – just give me slight advice, then leave the rest of the responsibility to me. Encourage me to come up with a solution to my problems. Don't do not take a decision for me.

SO: Doctors often say 'if you don't use it, you will lose it'. If we do not exercise and just keep sitting in front of the computer the whole day, then our limbs will not work efficiently. Similarly, if we do not use our original wisdom and powers and want others to decide for us, then our inner muscle will not be flexed.

SS: When someone else takes a decision for us, we may follow it, but we do not put in our hundred per cent effort since it is not our decision. As our full capacity is not utilised, we do not get the desired result, and this makes us feel weak. Then we blame the person who took that decision for us. And blaming others is the simplest way to deplete our power.

This way, instead of peeling off, our acquired layers are reinforced. And the more layers there are on us, the more scared we will be to take our own decisions. Once again, we will depend on others for decision-making.

Another important duty we have as parents is that parents empower children to take their own decisions, when they are still very young. Even if children make mistakes, the loss does not matter much, because in the process, the parents help them develop their decision-making power and innate wisdom. This does not mean that parents agree with everything their children do. But even if they are not in agreement with them, they should guide them instead of thrusting their decisions on them.

SO: When things go wrong, parents often tell their children, 'You did not listen to us ... now look what has happened!'
SS: This is so risky.
Children act according to their own sanskars and karmic account. Let them decide for themselves. Parents take decisions for them with the pure intention that nothing should go wrong. But over a period of time, they develop a sanskar of enforcing their decisions on them. This makes children dependent on their parents for decision-making, and they carry this sanskar into adulthood.

SO: A son who grows up in such an environment may later consult his wife for taking decisions. If the wife happens to disagree with his parents over various issues or vice-versa, it would escalate into something else.
SS: Yes, if the son's decision-making capacity is not developed, and he is used to following instructions, things could get difficult later. If he does not obey his parents or family members, they would be annoyed. He would not want to upset them, so he would be bound to accept what they say. He would be mentally programmed like that.
Even when parents take the best decisions, some of those are right for the children, others may not turn out to be so. It would thus be better if children decide on their own, and make their own right and wrong choices. In the process, they would develop their inner powers.
If others come to us for advice, we must not take a decision for them. If it is our role to guide them, we can introduce them to their own capacity. This will be our biggest gift to them.
Let us take an example. A daughter comes to her parents' home and complains to them about her husband and in-laws. She is

in pain. As her parents are attached to her, they too feel the same emotions. All of them are now in the same boat, so it becomes difficult for them to take the right decision.

SO: The parents have not yet heard the other side of the story. It is possible that the daughter exaggerated her problem. Or she may be too sensitive.

SS: Underline this – the daughter is not lying, she is only sharing her grief. Sometimes parents feel that she might be magnifying the situation, but she is not deliberately doing so. She would have really been hurt. Everybody's capacity to handle pain is different. If they already know that it is her sanskar to feel hurt easily, the first thing they must do is to make that problem look smaller. They can give her the right advice only if they are aware of her capacity and sanskars. Otherwise they might take her complaint on face value and base their advice on that.

SO: Sometimes parents tend to overreact.

SS: It is because they consume the pain of their daughter due to attachment with her.

SO: Yes.

SS: Parents accept the complaint as it is, and then go on to endorse what the daughter says. They say 'you are right, those people are wrong'. At the same time, they tell her that she still has to return to her husband and in-laws because they are her family. Because her parents have reaffirmed her pain and also told her that she has no other option but to go back, this time the daughter returns to her in-laws' place weaker than before. She is unable to bear the slightest challenge there because she is now living in victim mode. She again complains to her parents and this goes on to become a vicious cycle.

Here the intention of the parents is good but their way of resolving the issue needs to change. They must remember that they have to empower their daughter, not disempower her, before sending her back to her husband's house.

Now let us treat the same scenario differently. The daughter comes and complains to her parents about her in-laws and husband. She is very hurt. Parents already know that she is a sensitive person, so they are able to judge that the situation could be smaller than what is told. So they take care not to consume their daughter's pain because if they do so, they will not be able to help her in anyway.

SO: You had said in a previous conversation that a counsellor can give the right advice only because he does not consume people's pain and so remains stable.

SS: A counsellor can do it, and so can saints, philosophers and guides. But even family and friends can do it.

How many times can one seek help from outside? Will it not be better if we detach ourselves from our family and friends, and give them the right advice and support whenever they need? Whether it is an issue within a marriage or about their career, we can help resolve it by listening to them in a detached way.

SO: Many people complain that they have a strict boss, and their parents strengthen their belief.

SS: Not just that, parents tell them that whatever be the case, they have to return to their workplace because there is no other choice. This means they disempower their children, set them into victim mode, then ask them to go back.

Our every thought, word and vibration are important. As parents, family and friends, our role is to empower our loved ones before they return to face their daily challenges. We have to do whatever makes them a lot more comfortable, than they felt before, while handling the same situation. They are in pain because they can see only their own perspective. We can help them see the other side of the story.

We should listen to them but not stretch the conversation too far. Let them know that we really understand them. Never reject them as too sensitive or discard what they are sharing as untrue. Remember, they have come to us in pain. To heal them, we need to understand their pain. If we say 'you do the same thing every time so it is not them but you are at fault', this is also a way to discourage them.

When others come to us for healing, we have to be very careful that we do not add more pain to their pain because this will weaken them even more. Our every thought and word count at that moment and should be what heal them.

SO: If we accept everyone with their version of things, does it mean that nobody is wrong? Some people even make up stories and blame others.

SS: Yes, nobody is wrong. Even the ones lying are doing so through their sanskars and perspective.

SO: This is difficult for me to digest.

SS: When we understand that nobody is wrong, it becomes easy to manage relationships. You yourself had said in a previous conversation that all of us look at the world through the colour of the glasses we wear.

SO: True, but if everyone keeps justifying their point of view, we will never reach a solution. If one person says his sanskar is right, the other one will stand by his own.

SS: Spirituality teaches us to clean the glasses through which we see the world. If you say your glasses are unclean, I say mine are unclear too, then we will continue to have conflict over what is right according to our perspective. Now we are learning spiritual knowledge. Even if one of us uses it to clean his lens, and develops a broader perspective, our relationship will change for the better.

To discipline others or to control them is not our role. If we can give them our love and cooperation, that helps remove layers of dust that clog their original qualities. With that we have done a wonderful job.

SO: I am really enjoying this conversation, and it reminds me of a story. There was a lion cub that grew up amongst goats. When the lion parents found him, they did not ridicule his lack of strength or his similarity to the goats. Instead, they took him to a pond and showed him his reflection in the water. They told him 'look, you are one of us, so you are as powerful as we are'.

SS: They introduced him to his own powers by radiating love and power to him. This is the parents' role – to help the child let go of the acquired layers.

Getting back to our previous discussion, when the daughter comes home with her complaints, it is the parents' role to show her the other person's perspective also. Parents can say 'what you are saying is right, but the intention of your in-laws is not to trouble you, but they are only acting through their sanskars'.

The mother-in-law, for example, could be in her own pain because her son now listens to his wife more than her. There could be insecurity, jealousy and possessiveness for the son and the family. She could be acting under the influence of those sanskars. The parents can ask their daughter to heal her mother-in-law with so much love, that she gets over these sanskars. When parents have this approach to solving the problem, their conversation, vocabulary and vibrations will be of an altogether different quality.

Suppose the issue is that the daughter is in pain because her husband comes home late every night and yells at her. When she shares her grief with her parents, they should detach themselves from the scene and try to show her the husband's perspective. Probably the husband is facing a lot throughout the day at his workplace. They can tell her 'instead of expecting from him, you could try to heal him when he comes back home in such a turbulent state ... he is not criticising you but venting the frustration he had accumulated throughout the day'. By showing the daughter her husband's perspective and pain, the parents will be able to shift her mode of thinking. By encouraging her to adjust to others' perspective, they can empower her before she returns to the same scene.

SO: Now the attention of the daughter will shift from her own issues to her husband's.
SS: That's it. When the daughter understands that her husband or in-laws are not criticising her but reacting due to their own pain, she will feel better and have a clearer understanding to deal with the situation

SO: It is all about understanding things rather than reacting.
SS: Yes, and that is how our natural quality of love will flow in our relationships.

MANTRAS FOR BEING LOVE

- When others take a decision for us, we do not put in our best effort to implement it. We then blame them for failure of the decision.

- Instead of taking decisions for children, help them to develop their decision-making power. Parents' role is not to control their life but to empower them so that they are able to take charge of their life.

- When family and friends come to us in pain, we need to take care not to consume their pain. Remain stable and understand their perspective.

- Do not endorse people's victim feeling. Show them their own qualities using which they can cross the situation. Also show them the perspective of the others involved in the conflict.

Reaching the Child Within

**Suresh Oberoi: I am not able to consistently remember that
the other person is a soul full of love, just like me.**
Sister Shivani: We cannot consciously remember it all day that
we are a soul and love is our original quality. It does not work
like that. There are two ways of going about it. First, if we
remember that we are a soul, love automatically radiates from
us. The other option is – if our interaction is based on love,
we automatically become soul conscious. Interacting with love
means our every thought is clean.

**SO: Whenever I interact with a child, only love radiates from
me, there's nothing else.**
SS: What do you think is the reason behind it?

**SO: Maybe because one cannot ever have a clash of ideas
with a child.**
SS: We interact lovingly with a child because he always radiates
the energy of love. A small child is neither judgmental nor

critical of us. He does not see our mistakes, or feel hurt or angry by anything we do.

SO: A child also looks at everyone equally. He does not discriminate between a thief and a saint, never labels anyone as rich or poor, good or bad. He just loves unconditionally.
SS: A child does not label others or remember their faults. He simply does not know the concept of judging them even in the subtle sense, and is free from feelings of hurt, comparison and criticism. As he has none of these blockages, love naturally radiates from him. This then automatically draws love from others. This is the formula for being love.
A child makes no effort to radiate love to others. Love naturally flows through him.

SO: But I cannot go back to becoming a child.
SS: Yes, you can. The child is able to radiate love naturally because he is free from internal blockages and labels. If we also rid ourselves of these negative tendencies, our state too will come closer to a child's.
Remember, we do not have to work towards creating the flow of love. All we need to do is to remove our internal blockages so that the natural flow is restored. This is similar to the fact that blood flows in our body naturally but health problems occur when blockages in the arteries obstruct this flow.

SO: People say that a child is the image of God.
SS: This is because the child is pure. He has no acquired layers or sense of ego, so his energy field is pure and magnetic. Even if an adult enters this energy field with feelings of ego, hurt, criticism and other labels, he starts to receive pure vibrations

of love from the child. This brings out his original quality of love effortlessly.

SO: In this case, a small child is influencing an older person.
SS: Yes, why not? It is the impact of one soul on another. If elders can influence children, it can also happen the other way around.

SO: My son and son-in-law say that just being with the little one refreshes them after a hard day. Elders forget their tiredness and return to their normal state in the company of a child.
SS: Elders experience their own purity in the company of a child. At workplace, there is only interaction of egos – of position with position, senior with junior, employer with employee, and money with money. So elders usually operate in a body-conscious mode all day, and also receive criticism and other negative vibrations.

SO: With children they experience interaction of love with love.
SS: When we are in a child's company, we too become like him. This proves that the original quality of love is the same for both.

SO: We don't feel tired when we stay in our original quality.
SS: Because the soul is originally powerful.
We have complicated our relationships by interacting through our acquired layers.

SO: In a previous conversation, you had mentioned that we can recharge our soul battery by connecting to a fully-charged battery. A child is fully charged. He does not lose anything by giving to others, as love only grows.

SS: When a child radiates love, it triggers the energy of love that is already present inside us. Just like if I create a negative vibration for you, it will also hit something negative inside you.

SO: Can you explain this?
SS: If I am thinking negatively about you, it will reach you. You do have a choice of response but the probability of my thought touching a similar negative chord inside you is very high, especially if you are living in the unaware mode, where you are not choosing your thoughts consciously.

SO: If I am living in the aware mode, I can choose not to accept your negative vibrations or can convert them into positive.
SS: Yes. 'Being aware' means that we are able to change a negative thought into positive, simply by self-checking – by telling ourselves 'I need not think in this manner'. When a negative thought occurs to us, we do not know if it is our own creation or it has been triggered by someone else's negative thought. The important thing is that we have the power to change it.
In general, others reciprocate the energy we send them. Similarly, the vibrations of a child trigger the sanskars of love and purity within us. The experience is similar to meeting a saint.

SO: We experience the same calm in places of worship.
SS: When we go to a temple or meet a pure soul, we do experience peace because of the collective vibration of that place. But the fact is that such a place or person only trigger the peace already present within us. So they are only giving us the opportunity to experience it. That is why we feel like going to such people or places frequently. We think we experience

peace only in their presence, and when we are not around them, we get entangled in the same old vibrations. But the truth is that they are only a stimulus for us to experience our original quality of peace.

The opposite of this is also true – if someone sends us negative vibrations, those will trigger something similar in us, if that negativity is already present inside us.

SO: What if I have a negative trait in me but do not want it to be triggered? Can I control that?

SS: You can be aware of it and change it.

For example, when we meet saints, their purity triggers our purity. But our impurity does not influence them. This is because through years of practice, they have cleansed themselves of their acquired layers to quite an extent.

SO: Can we ignite our original sanskars without going to the temple, meeting saints or being in the company of children?

SS: Of course. If we check throughout the day, our original sanskars are awakened so many times. It is not that we live in a negative state all day. We often experience such pure love. Sometimes we see a stranger and go out of our way to help him. It is because our original quality is to give others.

SO: Some time back, I saw kids playing around. I sent chocolates for all of them.

SS: But when it comes to relationships, we think, 'Why should I cooperate with him when he did not do anything for me?'

Just like you randomly distributed chocolates to children, knowing very well that you will not get anything in return, we all have to distribute sweetness to others. We must do things for others without bothering about whether they will return the favour, whether we will meet them again or not. Even if we get negativity in return, we have to distribute sweetness to others.

SO: Once, while coming out of a restaurant, I tipped the doorman. A gentleman who was with me disapproved of it, saying it made no sense to tip someone who I would probably never see again. He said I should do it only at places I visited frequently, because I would get respect in return.

SS: In such a case, the act of giving is actually a means of taking. People tip the doorman or waiter so that when they visit the place next time, the staff takes better care of them, talks to them with greater regard, and wishes them in front of others. Their intention is to receive it all in return for a meagre tip. It is their way of buying regard. So actually, they are not giving anything at all.

SO: If we can calculate everything so minutely, why don't we use our faculties to develop our spiritual side?

SS: We usually calculate what we must receive from others. We are aware of what it takes to get love, respect and care from them. Now, all we need to do is to shift this awareness – think what we should do in order to give love, respect and care.

We are definitely living in the 'aware mode' but what are we aware of? We are always conscious of what people give us or how they behave with us. But this awareness is about everybody else, and it is difficult to keep tabs on so many people. If we are sharp enough to catch others' vibrations, it should be much easier to catch our own. We must check what our mental antenna is tuned to – the mode of giving or taking.

If we adopt the strategy of giving to others unconditionally, life becomes very easy. But when we give to others while seeking their appreciation or anything else in return, our mind keeps checking if that condition is fulfilled. In the process, we are unable to share anything. We go into the 'taking mode' and keep comparing our efforts with the returns. By following this approach, we block our energies. A child does none of this.

A child changes as he grows up. He is conditioned by others about good and bad, right and wrong. He learns the blame game and so on. Bit by bit, his innocence gets covered by acquired layers. Small deposits of negative traits start to obstruct his natural radiance. The child keeps consuming whatever he is fed by his environment. He also acquires the same attitude as his parents. Today, the loss of innocence in children is faster than before because of invasion of media in our lives. There is a flood of information through TV and the Internet.

Everybody is originally similar, but several layers have accumulated over our being because of these outer influences. Spirituality teaches us to reach the child within us again.

SO: When it comes to food, we prefer to eat natural and organic. We want our food to be cooked very lightly so that its original nutrients are retained. But as people, we are going away from our originality.

SS: We have moved far from originality, but it is not hard to come back. We need not make effort to become a being of love, as that is who we are. We only have to work towards removing criticism, blame, anger etc. from our being. We created these blockages, so we have to remove them ourselves.

MANTRAS FOR BEING LOVE

- A baby does not see people through their labels of relationship, profession or status. A baby is not judgmental or critical of people. He naturally radiates love, since he has a soul to soul connection.

- Love flows naturally through us if we remove the blockage created by ego labels, criticism, blame, control, comparison or competition. When we do so, we shift from ego consciousness to soul consciousness.

- Love radiating from us naturally emerges the original sanskar of love in every soul we interact with. We like going to places and meeting people that have pure vibrations because they help emerge our sanskar of purity.

- We are aware of the love, respect and care which we expect from others. We are aware of what we are getting and what we aren't. Now we need to be aware of the love and care we can give to others.

Ping Pong of Thought Energy

Suresh Oberoi: You had said that our thoughts and vibrations reach others faster than our actions.

Recently, a particular team member's behaviour was stressing out the rest of our team to such an extent that everyone wished he would go away. One morning, when a relative of his was going to Delhi, this team-member asked me if he could also leave with him. When I asked him why he wanted to quit, he said he just didn't feel like working with us anymore, although he could not quite explain the reason. All of us had internally wished for him to leave, and it was as if those thoughts and vibrations actually reached him!

Sister Shivani: Absolutely! How long had you been creating those vibrations?

SO: For two to three days.

SS: It works every time. Anyone can try it out.

SO: Earlier, I was not convinced that merely sending someone vibrations of love could improve relations between us. But this incident has completely changed my view. If our vibrations could have a negative influence in this case, they will definitely have a positive effect when we try to make things work.

SS: If a few people criticise someone and collectively send him strong negative vibrations, those will definitely reach him and make him feel uncomfortable and unwanted.

SO: It was strange to realise that our thoughts, which a couple of us had created in a closed room was far away, had reached our team member. And the only explanation he had for wanting to leave, was that he did not feel like staying with us anymore.

SS: He did not feel like staying on because he was constantly receiving something negative. As we discussed previously, the vibrations we send others create similar quality of thoughts in them. So we have a responsibility.

The heavy energy we create depletes us first.

SO: When I thought negatively about that team member, did I get depleted?

SS: How did you feel while thinking negatively about him? First, we create negative thoughts about another person and feel depleted, then those vibrations reach him and he is depleted, then our relationship with him weakens. Then, he may also create similar thoughts in response to ours, and those vibrations reach us and affect us. This game of ping-pong can continue for days, months, years, or decades.

As we had been discussing about energy exchange, you were able to put two and two together and make sense of why your team member had behaved in that way. Otherwise, we usually don't accept that we are the reason behind other people's behaviour. If we did not know the background about transfer of vibrations in this incident, we would have probably blamed the team member and said 'he must have his own reasons for leaving. We would even have said that he anyway was not behaving properly for so many days'.

SO: We would have assumed that his decision to quit must be due to his own guilt, and it was better for everyone that he had decided to leave.
SS: Even if we do not want the other person to leave because we need him at work, or want that relationship to continue, we do not change the quality of our thoughts. We simply ask him to stay back. In this case, the person may stay on for a few more days. But as the old pattern of energy exchange continues, eventually this same situation sunfolds.

SO: It is a half-hearted attempt at making someone stay, like doing things out of compulsion.
SS: First we justify our own thoughts, and then we blame the other person. The moment we point a finger at the other person, the relationship gets out of hand.

SO: What if we never wanted this relationship in the first place; what if we are never going to meet that person again?
SS: Relationship means we have a karmic account with that soul.

SO: Do you mean this relationship existed in the past lives and will carry forward?

SS: Not necessarily. Suppose we send the other person negative vibrations and he decides to go away. Since we are unlikely to meet again, we do not try to make things better. What does he take along with him while parting from us?

SO: He carries with him the experience of pain.

SS: So what quality of thoughts would he create in future and at whom would those be directed?

SO: Those negative thoughts will radiate to me.

SS: This can go on for long, and as many times as he thinks about you. You had once shared an experience when, just by looking at someone's photograph, you could feel the same negative feelings for him as you did twenty years before. This means you continued to send negative vibrations to him even several years later.

So a person who leaves because of you, will also think negatively about you later in life. Whenever he hears your name somewhere or watches you on TV, he will create the same quality of thoughts for you as he had done while parting ways. Just because you had sent him negative energy for three days does not mean that he will create negative thoughts for you for only 3 days. He may do it for much longer.

SO: He could even do it for three lives!

SS: Yes, it is possible that this account is carried forward.

SO: Is that why they say let's part as friends even if we can no longer work together?

SS: It is important to do so, but what does it really mean to 'stay friends'?

SO: It means we will continue to meet and interact.

SS: No, staying friends means we will not think wrong for each other despite our differences. Even though we have separated, we will remain cordial whenever we meet. However, two people will not be able to do so if there are unresolved issues pending between them.

SO: It reminds me of two business partners who decided to part ways but 'stay friends'. Soon after their split, each started calling their common business associates, asking them to do business only with him and not his ex-partner.

SS: So is this parting ways as friends? This is hard core jealousy and competition. The thought that they had for each other was 'you decided to split ... now I'll show you that I can do better than you'. To part as friends means that we will not think negatively about each other even if our relationship was not a success.

Coming back to your first example, if that team member leaves you because he felt hurt, he will send you negative vibrations throughout his life whenever he remembers you. So think about it – we meet so many people every day who are not our friends or family. They meet us and then are gone forever, but there is definitely an energy exchange between us. If this exchange is heavy then they feel uncomfortable while dealing with us. What are we actually doing? We are creating negative investments, the returns of which will keep coming to us for a long time and deplete our energy.

SO: I read a message 'A person will always remember the way you make him feel.'
SS: Yes, and the more important thing is that he will send the same quality of vibrations back to you many times over.

SO: It means a karmic account is created.
There are moments when I feel low and I think to myself 'Why am I feeling sad when I've got everything in the world?' Does it mean that at that moment someone, somewhere is sending me back the pain that I had once given him? Do I receive others' thoughts of pain?
SS: Yes, why not? You just gave an example of how someone in your office received the negative vibrations that you had created for him. Why will you not receive the ones he creates for you?

SO: I will have to be cautious now.
SS: On the contrary, the understanding of karma makes things very simple. All we need to remember is 'whatever be the situation, my thoughts create MY destiny'. The thoughts we have for others actually create our own karmic bank account.

SO: Once, I lost a very expensive watch that my son had gifted me. I told my wife that I suspected one of our house helps. She told me never to create such thoughts for others because they reach them. Was she right?

SS: If you assume someone to be a thief, you create strong negative vibrations for him. If you are simply checking in your mind who all came into the house after you left, that just creates neutral energy. But to pass a negative judgment on someone is a direct attack on that person and it will reach him through vibrations. Then he will revert to you in one way or another.

In our thoughts lie our relationships, karmic account and our destiny. Our karmic account is created on the basis of the quality of our thoughts. It is not about the other person, it is about us.

If we create negative thoughts about someone, for example in the given situation we assume someone to be a thief, then that person will no longer be able to think good about us, although he may not know the reason for disliking us. Sometimes we are unable to pinpoint a specific reason as to why a relationship is not working out because everything seems to be apparently fine between the two parties. It means that at some point of time, one of the sides had created heavy, negative thoughts for the other.

SO: This is such an interesting game.
One of my brothers once scolded our niece. She was really offended. Bhen she was never so upset whenever I scolded her. She said that she never felt hurt by me. So, 'intention' must be playing a role here.
SS: Both the intention behind the action and the vibrations that were sent to that soul for a long time, and not just during that particular incident, play a role in this case.

Your niece did not feel bad when you scolded her because you must have been sending her loving and accepting energy throughout. Your brother, on the other hand, might have been critical or judgmental of her in his mind and she must have received those vibrations over a period of time. So depending on the kind of vibrations she received from both of you over the years, her response was different. She was not hurt by those few words spoken to her, but because of the vibrations she had received in totality.

If a person can receive your vibrations in three days, as you mentioned in your initial example, how much negative energy would be accumulated over many years? To clear such a pile of negativity is completely in our hands.

SO: How can we do that? I really want to know.

SS: Instead of creating negative energy for someone when we do not agree with his actions, we have to find a solution for it. Even in the worst case when we can no longer work with that person or live with him, we must not give ourselves the liberty to label him or to keep pondering over his mistakes, because that accumulates negative charge. This negative energy reaches him and he throws it back at us.

In this way, a ping-pong of negative energy begins. We must avoid playing this game with anyone. If we at all want to, let us exchange only positive energy.

If we already know that someone has the habit of lying, we must find a way to work with him. If someone has the habit of insulting, we must prepare our response for it. If someone is not sincere at work, we should see how we can manage with that. We have to accept the other person and mould ourselves such that we can work out a solution for ourselves. But instead of doing this, we continue to work with such people while constantly sending them heavy energy. This depletes us and them, and our relationship with them weakens.

MEDITATION AND REFLECTIONS

Let me look at myself – I, the soul, am the power whose thoughts and feelings reach those for whom they are created ... whether I am sitting in a closed room or miles away, my thoughts for others reach them ... others create thoughts corresponding to the energy they receive from me, and that becomes the foundation of our relationship ... from today, I pay attention to the thoughts I create for everyone – be it friends, family or strangers ... I don't ponder over their behaviour and negativities ... I put a full stop ... I understand them and adapt myself to be with them ... I remember that though they carry certain negative sanskars, they are originally beautiful souls ... my thoughts are pure and I pay attention to my karma ... how I deal with others is my responsibility ... irrespective of how they behave with me, my each thought creates my destiny ... Om Shanti.

MANTRAS FOR BEING LOVE

- When we create heavy negative thoughts for others, they reach them irrespective of our physical distance from them. Even if we behave nicely with them, they will catch our negative thoughts.

- Our negative thoughts about people will vibrate to them and they will create similar thoughts and emotions about us. Souls catch our message and respond accordingly.

- Our negative thoughts first deplete our energy, then reach them and deplete their energy, and then have an effect on our relationship.

- When someone is hurt because of the thoughts or words we created for him and our issues still remain unresolved, he will carry the wounds. He will then create negative thoughts for us whenever he thinks of us. His thoughts will reach us and deplete our energy.

- Let us understand other people's sanskars and prepare ourselves to live or work with them. Let's take care that we are not thinking about their negative sanskar and depleting our energy.

It Is All About What You Behold

Suresh Oberoi: If there is a misunderstanding between me and someone, how should I stop that negativity from piling up within me? If I try to suppress it, it raises its head again. How can I convert it into something positive?

Sister Shivani: If we create negative thoughts for others for a long period of time – be it a few hours or years – those vibrations create heavy energy. Then we discuss the matter with our friends and family repeatedly, and collectively create very heavy negative energy.

It has been found that if a group of people meditate collectively, they create very powerful positive energy that has a good influence on the subject they focus on. For example, in pranic healing or reiki, positive emotional energy created collectively is concentrated on a patient sitting far away and is able to heal his physical pain.

SO: This is distant healing.

SS: All of us are souls having a subtle body and a physical body through which we operate. A disease does not affect the physical body directly. It first starts as an experience of pain or suffering in the soul. This causes blockage in the subtle body, and that is then manifested in the physical body.

In distant healing, the positive energy sent to the patient first reaches the soul. It then clears the blockage in the soul's energy field or aura i.e. the subtle body. This brings relief to the patient sitting far away as his physical body is healed. So, the power of mind works.

SO: It does work.

SS: Similarly, if we collectively send negative energy to someone, that also works. Today, a majority of us are able to create negative thoughts faster and more easily than pure and positive ones. The person for whom we create those thoughts could also be in an emotionally weak state. So he will be very vulnerable to the thoughts he receives from us. That is why in the present scenario it is easier for negative energy to have an effect on us as compared to pure energy.

SO: This is because we have a lot of negative energy within.

SS: Yes, even the other person has a lot of it. Just like we tune both the transmitter and receiver to the same frequency to make the connection work, similar is the case with two people. Even if we constantly create good thoughts for others, it may take longer to have an impact on them because they may be living in a state of anger, hurt or pain. So our frequencies may not match. For others to receive what we are transmitting, our frequencies should be the same.

SO: Each time we have a negative thought, we have to replace it with a positive one.

SS: If we send others positive energy when they are in their own pain, they may not be able to experience our vibrations immediately. We have to send them positive energy consistently for a long time, so that it overpowers their pain and anger, and changes the quality of their thinking. On the other hand, if we send them negative energy, it is easier for them to catch it because they are already on that frequency. Negative to negative energy exchange may happen almost instantly.

The answer to your question is that while others' mistakes and negativities may be visible to us, we have the power to decide how long to keep those on our mind.

SO: Do we have a choice over what to keep on our mind?
SS: Yes, it is our choice. This place we are at right now has natural beauty and serenity. But the same space is also littered and has insects. It is for us to decide where we want to focus. If we see the beautiful greenery and feel the lovely vibrations, then we are appreciating the good qualities of this place and those remain on our mind. It does not mean that there are no insects here or this place is not wet or littered. But what is the energy that we are absorbing? The moment we think good, we feel good.

SO: Suppose we first see the litter, then appreciate the beauty of the place and also propose to clean it. It means we are seeing both the things.
SS: The point is – where is our energy going first? You had once given the example of a black dot on a white board. One way of looking at it is – it is such a big mark. Though it is a white board the spot is so significant. The person having this perspective will always highlight negativities and take the positive things for granted. Another person may see the same thing as a beautiful white board with a small black mark. So the situation is the same but the view point is different.

Similarly, if we come here and say 'what a beautiful garden, it is hard to find such natural beauty in our city, there is so much fresh air here', our state of mind will be good and we will feel nice. After that, we also see that the place is wet, a bit dirty and cold. We accept that and take care not to step on the litter, but continue working here.

It is one thing to see what's around us and another thing to keep it on our mind. We cannot stop ourselves from hearing or seeing what is happening in the world today. But we can decide what to keep on our mind and for how long.

Spirituality teaches us that we become what we think, that whatever we keep on our mind becomes our property. Right now, the litter is on the ground. But if we keep churning that thought, our mind will soon become a garbage bin. If we churn others' weaknesses, that impurity will stay on our mind and soon become part of our thought process. There are negative things around us, but we need not absorb those into our system.

SO: If I have already absorbed someone's weakness and also created negative thoughts about him, what should I do now?
SS: We may think about others' weakness for a few minutes, a few hours, a few years or a lifetime – it is our choice. The more we think about it, the more it becomes our property. When we realise that thinking about others' negativity damages us, them and our relationship, we can stop and change it.

For bringing about that change, we must have the following understanding – When we tell somebody 'it is your fault', who is the one deciding what is wrong? What is wrong for you could be right for me. There is negativity around us, but we need not absorb it into our system.

SO: Yes, it is possible because we all have different sanskars.
SS: It is simple – we see things according to our perspective. If others do not work according to our definition of 'right', we label them 'wrong'. However, others will not change because of us as they may not share our perspective.

If we look for people whose definition of right and wrong matches with ours in every aspect, we will not find even a single person. The longer we hold on to this desire, the more difficult it will be for us to create smooth energy in relationships. So first understand that the other person is not 'wrong' but 'different' from us. There is a lot of difference between these two ways of thinking.

SO: Yes, everything and everyone in the universe is different from each other. A son is different from his father, so is a daughter from her mother and a brother from his brother.
SS: Every soul is unique and has its own journey. Each one has a long history of several lifetimes. The memories of experiences recorded on one soul cannot match with any other. One way of living is to recognise this truth.

The other way of living is to think 'I am right, you are wrong but I HAVE TO work with you'. If we work together or live together out of compulsion and continue to create such negative energy for each other, what will the foundation of our relationship be? When we keep sending the vibration 'you are wrong', what are we going to receive from the other side?

SO: They will think that we are wrong.
SS: If one 'wrong' is bonding with another 'wrong', what will become of that relationship? Let us look at this aspect in the

parent-child relationship. Parents must check how many times they create the thought that their children are wrong. They think it is natural for them to object to their children's 'wrong' actions, and it is their role to correct them. They find fault in many things that their children do – the time they wake up in the morning or sleep at night, the food they eat, the way they dress up, duration they watch TV, the hours they use the Internet, their chatting on social networking sites, the friends they make or the speed at which they drive.

When parents constantly send the 'you are wrong' energy to their children, they are bound to receive similar energy in return. When such negative energy is exchanged in the most beautiful relationship, we label the outcome as 'generation gap'. Eventually, parents tell their children 'we don't understand you' and children say 'neither do we'.

SO: We tell our children that they are wrong. Our parents told us the same thing too.

SS: Yes, it is true for every generation.

When parents start to disapprove of their children's actions, the children stop discussing things with them. How many children today share everything with their parents? We receive so many long e-mails from children discussing their personal problems with us. At the end of the e-mail they request us not to share it with their parents. When a child is in pain, who is in the best position to help him? The parents. But the child does not want to share his problem with them because he knows that after listening to him, his parents will label him 'wrong'.

When a child is young, he shares everything with his parents, even little details like what happened at school, what the teacher said and so on. The parents listen gladly to him and smile at him. So an environment of acceptance in the house helps the child to share. But when he grows up and is in his teens, he stops sharing things with his parents. Now, parents have to question him about everything, but the child does not share even when asked to do so. Even if they enter his room, he says 'please go out and close the door, I want my space'. This is because when the child was young, he was appreciated for whatever he shares. Later, it becomes a little difficult for parents to accept everything he tells them. For example, if a child tells his parents that he bunked his classes to go to the movies, what is he going to receive from them?

SO: A long lecture.
SS: They will get angry with him and say 'you are wrong ... how could you do this ... this is not what we taught you ... don't you know how much we spend on your tuition, and so on'. Hearing such things, the child feels rejected. He is unable to figure out what made the parents react, because he does not feel his action is wrong. To him, informing his parents is just a regular, everyday sharing that he is used to doing.
If this pattern of sharing and rejection goes on for a while, the child stops sharing anything, anymore with his parents. This creates a gap between them. The gap is created because parents stop accepting the child, and because they do not have the power to remain stable while listening to his truth.
Now we have reached a point where children seek help from counsellors instead of sharing their problems with parents. If children feel they would rather share their personal issues with a stranger, a professional, then it is a big question mark over our family set-up. Parents really need to think about it.

MANTRAS FOR BEING LOVE

- When a group of people, could be family and friends, create similar thoughts for someone, then powerful collective vibrations are created, which reach the person. Positive vibrations can heal and negative vibrations can cause pain.

- Since the creator and the receiver are generally in a negative state of mind, the effect of negative thoughts is faster. If we create pure thoughts for someone, it will take some time for our positivity to influence his mind.

- Focus on seeing and retaining the good qualities in people. Though their weaknesses are visible, take care not to churn them and consume that negativity.

- Different souls have different sanskars. Each soul's perspective and understanding of right and wrong are different. What we find wrong with their behaviour may be right and justified for them.

Let Parents Turn Counsellors

Suresh Oberoi: Children are going to counsellors today because they are able to share with them about things they fear discussing with their parents.

Sister Shivani: Very true. When children face problems, are in pain and need support, they go to others for help instead of confiding in their parents. In fact they ensure that their problems remain a secret from their parents. This is because, when they confess to a counsellor about the mistakes they have made, about a relationship they are in, or an addiction they have fallen prey to, he responds with understanding.

If an outsider confesses things to you, how will you respond?

SO: I will talk to him politely. I will be stable because it will not hurt me to listen to him since I do not share a close relationship with him. After that, I will advise him.

SS: Right. You will accept him and say 'It is okay if something went wrong, we will find a solution. Even if you've developed a wrong habit, it is okay, we can work on it and get rid of it.

If you failed an exam, it is okay, this year you can study more and pass'. So basically your approach will be one of acceptance, love and support and it will be solution-oriented.

SO: I will be stable and not get angry with an outsider. I will also not ask him questions like 'how did you get into such a bad habit at this young age' or 'who all do you hang out with'.
SS: Who would you ask these specific questions to?

SO: I would ask this to my own child if he came to me with such a problem.
SS: A child in pain comes to elders for love, support and acceptance, and also to find a way out of the problem he is facing. He may not need a solution immediately. Sometimes there is no solution at all in a situation, or the child may already have it. But at that particular moment, all that the child wants is that someone should heal his wound with love and understanding.

SO: That is why it is so important to listen to him patiently.
SS: Yes. If a child shares his problem with his parents, they usually react even before he has finished telling his story.

SO: The parents are not stable and create anger and pain.
SS: The actions of a child matter a lot to the parents, as it is a very important relationship for them. As soon as they listen to his mistakes, their own mental state goes down. They feel angry, irritated, hurt and let down.
Their first conversation with him is: 'How could you do this? What did we teach you? You have brought a bad name to the family. What will people say?' In this case, what sort of energy do the parents transmit to the child and what is their way of talking? Instead of giving love, support, care and healing,

they give him the opposite of that – criticism and judgmental behaviour. When the child receives such a reaction from his parents, it adds to his pain. Parents must think of themselves as doctors and treat the child like a patient who is injured. To heal him is their most important responsibility. They do not even need to know how it all happened. A doctor never wastes even a few minutes asking the patient 'but how did you fall', because healing him is his priority.

SO: But parents cannot behave like a doctor because they obviously get hurt.
SS: When a child is injured physically, what do the parents do? They give him first aid. Console him and then ask him what happened. Their instant response is to heal him. Some parents, however, are so taken aback on seeing the injury and blood loss, that they are unable to deliver at that time.
Just as parents' priority should be to tend to the child's physical wounds, they must heal his emotional pain immediately as a priority. When the child comes to them for support, that is not the time to question him about how he got into trouble, why he forgot to follow their instructions and so on. Otherwise the moment they reject his act or behaviour, a gap is created between them and the child.

SO: Sometimes, soon after listening to a fraction of the child's confession, the parents' reaction is so strong that the child is unable to tell them the whole issue.
SS: Suppose I accidentally break a glass in your room and also drop a piece of crystal placed there. If the moment I confess about the broken glass, I get a very long and harsh reaction from you, I would rather keep mum about the bigger loss of having dropped the crystal too.

If the child is unable to open up to his parents, his pain remains unhealed. He then looks for support outside, from someone who can accept him despite his mistakes and is willing to heal his pain. If a counsellor can help a child after listening to him in a non-judgmental way, can't parents turn counsellors for their children, family and friends? A counsellor can give advice, but the love and support for emotional healing can come only from parents.

SO: How will it be if parents do both the things – they act as a counsellor by patiently listening to the child and not reacting, and they also give him love?

SS: To listen to someone without reacting means we accept him and do not create even a single judgmental thought in our mind. When we react, it means we no longer have control on ourselves and are sending across the energy of rejection. This pushes the person away from us.

When we are judgmental, we get angry and hurt. This blocks our energy of love. At any given time, a person can radiate only one kind of energy. We can't be loving and reacting at the same time. Parents often tell their children 'I am angry with you because I love you'. But it is not possible to send two energies at the same time. Parents cannot love their children in the same moment that they scold them.

SO: Parents may not have loved their child at that particular point but they did love him before and after that.

SS: But that was the most crucial point when they needed to radiate love and acceptance to their child.

When a child comes to his parents in a state of emotional pain, his self-confidence is low. He may have made a mistake and could be feeling guilty about it. He could also be afraid of his family's reaction. If he is already in a negative state of mind, and the parents also give him the energy of anger and criticism, then his mental state will be pushed lower.

The parents' first responsibility is to bring the child's state of mind to normal, and later give him advice or solution. If they advise him when he is most depleted, the child will not have the power to implement it. This understanding should be applied by everyone – whether a parent, friend or boss.

SO: Usually, people waste a lot of time discussing the mistake and the circumstances leading to it. They do not focus on the solution.

SS: If someone has accidentally broken something, the solution for it is that he should be more careful the next time. So the solution lies in the future. But that person's self-confidence needs to be restored immediately, so that he does not develop a fear of handling things.

Let us fix this simple formula for life – the bigger the mistake a person commits, the more love we will give him. Only after that will we give him advice. First empower, then advise.

If a person is disempowered, he may be unable to rebuild his confidence for an entire lifetime, even beyond. Mistakes can still be amended tomorrow. Even if a mistake cannot be rectified, it is after all just one very small part of life. Let us not magnify things and make them so big. The most important aspect is to strengthen that person because he has to perform many tasks and cross many more situations in life. That should be our focus.

A counsellor listens to all the problems of his patients, including details of even a sin committed by them. But he does not pass a judgment on them. He dwells on the solution. When a patient receives the energy of respect from his counsellor – which the family and friends usually withdraw upon knowing about his wrong act – he is able to return to a normal state quickly.

We should be non-judgmental not just in words but also in our thoughts. Once that person is healed, he will be able to solve his problems. We cannot solve others' problems.

SO: There have been cases of honour killing.

SS: When people become too judgmental over a long period of time, it takes an extreme form. Honour killing is an example of that. Such social evils manifest rarely. But what happens commonly as a result of judgmental behaviour, is that parents snap all ties with their children and refuse to support them.

SO: And when their children's decisions go wrong, they tell them 'this had to happen as you did not listen to us'.

SS: All this is so subtle. So what happens to the parent-child relationship? The role of the parents is to take care of their children for life – to give them advice, and most importantly to continue giving them their love and support.

Suppose there has been a very long discussion in the family over the child's bigger decisions such as career or relationship. The parents warn the child with their best intentions: 'Do not do this because it will have difficult repercussions that you will be forced to bear lifelong and you'll never be happy.' Sometimes the child is so stuck on his decision that he goes ahead with it despite everyone in the family advising him against it. But once the decision is taken, the parents have to change their mindset completely. They must accept the situation and be there for the child. If they continue with the same old mindset and negative vocabulary, what would they be actually doing?

SO: They would be cursing their own child.
SS: So, once the decision is taken by the child, the parents' thought process should change. Instead of saying 'now wait and watch what happens next', the parents should say 'if you are still going ahead with your decision, our blessings are with you. You should get the best in life'. If family members give their good wishes, there is high probability that things will eventually work out for the child. But if the child's decision turns out to be wrong for him, what is the parents' responsibility in that case?

SO: To accept the child.
SS: Yes, but what is the usual response from parents?

SO: 'See, I had told you this is going to happen. Now regret'.
SS: So what were the parents actually waiting for?

SO: They were waiting for the child to make an error, regret and come back to them so they could prove themselves right.
SS: Yes. They wanted that to happen so that for the rest of his life, the child does everything according to them. Is this love and support? Is this a parent-child relationship? Is this a soul to soul connection? It is nothing but a power and control game.

MANTRAS FOR BEING LOVE

- When people share their problems or mistakes with a counsellor, he is detached and stable. Being stable means the mind is not critical or judgmental.

- On hearing the mistakes, family and friends get critical and angry, feel hurt and let down. With all these emotions, the energy of love and care gets blocked.

- The one who makes a mistake is in pain due to guilt and fear of facing the family. Family's role is to heal the pain and not add pain to the existing pain by getting angry with him.

- When someone is in pain, our role is to empower him, increase his self-confidence, and help him focus on the solution rather than discuss his past mistake.

Love Others
When They Least Deserve It

Suresh Oberoi: Someone messaged me a beautiful line – 'Love me the most when I least deserve it, because that is when I need it the most.'
Sister Shivani: That's what we have been discussing in this series so far.

SO: When a person makes a mistake, he is punished for it. But, actually, that is the time when he needs others' love and support the most because he is already burdened with guilt.
SS: The line holds true for every soul. When we think that someone does not deserve our love because he is wrong, that is actually the time when he is in dire need of it. Usually, if someone in the family makes a mistake, the entire family feels hurt.

SO: They criticise him and reject him.

SS: But why do they do so? If a person does something which his family or the society disapprove of – be it related to his choice of career, life partner or something else – they consider him to be the cause of their pain. That is why the energy of anger and criticism is directed at him.

The family members need to realise that the individual concerned experiences more pain than anyone of them. He feels he has let others down, so he feels guilty and thinks of himself as a failure. He is also afraid of facing others. If they consider him to be the cause of their pain, their energy towards him will be negative. But if they realise he is in greater pain, their energy towards him will change.

SO: Some people commit grave errors and then deceive others by pretending to be guilty, though they never mean to improve. Some borrow money and never return it. Should such people be allowed to repeat their mistakes?

SS: In such cases, often the individual concerned is carrying a wrong habit from the past. If we do not approve of his act, we should be strict with him. But creating anger, hate and criticism against him is not a solution. We should realise that he is originally a pure soul but is currently under the influence of a negative sanskar. So we need to have compassion and sympathy for him. We must keep intact our love and respect for him and assist him in transforming.

A couple shared that their son had a habit of borrowing money from them. He would invest in some business but it would never work out. A lot of money had been wasted like that. In such a case, parents need to be very strict and should not lend money to their son. This is because if they do so, they will end up endorsing his negative sanskar that they want him to get rid of. They should be assertive and not relent even if the son is stubborn or threatens them emotionally. This will require a certain detachment on their part.

SO: Some children even try to scare parents with suicide threats.

SS: A child will not take any extreme step if the parents continue to give him the energy of love and support. They must tell him that they do care for him, but they do not agree with him in that particular matter. So they must love and respect the child when he least deserves it. At the same time, they should deal strictly with his negative sanskar so that it is not reinforced.

SO: When students don't score well in exams, they feel afraid to go home. At that time, they are in pain and need so much love and care.

SS: That is why in a previous conversation we had discussed that the bigger the mistake a person commits, the more we need to love him. If we love our family and friends, it should mean we are ready to love them even when they least deserve it. If we love them when they are perfect and withdraw our support when they make errors, that's not love. Even if someone's decision goes wrong, that is not the time to tell him 'I told you not to do it'.

SO: If my son fails at something, I could say it happened because he did not follow my instructions. But the fact is that

my advice may also not always be right. A movie offer that I ask him to turn down could go on to become a super hit.

SS: All of us make mistakes and no one is an exception. What is a mistake, anyway? When we implement something with the expectation that it will work for us, but the result does not turn out to be favourable, we call that a mistake. It is not necessary that every decision of ours will bring the desired result. We need to understand this for ourselves and others.

We may advise our family members with the best intention. But once in a while, one of them may act against our advice, and may go ahead with his individual choice. If his choice turns out to be wrong, we should not use that as a chance to prove ourselves right. Instead of waiting for him to fall and then saying 'see, we were right and you were wrong', we should love him the most – at those moments.

SO: At the beginning of my career, I had not got movie offers. But I could not go back home because I was afraid of taunts from family, as they had advised me against taking up acting.

SS: Your journey was eventually successful. Otherwise, things might have become difficult. We must remember that whenever our loved ones fail at their decisions, we, as their family, must stand by them and help them rise again.

Let us take an example. We are at a hill top right now. Suppose I want to jump from this place. But you advise me against it because I would get hurt. You explain consequences and try to dissuade me from doing it. You rightly stand firm when it is time to give advice. But if I decide to jump despite all your efforts to convince me, then there needs to be a total shift in your energy that very moment.

SO: If I care for you I should say 'if you still want to jump, wear protection gear and secure yourself with a rope ... I will have people at the bottom of the hill to hold you and not you hurt yourself'.

SS: This is it. Once I have taken the decision, your resistance should change into support, love and blessings.

Suppose I do jump and even get injured. That is not the time when you should tell me 'this is why I told you not to jump'. That is the time to help me get back on my feet and to remind me that it is not the end of the world. That is the time to help me move on.

What will my state of mind be when I fall? I will think of myself as a failure and will be scared to face others. I will be in pain, and will feel guilty about not considering your advice. If, at such a time I get unconditional support, I will not experience fear or guilt. This is an example of loving someone the most when they least deserve it.

We should apply this understanding to bigger aspects of life, and while taking major decisions. Always remember that when someone makes a mistake, it is not the time to teach him, it is the time to heal him.

When a child is in pain, he should be able to communicate that to his family members without hesitation. This will happen only when they are, in general, not judgmental of him and they accept him.

Suppose a young boy starts to smoke or drink, or falls prey to an addiction. Instead of telling him that the habit is wrong, elders tell him that he is bad. This pushes him away from his dear ones and closer to the addiction.

In such a case, family members need to adopt another approach.

First, they should tell him that they do understand it is natural for someone of his age to want to try new things, and that his friends must be doing it too. Then they should gently convey to him the harmful effects of addiction. In this way, they can come closer to the child and help him push away his act.

If, however, the family members scold the youngster, he will move away from them and be drawn closer to his peers. It is then possible that at some point of time, his friends may ask him to do something that he does not want to do. But he would feel compelled to participate in it because their acceptance is important to him. This is peer pressure.

Today, there are too many distractions for children, and there is no way by which parents can keep tabs on them. Gone are the days when parents could check who their children talked to, over phone. Now there is unlimited access to all kinds of information, right at their fingertips. In this scenario, the only way parents can shield their children, is if the children themselves come to them and share their problems. This can happen only if parents assure the children of their unconditional availability and support. They must make it clear that they are ready to hear out even if the child has made the biggest blunder.

SO: If children are scolded whenever they share their secrets with their parents, they will not be able to open up to them when they grow up.

SS: A lady used to attend our programme along with her ten-year-old son. One day, we discussed that children lie to their parents because they are afraid of being scolded by them. She made a note of it. The next day she found that particular line underlined in her notebook. She wondered who did that. When she asked her son, he accepted that he had underlined it. She sensed that he wanted to tell her something. So she told him that he could freely confess anything and she would not be angry with him. The child told her that he had failed an exam, but did not have the courage to tell her earlier.

To hide things and live in fear is very difficult for children. So it's important that parents build confidence in children that they can come to them anytime for support. In fact, we must give such an assurance to everyone, not just children.

Even in the workplace, people lie when requesting for leave and in other matters because they are reprimanded for speaking the truth. A parent or a team leader must make sure that whatever be the situation, his first response is not one of disturbance. He should be stable, understand the situation and accept what the other person is saying. This is how we can create a culture of transparency where everyone can speak their mind. If we do not build an environment that allows us to share our thoughts, then the ones suffering will have to face it all alone.

Once a couple shared with us that their 17-year-old son had committed suicide. Only after the incident they came to know that he had faced a lot of difficulties at college. They said he had never discussed it with them. Had he done that, they would have helped him. If one is unable to share one's inner pain, it keeps piling up within and can reach such extreme levels.

SO: Many parents remain preoccupied with work or networking. They are too busy to talk to their children,

to appreciate their talents and achievements at school or to watch them perform. If the basic bond is not developed, how can children approach their parents in times of need?

SS: Right. So remember to love others when they least deserve it because that is the time when they need it the most.

The other thing to understand is that everyone's definition of right and wrong is different. So when we are discussing something, our words should be 'I am right, you are also right from your perspective. Now let's sit and talk'. If both parties think 'I am right, you are wrong', then no discussion can be fruitful because the judgment has already been passed. Remember to replace the label 'wrong' with 'different', as there is a lot of energy difference between these two. The former is disrespect for others, while the latter is respect. This changes the foundation of our relationships.

MANTRAS FOR BEING LOVE

- Family and friends need our love and respect the most at those times when we feel they least deserve it.

- When people close to us make mistakes and we get hurt or angry, we feel THEY ARE the cause of our pain. Truth is that they in more pain than the rest of the family.

- If we feel they are the cause of our pain, our love gets blocked. If we understand that they are in pain, our love, compassion and care radiates to them.

- If we withdraw our support and respect, they will not be able to come to us for healing their pain. This means we were not available for them when they needed us the most.

- Even if parents do not approve of it, once a child has taken a decision, their energy should shift from resistance to support and blessings.

Accepting New Family Members

Suresh Oberoi: We were discussing that it is better to label someone 'different' rather than 'wrong'. If everyone in the family has a different approach to life, then what about discipline?

Sister Shivani: We must think the other person is different because when we think he is wrong, the energy we radiate is very heavy.

SO: Suppose we have a new daughter-in-law in our family, and she has had a very different lifestyle in her parental home. Let's say that in our family, we have a habit of informing each other when we go out, but she is not used to doing this. Will that not be problematic for us?

SS: Who is to judge which of the two habits is right? Should one inform the family before going out or is it okay even otherwise? Usually, the habit that a person has been following for a long time seems right to him. It would be difficult for him to find anything wrong with it. In this case, for you the practice of informing others before leaving the house is an obvious 'right'. So you do not think there is any other way to be.

SO: We are more comfortable if our family members inform us before going out. In case of any emergency, it would be easier for us to locate them.

SS: You have been following this rule for a long time and cannot think of any other option as right. For your daughter-in-law, who has recently joined your family, a different lifestyle is 'naturally right' because she too has been following it for a long time. This is the point to be understood.

You will have several reasons justifying your 'right' habit. For example, you said that keeping family members informed of our whereabouts makes it easier for them to trace us in case of an emergency. Similarly, your daughter-in-law will have her own logic. If you label her action as 'wrong', she too will label you in a similar way. Then the energy in your relationship will become strained. She will feel that you are trying to control her so that she complies with your rules.

The moment we radiate the energy 'my method is right, you have to follow it', the other person will try to move away from us, as no one wants to be controlled.

SO: There must be a difference between control and concern. One could simply be concerned about one's family member.

SS: Yes, there is definitely a lot of difference. To express concern for your family member, you will have to remove the 'you are wrong' energy from the foundation of that relationship. Then your concern will be effective.

SO: If we are really concerned about someone, we will not lose our temper with him or her.

SS: Even if you are not angry with your daughter-in-law but you are thinking that her way of doing things is wrong, the energy of control is reaching her. If after sending such heavy energy you express your concern politely and say 'you must inform me before going out', she will defend her action immediately. You attacked her habit, so she will attack yours. Your right logic will be countered by her right logic, and the argument could go on and on.

So you can change your response a little bit. If a new member joins your family and she is 'different', accept that it is okay if she does not have the same sanskars as you.

SO: I should also not think that it is strange that her parents did not teach her such basic things. Otherwise, such thoughts would reach her before our conversation.

SS: Yes, it is not the words but the thoughts behind them that must be amended. After that, if you express the same concern, it will be taken positively by her.

SO: Once, after listening to a religious discourse, I was about to leave in a hurry. Someone told me that I should have taken leave formally. I was very annoyed at their expectation. But they too must have found it strange that I had left just like that.

SS: Both the parties must have found it equally strange.

SO: Why couldn't they understand that I was in a hurry?

SS: Because they were thinking using their own sanskars. They had their own perspective on how people should behave.

SO: How should I bring 'being love' into the picture here? I am taking up very small, everyday examples because that is where most of our problems lie.
SS: In life, it is always better to try out an equation in smaller situations. When we do so, our sanskars undergo a change. Once sanskars are transformed, the equation automatically gets applied in bigger situations. We face major challenges rarely while smaller ones happen every day. A sanskar is formed when we do something repeatedly, and so it makes sense to apply these equations while resolving everyday issues.

Getting back to our subject of discussion, when we label others as 'wrong', they feel they are being controlled by us. Criticism, comparison and competition block our love, and so does control. The feeling of control – the thought that others should listen to me – stays in relationships much longer than any of the energy blockers mentioned above.

SO: My friend would unwillingly attend family get-togethers that his grandfather had every weekend. Seeing his discomfort, I changed certain rules in my house so that no one felt compelled to do anything.
SS: This is an example where you let go of visible control. Control can be very subtle. It means that our actions are driven by the thought 'what I think and do, and my way of working are right. You should follow that'.

Why do parents like their child more when he is very young? Because he is under their control. At that age, the child just goes by what his parents say. Adolescence is considered to be a difficult time because the child no longer agrees to everything his parents say. He starts using his intellect and some of his actions do not match their definitions of right. That is the time parents say that their child is going out of control.

SO: Later, after the son is married, they say he has gone completely out of their control.
SS: A greater cause of pain for the parents is their perception that after getting out of their control, their son has gone under the control of their daughter-in-law. But actually, he is under no one's control. He acts according to his own definition of right. Sometimes that definition matches with the parents, sometimes it matches with his spouse.

If we have a sanskar of expecting people to act according to us, we will be in constant conflict with them. Our relationships will be founded on this energy of conflict.

Suppose I like to wear white and am comfortable with dresses of this colour. Slowly my belief system will become 'white is right'. Later, my thinking will be 'white is the only right colour'. This means that all the other colours are wrong. The thinking actually should be 'white is right for me, different colours are right for different people'. Whatever is right for me does not become universally right. It is only right for me. The lack of this understanding is the basic cause of conflict in relationships. When we think 'only I am right, the other person is wrong', both parties feel suffocated. We become so closed because of our opinion that we do not make room for the other person's point of view. We do not try to understand his sanskars or the reasons behind his actions just because his ways do not match with our definition of right.

We should do what is right for us, then advise others, and also give them love and support. Finally, they will act according to what they think is right for them. We cannot convince others beyond a point to do something.

If we base our love, peace and happiness on how much others act according to us, then these energies will keep fluctuating all day. We will constantly be anxious about whether others will do as directed by us, as that will become our stimulant to remain stable. If they do not agree with us, we will be disturbed. It is an addiction to want people to work according to us, and it causes constant conflict in relationships.

Taking your example again, the daughter-in-law comes in house from a completely different set-up and carrying a different set of sanskars. Why do the in-laws expect her to easily adapt to the sanskars of all her new family members? Till the time she adapts herself to their lifestyle, they keep putting the label of 'wrong' on almost everything she does.

Now we understand the journey of the soul. A soul comes with unlimited recording of sanskars acquired in past lives. A child, therefore, has a long past, but in the current lifetime he is conditioned by his parents' behaviour, and so he adopts several of their sanskars. But when the daughter-in-law comes into her husband's household at the age of twenty-five or thirty, her conditioning even in this lifetime has been different. To expect her to change instantly, and to put a label of 'wrong' on her till she adapts to her new environment sows the seeds of conflict. That is why the relationship between a daughter-in-law and her in-laws is generally strained.

These days, people say it is good for couples to stay separately from the very beginning because it is difficult for them to get along with their parents. But why can't they get along? Just because we are all different?

SO: But both the sides – the daughter-in-law and the in-laws – should be understanding.

SS: Who in your opinion should understand first? If any one side initiates a positive move, it becomes easier for the other one to follow in that direction. We cannot wait for others to change. It is not possible for us to change them.

SO: Is it possible to restore disturbed relationships?

SS: We can transform any relationship even after several years, simply by changing the way we think about the other person in that relationship. We have to change our vibrations.

In the situation that we have been discussing, instead of thinking that the son is under the control of their daughter-in-law, parents can think that after receiving opinions from both the sides, he is acting according to what he thinks is right.

Nobody is in our control anyway. It is only an illusion we create when others listen to us. They listen to us only because they are convinced by what we say. They could also obey us out of fear or because of our social position. However, that too cannot last very long.

If parents send negative energy to the daughter-in-law when they think their son has aligned himself with her opinion, then she too will automatically create similar negative energy when her husband happens to agree with his parents. The foundation of their relationship will then be based on turbulent energy. It will continue to be like that until one side takes the initiative to break this loop of negative energy exchange. So there needs to be a bit of change in the thought process.

SO: If we keep accepting that everyone is different, it will be so difficult to run the house.

SS: When we accept that others are different, we respect them and create the energy of harmony in that relationship. After that, if we convey our point of view, they will receive it with better energy. Then that person may take his own course of action. It is not necessary that the change we want to see in him will happen immediately.

SO: Our views may not be considered.
SS: Yes, it is possible and that's fine. Our relationship with others is more important than our points of view.

SO: Harmony within the household is more important than all the small differences.
SS: Difference of opinion will happen daily. But if that creates disrespect in relationships, then it leads to disharmony.

SO: I have seen in many households that parents become dissatisfied and say they've given up on their children. They no longer interfere in their decisions and just let them be.
SS: They may not be communicating with their children through words but they are definitely communicating with them constantly through thoughts. The arguments that used to happen may have stopped. But the exchange of negative, disharmonious energy continues. If one decides to be silent and non-interfering, then one should be quiet outside and within. But if that is not the case, then a lot of negativity flows to the other side by way of thoughts and then is reflected back in the same way. That is not good for the persons involved, for the relationship and for the entire family.

MANTRAS FOR BEING LOVE

- People's habits and sanskars can be different from ours. We can see only through the filter of our sanskars and so we feel our perspective is right.

- The other person's perspective is 'different' from us, let us not label it as 'wrong'. What is right for us may not feel right to them. They are different from us, not wrong.

- When we create a thought that someone is wrong, we are disrespecting them. When we understand that they are different, we are respecting them and their perspective.

- When we accept the difference, then they also accept our sanskar. We respect each other, are open to understanding the other perspective and may be even ready to change ours.

Connecting Truly In Relationships

Suresh Oberoi: I have an apt quote to begin with. 'We have a tendency to want the other person to be a finished product while we give ourselves the grace to evolve.'

Sister Shivani: We want others in our relationships – be it our spouse, children or colleagues – to be a finished product. But when it comes to us, we say 'it is okay, I am improving gradually'. We justify our actions by saying 'what to do, it is my nature' or 'these habits run in our family'. But we give no such liberty to others and want them to be perfect, and that too according to our definition of 'perfection'.

SO: Oh yes, I did not realise that. We want others to fit into our image of a 'perfect daughter', 'perfect son', and want them to be as we define them.

SS: We want others to be perfect according to our standards. It may seem to be a small thing, but this desire is the source of most of our conflicts. Others are perfect the way they are, with their own sanskars.

SO: This is a good point of view.

SS: Suppose I have a particular way of sitting and I am very comfortable with it. You are passing by and tell me 'don't sit like this, sit straight'. I will resist the change immediately as I may not be comfortable with the way you want me to sit. This is because my current posture is perfect for me. Many times parents say they know what is perfect and right for their children. But this may not be the case always.

When someone chooses a life partner, or a family welcomes their new daughter-in-law into their house, they already have an image in their mind about how that person should be. They have a preconceived image of a perfect person, which they create on the basis of the sanskars they have.

There are three images of a person for us. First, we create an image of how he should be. Then we meet that person and perceive him through our sanskars. That is the second image we create of him. And the third is what he actually is. People are not what we think them to be. We can never really know anyone too well because we know them only through the filter of our sanskars. We simply cannot see them from another point of view.

SO: We may not even know ourselves fully. Sometimes, I am surprised at my own reaction to various situations.

SS: Right. Because up until that point, you did not know that you had that sanskar.

SO: Yes.

SS: This happens because we souls carry recordings of several sanskars acquired in our past births.

Let us consider ourselves to be a CD with a hundred pre-recorded 'songs' or sanskars. In the current lifetime we may have played only fifty songs. This means the remaining fifty are yet to be played.

SO: We are not even aware of the remaining songs.
SS: Right. Then all of a sudden, some situation triggers one of those 'unknown' songs to play. That leaves us and others around us surprised. Looking at our own response we say 'this is not me'. But the truth is – this is the me that I did not know of.
So we have to be aware that there are still many songs recorded on us that have not played in this lifetime but could get played any time. And when that happens, we must take responsibility for whatever sanskar emerges – whether negative or positive. Accept that the sanskar is our own. If it is a positive sanskar, we should hold on to that speciality and use it again and again in our life. If, however, a negative sanskar emerges, we must take care not to replay it if a similar situation arises in future.

SO: But we are so busy watching others' sanskars that we do not look at our own.
SS: We cannot really look at others' sanskars. Even if we claim to know others well, that may not be the case.

SO: We at least know them from our point of view.
SS: Our point of view could be completely different from who they actually are.
Suppose you are a very sincere person. I, on the other hand, have the sanskars of doubt and criticism. You may do your work with utmost sincerity, but since I do not possess the sanskar of appreciation, I will always criticise you irrespective of how much effort you put in. As I have the sanskar of doubt, I will think, 'Did he really do his work honestly? Maybe he had a selfish

motive behind doing it.' I may never be able to truly see your sanskar of sincerity because I always view you through my filter of doubt. So can I really know you? No, I cannot.

The first image that we create of a person is how we want him to be. The second image is how we perceive him to be. The third is what he actually is. And these three images could be completely different from each other. We may probably never come to know about the third image – how a person actually is – while we constantly try to match the first two images. When we attempt to change the person as we perceive him into the person we want him to be, it can be very damaging for us, the other person and the relationship.

We create a relationship in our mind, it does not exist outside. We do not have a relationship with others, but with their image that we have created in our consciousness. If you are an absolutely dishonest person, but the mental image I have of you is that of an honest person, then despite everything you do, I will continue to see you through that filter.

SO: I have experienced this myself. A man used to visit us. He looked like a cheat to me, but my son would always praise him.
SS: Both of you can form a different image about the same person in your consciousness. You will go by your perception and may not be able to understand your son's perception.

SO: And he will not understand mine. He will think that I doubt everyone I meet.
SS: Right. We should not try too hard to change the other person's perception because it may not be possible for him to see with another view point. The earlier we realise this, the better it will be for us.

The fact is that the hundred song recordings on me may not match with yours. You may take a lifetime to convince me to play a song that is recorded on you, the CD, but it cannot happen because that song is not recorded on me. I simply will not know how to play it.

Understanding each other becomes difficult at times because we do not see through the same filters. We should not try too hard to convince others to our point of view because it creates conflict in relationships.

SO: Do you mean to say we should have no expectations from anybody at all?

SS: If you and I have different sets of songs on our CDs, and I expect you to play from your CD a song which is recorded on mine, what good will that expectation yield?

SO: But people must have something in common – like respect for each other – on the basis of which they can live comfortably.

SS: They may not have even a single song that is common between them. Look at the journey of the soul. Everyone has experienced different lives – some may have taken fifty births before this, some may have taken seventy. In all these lives, each one has had different sets of parents and faced different situations. Even if we look at the current lifetime of two souls that have been in their present bodies for the past fifty years, their experiences could be completely different from each other. Hence their recordings would be different too. It is possible that not even a single situation that one faced occurred in the other's life. Their cultures, family values, conditioning, religion and even countries could be different. If there can be so many differences between two people in just the last fifty years, then imagine the enormity of differences they are bound to have in fifty lives. There is unlimited recording on us souls.

One person's definition of trust and honesty will be different from another, and even such minor differences could create conflict. For example, you may respect me, but you may not respect me in the manner I want you to. I will expect you to respect me according to the sanskars recorded on me.

SO: Then why do different people pay respect in temples in the same manner?
SS: People perform the same rituals in temples, though their thoughts will remain different. There are so many people who do not even go to the temple. You are looking at those whose one 'song' or sanskar is common.

SO: They are somewhat similar.
SS: Even among those who go to the temple, they all do it with a different feeling.

SO: Some might be going to the temple out of fear, others due to greed, and some others due to family's insistence.
SS: Even if all the people going to the temple do so as a mark of respect, there will still be a difference in the level of respect. We are sitting amidst greenery and you may not find even two leaves here that are completely the same.

SO: So it is my fault if I am looking for identical leaves.
SS: Beautiful! This is it. It is our fault that we look for identical

leaves and we can waste our whole life doing that. If we decide to be happy only when we find two identical leaves, what are we writing in our destiny? Sadness, anger, irritation, dissatisfaction and never-to-be-fulfilled expectations. All conflicts will be resolved when we understand that our definitions may not match.

SO: I agree with you that no two souls can be alike when two leaves cannot be. How should I bring 'being love' into the picture?
SS: Being love can work when we love and appreciate each leaf as it is, however it may be.

SO: Suppose we only acknowledge that this is a leaf of one kind and that leaf is of another kind.
SS: Even in that case, love will flow because there is no blockage for the energy of the soul.

SO: We are not labelling them as 'good leaf', 'bad leaf', 'small leaf' etc.
SS: Right. If we look at something as it is, our energy blockage gets cleared and our love begins to flow.
People are different, so we should have no problem with it. If we keep trying to match our definitions of 'right' with others', it is a never-ending game. By doing so, we will only create for ourselves a destiny of struggle. When the sanskars of even parent and child are different, how can we expect others to be like us? You had said in the beginning of this conversation that you are at times surprised at your own unexpected reactions. Anybody's latent sanskars can get activated any time. People will not stay the same as we have known them to be, for years. Even

beautiful sanskars can get activated of a sudden. For example, somebody we considered weak may suddenly show tremendous willpower in a particular situation and surpass our expectations. The opposite is also possible.

One small effort we all have to make is to let go of the past. It is possible that people acted in the past under the influence of some latent sanskar.

SO: Almost every sanskar is there in all of us, and we do not know what gets activated when.

SS: Yes. Most importantly, all souls have the seven original sanskars of wisdom, purity, peace, love, happiness, bliss and power. This is true even for those in whom we are unable to spot a trace of these. Remember that irrespective of the songs a person is playing currently, he surely has these seven recordings. We should try to look at others in this consciousness. If we focus only on a person's current sanskars, which are acquired, rather than his original sanskars, we will form a very different image of him.

SO: I have to be playing one of those seven original songs myself to be able to see others in that light. If I am on another track, it is not going to work.

SS: Absolutely. Unless we ourselves are using those seven qualities, we will not be aware that others have them too.

When we look at another soul with the consciousness that it has those original qualities, there is high probability that our vibrations will activate those in it. This is why soul consciousness is so important. Raj Yoga teaches us to make inner effort so that we are able to create a consciousness that allows us to see others as pure, peaceful, loving souls.

If someone is shouting at us but we create a thought 'he is originally a peaceful being' then, firstly, we will be able to play our original song or sanskar instead of reacting at him. Secondly, the vibrations of peace and love that he receives from us will silence his anger and activate his sanskar of peace.

SO: We will do this homework – to see everyone in the light of our seven original qualities.

SS: Let's at least do this much – whoever we meet during the day, the first thought we create for him is 'this is a pure, beautiful, loving, peaceful and powerful soul'.

If someone is very weak as he is unable to do what he decides to, then instead of looking at his weakness let us send across a pure thought 'he is a powerful soul'. Basically, we are sending him the vibration that can trigger the beautiful song recorded in him, of which he has lost awareness. There's high chance that our pure vibrations will be able to activate his original sanskars.

MANTRAS FOR BEING LOVE

- We normally carry a preconceived image of how we want a particular person or relationship to be. We then keep comparing that person to the image in our mind and try to make him like that image.

- We never really know people as they truly are. We know and understand them through the filter of our sanskars.

- Each soul is a bundle of many, many sanskars created in all their births. We are not aware of all our sanskars. We are aware only of the sanskars which come into action repeatedly.

- We may not understand other people because we do not have the same perspective as theirs. We need to accept that they have a different perspective and not try to control or change them.

Feed the Wolf
You Want to See Grow

Suresh Oberoi: I used to constantly complain to my Guru about others. He would respond by saying, 'A crow caws, a cat meows.' But I did not know that it was his answer for me. Now I understand that every leaf is different. Now the crow is cawing and other birds are chirping, but that is not disturbing me. It is so clear to me now that every soul is different and has its own point of view, and there is nothing wrong with that.

Sister Shivani: You just shared something important – when a crow caws or a bird chirps, it no longer disturbs you. Why not?

SO: Because I know they will surely do it; it is their nature.

SS: This is acceptance, it makes our mind stable.

SO: Acceptance is considered more of a weakness than a virtue. A person who accepts others, often looks at himself as a victim who is forced to do so.

SS: If someone thinks in this manner, it means he has not used the virtue of acceptance at all. When you say you do not get disturbed by the birds, all it means is that you do not create any thoughts questioning their act or nature. You accept that they are birds with their own voice, and that's what comes naturally to them.

God teaches us a beautiful thing: *'Jo aatma prashnachit hoti hai vo prasannchit nahin ban sakti'* [the one who questions everyone's sanskars can never be happy]. If we want to experience love, bliss and happiness, we have to be free of judgmental thoughts. And that will happen when we accept people and situations as they are. The moment we have questions about them, our happiness disappears. Others will be what they are. Our focus should be on keeping our mind silent. Today, if we check, our mind is always questioning everything and so we hardly get to experience peace. Now we have to change from being *'prashnachit'* [judgmental mind] to *'prasannchit'* [blissful mind], and acceptance is the key to it.

What does acceptance truly mean? Should we not interfere in others' business even when they act against their own well-being? Acceptance simply means to be first at peace with ourselves. If, for example, I think your chair needs to shift, there are two steps to go about it. First, I accept that it is your sanskar to sit like this and that you are comfortable in this position. It means I do not create these thoughts – 'why is he sitting like this ... he doesn't even know how to sit ... he should have at least moved a bit ... can't he understand even if I correct him everyday ...

he has become very stubborn'. As these thoughts lead us to reject the situation or person, we should not create them.

When we are peaceful and stable, we must take the second step and convey what we want to. We may have to repeat the same thing to our family and friends every day, if it is for their betterment. We could say 'I feel it would be better for you if you do it like this'. Once we convey this, we should put a full stop to our thoughts. We should not expect the other person to accept it right away. That's because he will accept it only when he is comfortable with it.

We should be very clear about our role as a parent, friend or senior in the organisation. Our role is only to empower others through our vibrations so they can grow. Parents must give emotional support and polite advice to their children. After that, they have to let them be.

It is just like taking care of a plant. First we check the quality of seeds and the direction of sunlight. Then we sow the seeds and water them every day. Then we patiently wait for nature to take its own course. Sometimes, if the sapling does not appear in a few days, we dig up the seed. It will not grow like that.

After giving advice, we have to just leave it there. We can give the person strength through our pure vibrations, but we should not keep checking every day if he has changed or not. Let us not get worked up over delay in response from the other side or else we will begin to complain about him to others.

SO: We may even say 'he will never change'. If we keep sending such vibrations to him, he will not be able to make any progress at all.
SS: Very true.

SO: If there is no change in the other person, it could also mean that something is lacking in our prayers and vibrations.

SS: Usually, when things do not go our way, we change our vibrations immediately. When we tell someone 'you will be able to do it', it is a powerful blessing. But if we later create thoughts of doubt, such as 'I don't really know if he will be able to do it ... he has never succeeded so far', then our best wishes will not work even though our words are positive. Our role in every relationship is to empower the other person, and to accept him instead of questioning him.

If the family collectively sends positive vibrations to one of their members, that soul can create miracles as the positive sanskars recorded on it will emerge. Remember, every soul has pre-recorded original sanskars of purity and power.

Suppose a child has a habit of lying. Parents ask us if acceptance means that they let their child be the way he is. No, acceptance simply means that for the present moment the parents accept the child with that sanskar, and they do not create a single question in their mind such as 'why does he lie'. When their mind is silent, it will play a huge role in the child's transformation because they will be able to send good vibrations to him. Their focus will change to awakening the child's positive sanskars.

In our family, we usually look at others through their prominent sanskars, and everyone discusses those constantly. If a family member already has a dominant negative sanskar, and everyone keeps talking about it, then we end up giving more energy to that sanskar. Where attention goes, energy flows, and where energy flows, things grow.

SO: I read a beautiful story. A son tells his father that he has noticed two wolves inside him who are in a tug of war with

each other. One wolf pulls him towards goodness, and the other pulls him towards evil. 'Who will win?' he asks. The father answers, 'The one you feed more will win.'

SS: So beautiful! Most importantly, the wolf that is fed by the entire family will win. Suppose you are feeding the wolf of anger inside you, but the rest of your family is feeding your good wolf, then the latter will become strong. This is what we have family, friends and relationships for.

Every person has shortcomings, and they can become worse if they repeatedly act according to those flaws. So, it is the role of the family members to feed the good wolf in each other. But unknowingly, they too keep feeding the bad wolf. That's why it keeps getting stronger day by day.

Always remember – 'where attention goes, energy flows, and where energy flows, things grow'. Instead of paying attention to others' negative sanskars, we have to focus on their positive sanskars that may not even be active at the time. For example, when we look at someone who is short-tempered, we can think – 'even though he gets angry these days, he was not like this always ... he is originally a peaceful soul ... even though his dominant sanskar is that of anger, he uses the quality of peace many times during the day ... he does not stay angry all through the day ... it is just that he is using the sanskar of peace less, that of anger more'.

SO: That's a very good point!

At times we think that despite all our efforts we are unable to bring out someone's good qualities. The reality is that when that person displays a positive sanskar, we do not pay much attention to it, as we are expecting a total makeover.

SS: It is easy for us to spot a sanskar that is more prominent. As it is, we do not pay much attention to goodness; it is taken for granted. For example, if you face a situation calmly, I may not appreciate it because nothing much happened apparently. But when you are angry with me, it upsets me, and leaves me wounded. So I will keep pointing out that you are short-tempered. Our role now should be to spot that one rare time when someone crosses a situation calmly or when he attempts to change.

SO: When we notice a change in someone, instead of appreciating it, we say things like 'the change is temporary ... he will soon show his true colours'.
SS: By doing that, we reinforce that person's negative sanskars yet again. We do not realise that in the name of love, we really strengthen each other's weaknesses. We keep discussing those even with outsiders.

SO: I love this expression – we ourselves strengthen each other's weaknesses. We feed the negative wolf inside others.
SS: We must decide to stop feeding the negative wolf completely. This means we should not think or talk about negativities of our family members, especially not discuss them outside. When we discuss about our close ones with others, we give out inside information to them. Secondly, those people may share it with others. That way, a lot of people may end up talking about the negative sanskars that we want to get rid of. So contrary to our intention, the negative energy will multiply manifold.

SO: As they say, use it or lose it. We should use our good sanskars so that they are strengthened. We must also stop feeding the bad wolf inside us.

SS: If we do so, our negativities will finish. However, if we are unable to do so ourselves, our family can support us by not giving any more energy to our negative sanskars.

SO: In the process, the family members will be helping themselves too. In reiki it is believed that when we heal others, we heal ourselves.

SS: Beautiful! That happens because the positive energy and vibrations that we create work for us too. In the beginning of the series, we had discussed the same point – when we think good about ourselves, it reaches others, and when we think well of others, we automatically do good to ourselves.

So, if we want to change a negative sanskar in someone else, we must stop thinking and talking about it. The more we discuss it, the more difficult it gets for that person to change it. This is because when everyone's thought energy is focused on a person's negative sanskar, it fuels that negativity. If there are two plants and we do not want one of them to grow, we need not uproot it. All we have to do is to stop watering it. It is that simple.

It is our responsibility to help our near ones overcome their weaknesses. Instead of continuously blaming them and considering them to be the cause of our misery, we must help them rise above their shortcomings. A person who has anger, jealousy or any other negativity is already in pain. His self-esteem could be low. So let's not water the plant of his weakness.

Similarly, even if we see only one speciality in our family member, we must start watering it appreciating it and giving it attention. Within a few months, we will witness a completely transformed personality because we cooperated with that person to grow one of his positive sanskars that he wasn't even aware of.

MANTRAS FOR BEING LOVE

- Accepting another person means understanding that he has that set of sanskars at the moment, and not creating any negative thoughts about them. Acceptance lets the mind remain calm and stable.

- The mind which is always questioning others' sanskars by thinking 'why are they like this they should change, I am in pain because of their sanskars' cannot be happy.

- If we find that a family member is doing something which is not right for him, first we need to accept him, which means not to get disturbed by his behaviour. Then we should give him advice but not expect that it will be implemented immediately.

- Where attention goes, energy flows. Where energy flows, things grow. Do not think and talk about others' weaknesses. Give attention and appreciation to their qualities and empower them.

Change Your Glasses
to Change Your World

Suresh Oberoi: I would like to share two quotations that I read. 'Whenever you are in conflict with someone, there is one factor that can make the difference between damaging your relationship and deepening it. That factor is attitude.' The second one says, 'When you judge another, you do not define them, you define yourself.'

Sister Shivani: These are powerful statements. When we pass a judgment on others by saying 'they are like this', we think we are defining them, but who are we actually defining?

SO: Ourselves. I would like to understand this a bit more. I had earlier discussed about a colleague with whom we had some issues. We all wanted him to leave. Those vibrations reached him and he eventually decided to quit work.

SS: What happened after that?

SO: That person was upset and wanted to leave. At that time, I thought to myself that we discuss about being love on our show, let me try it out in real life. So I apologised to him through my thoughts, and sent him good wishes and vibrations. Later, when I spoke to him over lunch and apologised in person, he was moved to tears. He suddenly became so warm and was a completely changed person. He decided to stay with us.

SS: The thought we were discussing was – 'when you are in conflict, the one factor that decides whether you damage or deepen the relationship is YOUR attitude'. Here conflict could refer to even a mere discomfort between the two people.

SO: Conflict could even mean cold relations, when two people do not share cordial vibes.

SS: The energy exchange is not in harmony, and so there is an uncomfortable feeling between two people. One could have such an experience with a neighbour, a colleague, relatives, or even with one's family members.

If we wish to check the quality of our relationships, we need not look outside. Just by monitoring the quality of our thoughts for others we can know the kind of bond we share. Those for whom we think good most of the time are beautiful relationships, and those for whom our thinking is mostly cluttered are the relationships that have conflict.

We can move closer in our relationships or drift apart depending on our attitude. You have already experienced it practically. Initially you thought negatively about your colleague because you did not agree with his actions. But your relationship with him improved later because you changed your attitude towards him, even though he did not change as a person.

SO: His actions do not offend me so much now. Earlier, I used to keep judging him. Now, he has changed and so have I.
SS: It is actually the other way around. You changed your thoughts for him, that is why he changed. He was about to quit because of the initial wave of negative energy that you had sent him. Later, you changed your thoughts, which means that you sent an altogether different energy towards him.

SO: I even apologised.
SS: Sometimes we say sorry when we don't mean it. In that case, we do not get the desired result because the conflict in relationships is not external but internal. When we are in conflict with someone, the chords inside our mind are badly entangled. Once we unwind there, the external apology is accepted immediately. But if we say sorry when our thoughts do not agree with it, the same person will reject our apology. Even if we request him to stay, he will be adamant about leaving because he would not have received the vibrations of apology.

Things got resolved in this particular case because you first sent positive thoughts to your colleague, then talked to him. The important thing to understand here is that he continued to behave like he did before. Nothing changed from his side, not even his behaviour which you initially found uncomfortable. This proves that our choice to maintain harmony in a relationship is independent of the other person's behaviour.

We create repetitive negative thoughts about someone when we are not comfortable with a particular personality trait he has. This causes our mind to get entangled in those thoughts. But when we stop focussing on that sanskar, there is no further accumulation of heavy energy within us, even though that negative trait is still present in that person. This means that our relationship – the quality of energy exchange between two souls – is independent of the other person's behaviour. This is the secret of creating harmony in relationships.

This aspect is important to understand because every day we meet a lot of people whose sanskars do not match with ours. If we continue with our old pattern of thinking, we could come into conflict with so many people.

SO: As everyone in the universe is different, we are bound to have conflict in relationships.

SS: There are some people with whom we are simply unable to bond because their nature does not match with ours. Your experience has confirmed that we can be in harmony even in such cases. Their flaws may be visible to us, but if we do not keep that negativity on our mind, our relationship can still be in harmony. That is why that message says 'conflict is only in your attitude' and not in the other person's behaviour.

SO: Can you explain the word attitude?

SS: Initially you were thinking negatively about your colleague because that was your attitude towards him. When such an attitude is formed, one tries to find fault even in the other person's good acts, because that is the filter through which one views him.

Relationship is a soul to soul connection. Whenever we come into conflict with another person, it means both the souls get disconnected from each other and from their original good qualities. Their energy gets blocked.

We come into conflict with others either because of something that happened in the past, is taking place currently, or we anticipate it in future. Hurt created due to a past interaction gets registered in our memory with the mental programming 'I was hurt because of him'. This thought and feeling get triggered each time we think of that person. Once this programming is done, it is not possible for us to connect to that person soul to soul because we hold him responsible for our pain. How can we like anybody who is the cause of suffering in our life?

SO: It is like loving an illness.
SS: Yes, so it is not possible. The relationship will remain conflicted because that negative memory is deeply ingrained in us.

Some conflicts arise due to present situations. We are very quick to label others by thinking 'they are like this', because that is what we have grown up watching. We have come to believe this to be the normal way of being.

So, we first put labels on people. Then, we like or dislike them according to those labels. We create an image of them in our consciousness with the sanskars we have. That is why that quote says that when we judge someone, we do not define them, we define ourselves.

Suppose four artists are making your portrait. They will eventually come up with different portraits even though the subject is the same, because each one paints according to his personality.

SO: Each one would use a different medium to make the portrait – charcoal, watercolours or oil paints.

SS: That choice also depends on the personality of the artist. So, the painting defines the artist and not the subject. If the painting defined the subject, then all the four artists would come up with the same painting. Therefore, we judge others according to the colours of our own thoughts.

SO: That is a beautiful expression!

SS: When we say something about another person, it highlights our personality, not theirs. Different people perceive the same thing differently based on their personality.

Suppose you have five beautiful qualities and five strong weaknesses. One person will create an image of you on the basis of those five flaws. Another one will take one weakness and four qualities to create your image, and the third one may do the opposite of that. And someone else may create your image based on all your good qualities.

The person who creates your image based only on your weaknesses has a sanskar of criticism. The one who creates the image using your five good qualities has the sanskar of appreciating others. So the artists are not defining their subject, but defining themselves. How the subject actually is, we are not yet discussing that.

The quote you shared gives us a very powerful tool – if we have created a negative image of someone in our consciousness, we have the power to change that image today without that person changing himself. It is all about changing our perception. Usually, we keep waiting for others to change so that we can change the way we think about them.

SO: My guru used to say, 'The one who lights the fire will douse it.' This means if I think negatively about a person, I have to change my thought pattern to resolve that conflict.

SS: This means we have the power to change the images of other people that we have created in our mind. We could change the colours we use, our medium or style of painting, even when the subject remains the same.

Only we get to see the images that we create in our mind, and we see those every day. So let us start to create the images that we would like to see. If we do not like our creations, a very heavy energy accumulates inside us.

We do not have a relationship with other people but with the image we create of them in our consciousness. If we want our relationships to be more beautiful, we must keep enhancing the images we create inside. Others will not change, neither will we ask them to change, nor expect them to change. We will only change our colours and strokes. When the creations in our consciousness change, the energy inside us will be transformed, and we will start to move from conflict to harmony.

SO: When we change, the world changes.

MANTRAS FOR BEING LOVE

- When we judge others, we do not define them, we define ourselves. We perceive others only through the filter of OUR sanskars. So when we define them, we are actually defining OUR filter, which is our sanskars.

- Different people create a different image about one individual depending on THEIR OWN sanskars. Let us focus our attention on people's qualities when we create an image of them on our mind.

- When we are in conflict, the one factor which decides whether we will damage the relationship or heal it is OUR ATTITUDE. Our relationship will be in harmony with those for whom we create beautiful thoughts.

- Even if we do not approve of others' behaviour, let us not criticise them in our mind. Even if our sanskars do not match, we can still be in harmony if we refrain from thinking negatively about them.

Do Away with Labels

Suresh Oberoi: In our previous conversation we discussed that our attitude shapes our relationships.
Sister Shivani: We must hold on to this thought and use it in every relationship. We also talked about the three aspects of time – past, present and future. Some conflicts arise due to things that happened in the past. In most households, people spend a lot of time discussing the past. They don't let go of what their relatives or friends had said or done to them because they were hurt at that time. It could be even several years ago. At that moment, their mind got programmed with the thought 'I was hurt because of them'.

Whenever we feel hurt, we must programme our mind with the thought 'this hurt is created by me'. This may seem to be a small thing but it is not so. If, the moment we are hurt, we programme our mind with the thought 'what the other person said or did was not right, but the feeling of hurt is my own creation', it will become a lot easier to finish it and heal ourselves. If, however, we programme our mind with the thought 'they hurt me', the energy exchange between the two parties will be one of conflict, and it could remain so for years. There is a world of difference between taking personal responsibility and blaming others.

SO: True.
SS: Now, let us revise our past memories and simultaneously re-programme our mind. It will be easier for us to do it today because a situation that seemed overwhelming once upon a time may look insignificant today. So, it will be much easier to let go of it.

Re-programming the mind changes the energy that we radiate to others. If we don't do it, we may hold on to the past for very long, which means our relationships will never be in harmony. To let go of the past, let us re-emerge those scenes and re-programme the mind with the thought 'even if their action was not right, it was I who created the hurt in response to it, so I will finish the hurt myself'.

SO: Even the label of 'wrong action' was given by us.
SS: Yes, we have already discussed that everyone's definition of right and wrong is different.

SO: 'They are wrong' is our point of view and the feeling of hurt is also created by us.
SS: That is why we have to take charge of healing ourselves.

SO: The other person may not even know that we were hurt.
SS: Yes. Similarly, many people could have been hurt by our

past behaviour but we may not know about it. This confirms the fact that the feeling of hurt is an individual's own creation in response to a situation. Issues of the past must be resolved to finish our internal conflict.

Now let us bring our attention to the present. Be careful not to judge others by thinking 'this person is like this'. The moment we label someone, the energy of that relationship changes. Suppose I say 'this person lied today ... he also lied yesterday'. But if I go on to say 'he is a liar', then I will see him only through that label.

SO: Are these three statements so different from each other?
SS: The first two statements are talking about an incident that happened. But when we label the person as a liar, it limits our view point. Henceforth we will see him only through that filter. That's why there is so much difference between these two ways of thinking.

SO: One of my drivers used to cheat while refuelling the car. I did not fire him, but I told him that the other driver would get the job done in future. So it was definitely on my mind that he was a thief.
SS: It is okay to find a solution to a situation. We definitely have to protect ourselves from others' negative sanskars.

SO: What is wrong in calling him a thief?
SS: Once you put that label, you will always doubt him. So there will be constant conflict.

SO: To see someone commit the same error repeatedly and to look at each of the incidents separately is impossible.

SS: If you think that someone has a negativity due to which it is becoming difficult for you to work with him, you can stop working with him. This is better than creating constant conflict in the mind because that is good for neither of you. If you are unable to think positive about him, he too will have similar thoughts for you. Many of us live with such negative energy exchange for years.

Many people complain that they are unable to feel constant peace, happiness and bliss though everything is going on fine in their lives. If we find it natural to label others, it means we are constantly radiating negative energy. As a result, we won't be able to experience happiness.

SO: Is the label a blockage for being love?
SS: Yes. If I label someone, my love is blocked not for him alone, but that blockage depletes me and becomes my reality.

SO: Can you explain this again?
SS: If I put labels on people around me – 'this person is a liar', 'this one is always late', 'that one is lazy' and so on – then we may be living or working together, but the energy exchanged from both the sides will always be heavy.

SO: So, instead of labelling someone, should we just say that he has a particular negative sanskar? Is that okay?
SS: If we see a person through a label, we reinforce that label on him every time. For example, if your driver stole petrol once, it does not mean that he will steal anything that comes his way. Yes, it is true that he has a tendency to steal. But when you put a blanket label on him by thinking 'he is a thief', you assume

him to be doing something wrong all the time, which is not true. After putting a negative label on him, you will find it difficult to create positive energy for him. So, if you feel the need, you can take the required disciplinary action against him. But there is no need for you to stay in a negative energy exchange for years, as it is damaging for you.

You do not know whether that person will steal again or not. But if you continuously think about him through that label, you will keep losing your precious energy and deplete yourself. You will also interact with others through the same discharged soul battery.

SO: So, this approach is not worth having as it makes one lose out on good karma and health.
SS: Yes, that's true. Most importantly, you will develop a sanskar of putting labels on others.

SO: Then I might put a similar label on the other driver too.
SS: Yes, you might even start labelling your family members!

SO: I will get into the habit of doubting others.
SS: Yes, that's true. Even if the other driver is trustworthy, you may become doubtful of him. So what kind of energy will you send him?

If we doubt others, it is our loss; if we trust them, it is our gain. Instead of constantly being suspicious of others and discharging our energy, a better option is to trust everyone. Out of ten people we meet, nine will be trustworthy.

SO: When I had just started managing my own house, I would sometimes doubt my staff if I could not find my stuff. At that time, my mother told me 'Take care of your belongings, never blame others.'

SS: She asked you to protect yourself and not blame others. This is wisdom.

When nine people are honest, but one is not, it is okay. Let our trust not shake because of that one person. We are anyway going to meet one out of ten people who will do something that is not right. But if we lose our faith on everyone because of that one isolated experience, we will lose something far more valuable than the thing we have lost.

SO: If we trust everyone, our positivity may encourage even that one person to improve.

SS: In fact, we should trust that one person the most. When we keep sending the vibration 'I trust you', that energy triggers the honesty inside that person. Remember, the soul's original sanskars are recorded on it, and they remain present irrespective of its current action.

The opposite of this could also be true. Some people are honest, but they constantly receive the energy of doubt from others. As a result, they end up doing something they did not intend to.

SO: A story explains this. Once, a saint went to a businessman's house for dinner. It got late, so he stayed over for the night. He slept in the room where the businessman had stashed a lot of money. He thought to himself 'if I take away just one bundle, nobody will notice'. So he stole a bundle and left the next morning. Later, he ate some food bought with that money. But soon he felt sick and threw up. He realised what he had done and went back to the businessman's house with the remaining money.

A member of the staff was being beaten up there on suspicion of theft. The saint confessed that it was he, and not that man, who was to blame. But the businessman did not believe that a saint could do such a thing. The saint reiterated the truth and asked the businessman whether that money had been earned through corrupt means. The businessman was surprised as to how the saint knew about it. The saint said there was definitely something about that money which had influenced even someone like him into doing wrong. He said when he got back home, there was a change of environment, and that had helped him realise his fault.

SS: Such stories teach us the importance of our vibrations. The moral of the story is that even a saint will be forced to commit a wrong action if he consumes negative vibrations. And a thief can become a saint if he receives high-energy vibrations.

SO: It is such a vicious circle. The quality of our money influences the food we eat.

SS: And that influences our mind, body and relationships. All this goes on to determine the energy of our home, collective energy of our society and the world.

That is why at the Brahma Kumaris we say 'when we change, the world changes'. If each one of us elevates the quality of our thoughts and vibrations, the world will definitely be transformed. The world will change because it is made up of our vibrations. If we want a new world that is clean and pure, we have to create it in our mind first. If we cleanse our inner world, the world outside will automatically be purified. Each one must try this out.

SO: One should not hurt or cheat others while achieving goals in life.

SS: If we do not take care of ourselves while we are on the journey, we may earn money but would simultaneously deplete ourselves. If we cheat others, shout at them, or create hurry, fear and anxiety at our workplace in order to reach our goals faster, we are on the wrong track. If we deplete others' energy by any means, our energy will also deplete. Spirituality means following it in business and family life. This means that we should accomplish our goals ethically and stay in harmony with our colleagues and family. While doing everything else, we must take care of our state of mind. If our thoughts are clean, we will be able to achieve a lot, and our inner battery will remain charged.

Instead of getting angry with others at our workplace, if we speak to them politely, we will be recharged through the good wishes we receive from them. Instead of cheating others in business, let us cooperate with them. Instead of exploiting our clients, let us work for their benefit be blessed by them. The money that we earn through this approach will bring us love and good health.

SO: People say they work hard to earn for their children. But if they use corrupt means for it, the karmic result will definitely influence their children as well.

SS: Take a simple example. You go to the market and buy apples. The vendor slyly slips two bad apples into your bag, underneath the rest of them. On reaching home, when you find that out, you will definitely have negative thoughts about the vendor. The value of those two apples is insignificant for you, and may not be a big deal to throw them away. But the vendor has just earned the energy opposite of blessings.

If we cheat someone even slightly, we will bring home money but not blessings. And if we do not receive blessings, how will we get happiness, love and health?

Our homework is: not to label anyone because that makes conflict natural. When we take off the labels, harmony becomes natural and the blockage of our energy is cleared.

MANTRAS FOR BEING LOVE

- When we hold on to past hurt, we create energy of conflict in relationships. Each time we create hurt, we have to take personal responsibility for the creation of our emotion and heal ourselves.

- Let us re-programme our mind about the past situations. Understand that what they did was from THEIR sanskar and perspective, the hurt was created by us. They DID NOT create our hurt so we do not need them to heal us.

- If we put labels on people, then we will always see them through those filters. We will always radiate negative energy to them and receive the same from them. This will deplete our power.

- We should be aware of people's sanskars and protect ourselves while working with them. If we put labels on them, we will start seeing other people also through those labels.

Translating Knowledge
Into Wisdom

Suresh Oberoi: The words of wisdom spoken by elders make more sense to us as we evolve and grow older.

Sister Shivani: Elders or wise souls share deep insights in the form of essence. We later discuss those words, open them up and delve deep to understand them. We then apply that knowledge in our lives – experiment with it and gain experience. It is only after we experience those truths ourselves that we are able to realise what they truly mean.

SO: My guru also taught me something similar. He said that one may read many books, but the personal experience of that knowledge is one's actual property.

SS: This is because only when we experience that knowledge, it becomes our sanskar. When we hear a point of knowledge and discuss it with others, it exists only at the thought level. It becomes a sanskar – an impression on the soul – only after we bring it into action. If we do not use knowledge in our practical life, we will not have the conviction that it works. So we will not be able to use it when we face a challenging situation.

It takes more effort to apply knowledge for the first time because we have our inhibitions and need to push ourselves. Once we get the result, the process becomes easy and enjoyable. We are convinced that a bit of change within the self will give us the same positive result that we got last time.

Suppose you have put on a lot of weight. If you are able to lose those extra kilos by following a particular diet and exercise regimen, it will not be difficult for you to repeat it in future, because you have already tasted the definitive result.

SO: And one feels so light – both physically and mentally – after going through this process.

SS: Till the time we experience something, it does not become our property. Only when we use a point of knowledge does it translate into wisdom. Somebody can be very knowledgeable but not necessarily wise. These are two different things. The one who brings knowledge into practical life is wise.

Anything that we read in religious scriptures and spiritual books, or as a thought for the day, is knowledge. It does not turn into wisdom until it is practised. So when we receive some knowledge, it is good to try it out at the earliest.

SO: My guru used say that _tapasya_ means 'tapa hua gyan' [knowledge which has been used and refined]. He would say, 'There's no need to go to the mountains for _tapasya_, just take one point of knowledge and churn it in your mind.'

I have noticed that when I share my personal experience, it touches people deeply, but when I narrate someone else's experience, it has little impact.

SS: Experience brings result. When we share our personal experience with others, the vibrations we radiate are very different from those we radiate when we share someone else's experience. If we tell someone about a point of knowledge written in a book, it is more like sharing information. But when we use that knowledge practically and share it, that person receives the vibration of our conviction. He gets a feeling that THIS WORKS.

SO: It convinces the other person.

SS: The other person needs power to bring about a change within. If you do something practically, then share that personal experience with him, it gives him a very powerful vibration – 'this works, go try it'. Though that person may have heard the same thing many times before – for nothing that we hear is new to us, as all knowledge is accessible these days – that vibration touches him and inspires him to try it out himself.

SO: If someone tells us that he was cured of his illness by a particular doctor, we would want to see that doctor.

SS: Similarly, if parents demonstrate what they preach to their children, it will become very easy for children to follow them.

SO: What should parents do?

SS: They should implement the religious or spiritual knowledge that they teach their kids. Spirituality means to use every day the knowledge we have. However, today many people think that spirituality and life are separate from each other.

The other day I met a businessman at the airport. He said his business was flourishing and had spread to many cities. But he was very keen on taking a break from materialism and exploring the path of spirituality. I told him that he did not need to shift from business to spirituality. In fact, he could expand his business further. But he needed to make it clean, run it ethically and with his purest energy. He said that was not possible. Then, I said, spirituality would not work. Spirituality does not mean that we leave our current challenge and sit and meditate. If our spirituality does not work in practical life, what purpose does it serve? Use spirituality in your life, it will work.

SO: I also met a highly-accomplished businessman who wanted to shift to spirituality. For that, he said, he was opening three new factories. I asked him how further expansion of business was going to help him spiritually. He said he was doing it not to make money but to give people jobs.

SS: How sweet! His intention had changed from taking to giving. This is spirituality.

Spirituality is not separate from our lives. Rather, it is a tool to be used in all aspects of life. There is a myth that the one who practises spirituality gets disconnected from his family and friends. In this series we have discussed that we in fact remain disconnected from each other till we do not use spiritual tools. Spirituality does not make us drift apart but bridges the gap in our relationships. It works only if we use spiritual knowledge practically, and not just read it.

Sometimes people look at those meditating for years and come to the conclusion that spirituality makes little difference to practical life.

SO: When we don't want to do something, we look for excuses and count those who have failed at it.
SS: Our way of applying spiritual knowledge could be completely different from others. So we need not look at others. We are nobody to judge anyone because we have no idea about their internal transformation.

SO: Exactly. Somebody could have been spiritually weaker than us. He might have worked hard to come to our level.
SS: We can know and check only ourselves. So there's no point looking at others or getting affected by their opinions. We alone know what our thinking was in the past, how it is now, and what we need to make it in future. So we should not compare ourselves with others or get swayed by their opinions. Let us not be too happy if someone says 'you have changed a lot', because they do not know us at all. They are not able to see our thought process.

Whatever we are learning, it is good to use it in our practical life immediately. If we spot our weaknesses, we should give them away soon. This is called 'turant daan mahapunya', which means that prompt, immediate donation is the highest positive karma.

SO: Does *daan* here mean to give away our weaknesses?
SS: Yes, what other form of donation or surrender would be called the highest positive karma? Sharing what we have in surplus, such as money or clothes, is good karma. But to give away our weaknesses, negative habits or addictions is *mahapunya*, because after that donation our life changes forever. The life of those around us is also affected in a positive way.

SO: The truth is that our actions do affect others, so we cannot be too individualistic. For example, if I smoke here, others around me will be forced to consume those toxins; they will become passive smokers.

SS: Right, our habits affect those around us. And if our actions have a negative effect on others, we are creating a karmic account between us.

SO: Could you explain this?

SS: If your act of smoking affects my health, or any of your actions hurt me, won't that create a karmic account between us?

SO: Maybe we shouldn't do anything at all, as everything seems to be creating a karmic account.

SS: Why not? The understanding of karma is in fact an inspiration for us to cleanse ourselves. We are initially hesitant of going to a swimming pool because we find swimming difficult and are afraid of drowning. So we feel it is better not to try. But we must take the plunge and also face the initial struggle period. After that, it is only fun.

Similarly, when we try to give up a weakness, we do face initial trouble, but after that our karmic account changes completely. It also benefits others, because of which we receive their blessings and our account of *punya* [positive karma] goes up.

The points of spiritual knowledge that we have discussed in this series are easy to do – such as 'to think good about others', 'to do away with labels', 'to change the image we create of others in our mind'. Every day, let us pick up one image we have created in our mind and change it. That will be a *mahapunya* because when our mental state changes, the energy that we radiate becomes positive.

SO: We think much more about the people we dislike than the ones we like.
SS: One or another person is always on our mind. But if we do not think about them with the right awareness, most likely a negative mental image keeps forming on its own.

SO: What happens when we send love and blessings to others, think well of them, and focus on their specialities?
SS: When we consciously intervene like that, the image that we had created of them in our mind is positive. Since these images are visible only to us, it is important that we store something pleasant.

SO: Sometimes, when we consciously choose positive thoughts for others, it looks like we are lying to ourselves.
SS: There is nothing false about creating a nice image of a person by thinking in this way: 'I do not agree with your view point, but you will have your own reasons for behaving in this manner. You are acting according to your sanskars, and even if I am not comfortable with those, it is fine.' But if I think that the other person is bad, how could he behave like this and so on, it creates an altogether different image of him.

SO: If everything happening around me is perfect, such as the movement of the earth, the change of seasons and so on, it means that things happening to me by way of my

karmic account are also justified. First, I should accept my situation as it is, and then think of how I can improve it further.

SS: This is a better option than feeling sad about the situation or labelling others as bad.

SO: Actually, other people are just like postmen. They are mere instruments that bring us our due.

SS: Absolutely. We receive negative energy from others only because they have received the same from us in the past – could be yesterday, a few years ago or in a past life. So we ourselves are responsible for our current situation. The important thing is to send them positive energy in future.

SO: But we may not know who sent the negative energy first.

SS: Whether we have received the negative energy for the first time or it is a return of our own karma, we can still choose the energy we respond with. Whatever the case may be, the solution is always to change the energy that we express, irrespective of what the other person is doing. We should hold on to this point of spiritual knowledge like a mantra. To have a mantra means to use such formulas to turn our life around.

Let us remember, irrespective of how others behave with us, our thoughts are still our choice and responsibility. That power is completely ours. When we are faced with a difficult situation or person, we must use this mantra. It will beautify our relationships. Our inner self becomes clean because we will not hold on to any negativity, nor blame others for anything. We will then be able to transform our thoughts and settle our pending karmic accounts gracefully.

MANTRAS FOR BEING LOVE

- When we listen to and read spiritual knowledge, we become knowledgeable. When we implement that knowledge in our karma, it becomes our sanskar and we become wise.

- If we experiment with the knowledge and experience it, we get convinced that it is the truth. It then becomes part of our vibrations and the conviction with which we share it with others inspires them to experiment.

- Spirituality is not separate from our day to day life. It gives us the tools which we use in our family, professional and personal life. Karma done using the original qualities of the soul is spirituality.

- Our journey of self-transformation is personal. Only we know what we were, what we are now and what we want to be. We cannot compare with others or get affected by their opinions.

Life and Spirituality Go Hand-In-Hand

Suresh Oberoi: I was thinking whether someone like a businessman, who has to deal with all sorts of people, may not be able to follow the path of spirituality.

Sister Shivani: Today, every field of work – be it business, administration, education or health care – has challenges. There are all kinds of people everywhere. And a lot of things are happening that we may never have heard of before. But if we start to think about them, our mind will wander in that direction.

The weather could turn bad, there could be an outbreak of infection, or the water could be contaminated, but none of these is an excuse to allow ourselves to fall ill. If we believe it is natural to fall ill because of the weather outside, we will lead a life of suffering. This is what we are doing today.

Take a simple example. Many of us use anger in our day-to-day life. We picked up this habit from our environment. When we saw that anger got people quick results, that lying saved them from difficulties, and that corruption accelerated their work progress, we started using these methods in our life too. This is because our only aim was to get our work done. In the last 20-30 years, we have achieved a lot in life. However, the other fact is that we souls have become weak because of the way we have gone about achieving things.

SO: People use different tactics to get their work done. Some threaten others or frame them. Even a child has his way by crying.
SS: Those of us who have allowed ourselves to become part of such a system have to sit back and check the quality of our life and the state of the soul. If by using these means we are happy inside, love is still our value and health is natural to us, we need not change anything in ourselves.

SO: But all these tactics do work as weapons for people.
SS: Suppose I flaunt a weapon, people get scared of it and so that weapon makes it easier to get my work done. I may have been 'successfully' using this weapon for a long time. But today, I need to check if holding this weapon has injured my hand. I may have accomplished a lot but my method of working could have wounded me. The healing process will take time, and it will not begin till I let go of the weapon.

SO: If someone is achieving his purpose by using a weapon, why would he consider giving it up?
SS: Because in the process of using the weapon against others, his own hand may get cut and he may never get a replacement.

SO: Could you explain that point?

SS: It means that our ways of getting our work done – be it the habit of using anger, criticism, manipulation, or control – could injure us so badly that we may never fully recover from it. Repeated use of negative emotions depletes soul power. They weaken our mind, which in turn influence our body and relationships. If our spiritual health is weak, there's a high chance that our emotional, mental, physical and social health will get affected. This will create a life of pain. So we all have to choose our priority.

People use these tactics so that they can achieve more in life for the sake of their family, so that they can earn respect in society, and experience love and happiness. But by adopting a 'by hook-or by-crook' approach, they land in the opposite direction. They end up doing irreversible damage to their mind, health and relationships. They now need to pause and ask themselves if it was all worth it.

If we live in a mansion but cannot stay together as a family, then what's the whole point?

SO: I know of a millionaire whose children stay abroad. He keeps requesting them to come back but they refuse to live with him or use his money.

SS: That person needs to check the means he had used to earn wealth and what sort of energy he had earned along with the money?

If he used the sanskar of anger at work, he would probably have lost his cool even with his kids. That would have created a gap in the family during their childhood. Now, when the children are all grown-up, they don't have a strong bond with him. They do not want to come back because they did not like the heavy energy in the house.

We really need to ask ourselves if we want to get our work done at the cost of everything else. What will we do with all the money earned if our health is so bad that we can no longer enjoy a good meal or get a good night's sleep?

Today, we can hardly find a family where everyone is happy, and enjoys good health and relationships. That is why this age is called *Kaliyug* or Iron Age – a time when chaos, despair and unrest are dominant. We are not sad because of the times we are living in, but it is the other way round – we are in *Kaliyug* because we are sad.

If we want to alter our situation, we have to let go of our old belief systems. Even if everyone around us is still using the old beliefs, we must make our personal choices based on what we want from life. If a happy mind, good health and beautiful relationships are our priority, we have to take care of all of them consistently.

SO: By making a positive inner change, we will also earn a good night's rest. These days some people cannot sleep even after popping a sleeping pill.

SS: Yes, very true.

We had been searching for happiness outside and we have managed to achieve a lot outside. In the past few decades, science has given us so many facilities and mediums of communication that we should actually have been leading very comfortable lives by now. But the fact is we are far more stressed today.

SO: Comforts were so few.

SS: There were no sources of entertainment either.

SO: We used to listen to the radio or watch the only TV channel available at that time.

SS: Our kitchen today is fitted with so many gadgets that we can wrap up cooking in no time, and that too just at the push of a button. Our grandparents had none of these luxuries – which have become our necessity today – but probably their generation was much happier than ours. Not many medical treatments were available to them but they were far healthier than us. There are many grandparents and great-grandparents even today leading healthy lives.

SO: We had never heard of the word 'cousin' in our childhood. We always looked at each other as brothers.

SS: There was a common desire to bond together. In fact, people used to think of the entire village as their family. And today, we find siblings fighting legal battles over property.

From a stage where we did not have much, we have come to a point where we have all comforts we can think of. We have earned it all through our efforts, but along our journey we have also earned pain, anxiety, anger and stress. That is why we have with us today the entire package – including wealth, difficult emotions, entangled karmic accounts and an energy that is opposite of blessings.

SO: We never looked at things from this angle as our focus was always on earning money and reputation.

SS: The past is past, but are we ready to change now? We need not give up the comforts we have earned for ourselves. We only have to bring about a change within. Some people say that inventions like the mobile phone and internet are the cause of stress, but they are actually the cause of comfort. Our lives have become so much easier ever since we had these facilities. A mobile phone does not cause any stress on its own. It becomes a problem when we get addicted to it or we misuse it. Spirituality teaches us *'saadhan bhi istemaal karo, saath mein saadhna bhi karo'*. It means we must enjoy all the means of comfort but not abandon our inner world.

When we set out on the journey for change, we may be alone. There will be challenges, and simple things may get a bit difficult and time-consuming initially. But if our approach is right, our spiritual energy will increase. If our methods are not right, our soul power will go down. God teaches us *'satya ki naav hilti hai dolti hai, lekin kabhi doobti nahin'* – the boat of truth rocks but never sinks. So, we must tread the path of truth, stand by our values and keep increasing our willpower.

SO: There are many corporate houses even today that follow ethics.

SS: We must stand by our values not just in financial matters but also while dealing with people. We must interact with others with the purest energy.

SO: But the belief is that one cannot work done without using anger.

SS: It is really a matter of personal choice. If we use those means, we should be ready to face the consequences too. It is up to us.

SO: What if it is too late before someone realises his mistake? For instance, a person may keep achieving success

by suppressing others. But he may not know until much later in life what repercussions it has had on him.

SS: Repercussions of our actions will not appear much later in life; we will get them every day. We should check for the result of our actions beyond our field of work and bank balance.

SO: A person who supresses others at work may feel restless when he goes back home.

SS: He does not even have to wait till he goes home, to realise that he is not at peace.

SO: But he may not realise it himself. If he visits a doctor, he will tell him that it is the nature of his business that compels him to do all the bad stuff. The doctor will not give him any spiritual tools for self-empowerment; he will only write him a prescription.

SS: A psychiatrist or medical practitioner cannot give a medicine that can make the mind peaceful. He can give a medical cure for a particular ailment such as depression, but that is no guarantee that the mind will become peaceful. There are so many people today who do not suffer from depression but their mind is not at peace. Their mind is so restless that they cannot sit in solitude. That is why they switch on the TV or consume alcohol after returning from work. By choosing these means of escape, they temporarily withdraw from their noisy mind. They distract their mind because they know no other way to separate themselves from their own thoughts.

Their mind is not at peace because the actions they performed during the day, had actually stolen others' mental peace. If we cause unrest to others, no medicine, technology or addiction can help us. These are only temporary measures.

SO: Will it not help if they meditate or seek advice from gurus?

SS: They might not be able to meditate because spirituality and practical life go together.

If I start to practise meditation but my approach towards life remains the same, and I continue to use anger in my interactions, I would create heavy energy and earn the same for myself all through the day. If I try to meditate the next morning, it might not work. One who shouts at others cannot meditate well the next day. It is not possible. That is why we have to take care of our spiritual well-being through meditation and practical well-being through good karma, simultaneously.

Meditation is like filling up our bucket with the power of the Supreme. We learn to connect to Him, and His powers flow in, filling up the bucket. But if the bucket leaks all day through our negative thoughts and actions, it will never get filled, however long we may leave it under the tap. We have to plug the leakage and keep attention on ourselves throughout the day.

Doing our business ethically and honestly is an obvious component of plugging this leakage. We don't even need to discuss it, because if we are not being fair at work, it means spirituality has not sunk into our lifestyle at all.

If the discharge of energy is far more than the recharge, no energy is accumulated. So, spirituality goes hand in hand with practical life. It will work for us only if we charge ourselves not just during meditation but throughout the day.

SO: True.

SS: When we go to a meditation camp, a temple or a mosque, or when we meet an enlightened soul, we feel good. But for how long does that last? When we come back home, we are the same person again.

We stay much longer in our practical field. If, in our daily life, we do not express the same vibrations that we experienced at a spiritual place, then the experience of peace and happiness will be transient. We will then feel good only as long as we are in that positive company or place.

The purpose of meditation is not to feel good and peaceful only while meditating. It is to accumulate spiritual power that can be used in our actions during the day, so that we remain peaceful throughout.

SO: It is like recharging our mobile phone in the morning so that it works all day.

SS: If we can talk over mobile phone only as long as it is connected with the charger, then it is of little use. We cannot stay next to the charger all day.

Similarly, we cannot meditate all the time. Only that method of meditation is correct which empowers us for the rest of the day. If we remain healthy only as long as we stay with the doctor, what's the point of that treatment? The treatment is fine only if it makes us fit in general.

Meditation and study of spiritual principles every morning empowers us. They give us the tools to be used during the day in our every thought, word and action – whether in personal or professional life. When we create pure thoughts and actions, it further increases our soul power. And this daily practice keeps us stable and in-charge of our emotions even in a crisis.

MANTRAS FOR BEING LOVE

- When we use the weapon of anger to get our work done, our work gets done but our energy gets depleted. Repeated depletion affects our happiness, health and relationships.

- Everything that we experience today, we have earned that in our interactions. Today we have earned wealth, but we have also earned stress, anger and disease. We need to earn but should also keep attention on our state of being.

- While at work, if we are compassionate towards working with us, if we cooperate with everyone, then we are not only earning money but also earning blessings and good wishes.

- Today we experience restlessness in the mind because we have caused restlessness to people in our interactions.

About BK Shivani

SPIRITUAL GUIDE & MENTOR
SPEAKER & WRITER

Since 1996, BK Shivani has been a practitioner and a teacher of Raj Yoga Meditation, which is at the heart of the teachings of the Brahma Kumaris World Spiritual Organization. Intent on transforming human consciousness through spiritual education and meditation practice, she has been empowering millions across the world to experience their innate peace, happiness and love.

First telecast in 2007, her widely popular television show aimed at self-transformation, *Awakening With Brahma Kumaris* enjoys the rare distinction of having completed 2,000 episodes. For over a decade, the show has empowered individuals from all walks of life in India, USA and Canada, UK, Africa, Australia, New Zealand, Middle East and South-East Asia. Viewers have overcome mental stress, depression, addictions, low self-esteem and unhappy relationships, by taking personal responsibility of their emotions.

In March 2019, BK Shivani was awarded the prestigious *Nari Shakti Puraskaar*, the highest civilian honour for women in India, for her role in transforming human behaviour. Since 2017, she has been appointed as a *Goodwill Ambassador* by the World Psychiatric Association. For her excellence in empowering Spiritual Consciousness, she was honored with the *Women of the Decade Achievers Award* by ASSOCHAM Ladies League in 2014.

BK Shivani's TV show *Happiness Unlimited* was adapted into a book in 2014owing to its success. The book in India qualified into the Amazon Best-Reads List and went on to be the No.1 bestseller in the Religious and Spiritual section.

Having travelled to over 35 countries across the globe across USA, Canada, United Kingdom, Europe, Australia and New Zealand, Africa, South-East Asia and Middle East, she has delivered over 3,500 talks overseas and in India. She shares simple, practical wisdom through diverse platforms like public programs, television shows, discussion panels, interactive workshops, retreats, seminars, corporate events, social and community development initiatives, radio shows and social media outlets.

At Silicon Valley, USA, she has addressed corporate giants such as Google, Microsoft, Cisco, Amazon and Intel. She has also spoken at business houses like Reliance Jio, Maruti Suzuki India, Indian Oil Corporation, Godrej Industries Ltd., Sony Entertainment Television, Airtel Mobile Services, GE Energy, Asian Paints, Jet Airways, Singapore Airlines and Times Of India, to name a few. Apart from the YPO, FLO and EO Chapters, Indian Armed Forces, she also speaks at the Rotary International and Lions Clubs International. She has been invited by pan-Indian premier schools, colleges, management institutes and leadership institutes like IIM, IIT, AIMA and so on.

The Indian Medical Association of all the major cities of India have invited her for talks on mind-body-medicine. BK Shivani actively promotes Organ Donation initiatives every year. Besides, she is part of a team which along with FOGSI, has developed 'AdhbutMaatrutva', a unique programme that explores scientific & spiritual principles of Garbh Sanskar, for expecting parents.

BK Shivani advocates the importance of transforming consciousness through spiritual education and Raj Yoga Meditation, to embrace principles of health, happiness and harmony. She analyses and addresses a wide spectrum of topics like self-transformation, self-empowerment, life skills, emotional and mental wellness, karmic philosophy, harmony in relationships, parenting, value education, leadership skills, overcoming addictions and many more.

A gold medalist in academics, BK Shivani holds an Electronics Engineering degree from the Pune University, India.

She regularly interacts with over 5 million followers on social media.

Connect with her on social media:

    /BKShivani

The Brahma Kumaris

www.brahmakumaris.org

The Brahma Kumaris is an international NGO in general consultative status with the Economic and Social Council of the United Nations and in consultative status with UNICEF. With its global headquarters in Mt Abu, Rajasthan, through more than 4,500 centres in over 140 countries, the Brahma Kumaris offer a wide range of courses and programs to create positive change.

The Brahma Kumaris teaches Raj Yoga as a way of experiencing peace of mind and a positive approach to life. The organisation provides opportunities to people from all religious and cultural backgrounds to explore their own spirituality and learn skills of reflection and meditation derived from Raj Yoga, which will help develop inner calm, clear thinking and personal well-being. Since its inception, the organisation has made values like purity, peace, love and joy a practical and sustainable experience in the lives of millions of people worldwide.

At the heart of the organisation's teachings is the foundation course in Raja Yoga Meditation. This course provides a logical and practical understanding of the relationship between spirit and matter, as well as an understanding of the interplay between souls, God and the material world. All courses, seminar and workshops are offered to the public free of charge, as a community service.

The Foundation Course in Raj Yoga Meditation is offered free of charge at every centre of the Brahma Kumaris. It is a 7-day course, 1 hour daily. To know your nearest centre visit

https://www.brahmakumaris.com/centers/(India)
http://www.brahmakumaris.org/centre-locator (International)

AWAKENING channel is a 24–hour TV channel of the Brahma Kumaris.

WINGS OF BRAHMA KUMARIS

Brahma Kumaris has set up various Wings that conduct customized services and courses for different sections of the society. Seminars, workshops, conferences, research and several creative activities are held from time to time by each wing in the direction of 'Applied Spirituality'. Wings at a glance:

- Administrators' Wing
- Art & Culture Wing
- Business & Industry Wing
- Education Wing
- Jurists Wing
- Media Wing
- Medical Wing
- Politicians Wing

- Religious Wing
- Rural Development Wing
- Scientists & Engineers Wing
- Security Services Wing
- Shipping, Aviation & Tourism Services Wing
- Social Service Wing
- Sparc Wing
- Sports Wing
- Transport & Travel Wing
- Women's Wing
- Youth Wing

COURSES OFFERED

- Self-Management
- Stress-Free Living
- Values In Action
- Emotional Intelligence
- Mind Management
- Harmony in Relationships
- Self-Empowerment
- Enhancing Self-Esteem
- Exploring Inner Powers
- Values in Health Care
- Leadership Skills
- Work-Life Balance
- Karmic Principles
- Art Of Right Thinking
- Effective And Good Parenting
- Spiritual Advancement

In addition to the institution's centres, these courses are conducted at the workplaces,offices of private and public firms, hospitals, schools, other community settings and prisons.

RAJ YOGA MEDITATION COURSE

Raj Yoga Meditation – A form of meditation that is accessible to people of all backgrounds. It is a meditation without the need for rituals or mantras, and can be practised anywhere at any time, with 'open eyes'. Regular practice helps us to respond to situations, rather than just reacting to them. We begin to live with harmony, we create better and happier, healthier relationships and change our lives in a most positive way.

8 Spiritual Powers – With self-transformation as a goal, life becomes a great journey of discovery. We discover how to cope with every challenge and how to live well in every situation using the 8 powers of Raja Yoga: the power to withdraw, the power to pack up, the power to accommodate, the power to discriminate, the power of judgment, the power to face, the power to co-operate and the power to tolerate.

Spiritual Lifestyle – By remembering our spiritual powers and learning to adapt, tolerate and be ever alert, we create a non-violent, responsive, rather than reactive, relationship with life. We move from rejecting people and situations, to welcoming them. Such a lifestyle makes understanding of inner peace, the sweetness of love and the power of bliss remain alive within us.

Self-Realisation – Recognising the self as a spiritual being, an infinitesimally tiny star, point of light – a soul. The intrinsic nature of the soul is that of love, peace, happiness, truth, bliss, purity.

Knowing God – Like us, God is also a soul, the Supreme Soul

– who never takes a body of His own. He is the Almighty Authority, the Ocean of Love, Peace, Power and Purity.

Relationship with God – When you learn to tune your mind in meditation to the mind of God, then whatever the situation, you always have a source of help and strength to draw upon – an infinite reservoir of power and virtues that is only a thought away.

Law of Karma – Every action has an equal and opposite reaction. This means whatever we are presently experiencing is the return of what we once sent out. Our every thought, word and action is the energy we create and radiate – this is our KARMA. Situations and people's behaviour is the energy we receive – this is our DESTINY.

AWAKENING
To A New Way of Living

AWAKENING

The Brahma Kumaris TV Channel

Awakening, the TV Channel by the Brahma Kumaris is created with the understanding that 'When We Change, Our World Changes.' It showcases:

(1) Chat shows and talk shows on emotional health and lifestyles issues such as Stress, Anger, Fear, Relationships, Professional Issues and Work-Life Balance.

(2) Programmes on the Mind-Body connection: Programmes on De-addiction, Reversal of Coronary Artery Disease,

Diabetes, Yoga, the role of emotions in creating good health and healing a disease.

(3) Programmes on Mental Health issues: Depression, OCD, Hyperactivity in children and all mental health diseases prevalent in today's times.

(4) Programmes on the application of Spiritual Principles in every profession: Doctors, Jurists, Politicians, Administrators, Business & Industry, Media, Art & Culture, Scientist & Engineers, Security Services, Travel & Tourism and many more.

(5) Cookery shows presenting sattvic recipes and also sharing the role of mind during cooking and eating.

(6) Special programmes on holistic parenting.

(7) Guided meditations throughout the day to help people to meditate sitting at home.

(8) Devotional songs

Watch *Awakening* on:

BRAHMA KUMARIS CENTRES

INDIA

SPIRITUAL HEADQUARTERS
World Headquarters, 'Pandav Bhawan',
Post Box No. 2, Mt. Abu – 307501
Tel: (+91) 2974-238261 to 238268

Om Shanti Retreat Centre,
Gurgaon, Haryana.
Tel: (+91) 124-2667000, (+ 91) 96506-92000
Email: orc@bkivv.org

Shanti Sarovar Retreat Centre,
Hyderabad.
Tel: (+91) 40-2300-1234, (+91) 9396503335
Email: shantisarovar@bkivv.org

25, New Rohtak Road,
Karol Bagh, New Delhi.
Tel: (+91) 11-2355-0355

23, Dar-Ul-Muluk,
Gamdevi, Mumbai.
Tel: (+91) 22-2380-5873
Email: bkgamdevi@gmail.com

81/1, Bangur Avenue,
V.I.P. Road Side, Kolkata.
Tel: (+91) 33-2574-7863

3702, Annanagar,
Block Q–96, Chennai.
Tel: (+91) 44-2626-7441, (+91) 44-2626-6765

INTERNATIONAL CO-ORDINATING OFFICE AND REGIONAL OFFICE

FOR EUROPE AND THE MIDDLE EAST

Global Co-operation House,
65-69 Pound Lane,
London, NW10 2HH, UK.
Tel: (+44) 20-8727-3350
Fax: (+44) 20-8727-3351
E-mail: london@brahmakumaris.org

REGIONAL OFFICES

AFRICA

Global Museum for a Better World,
Maua Close,off Parklands Road, Westlands
PO Box 123, Sarit Centre,
Nairobi, Kenya.
Tel: (+254) 20 374-3572
Fax: (+254) 20-374-3885
E-mail: nairobi@brahmakumaris.org

AUSTRALIA AND SOUTH-EAST ASIA

A181 First Ave,
Five Dock,
Sydney, 2046 – Australia
Tel:(+61) 2-9716-7066
E-mail: fivedock@au.brahmakumaris.org

THE AMERICAS AND THE CARIBBEAN

Global Harmony House,
46 S. Middle Neck Road,
Great Neck, NY 11021, USA
Tel: (+1) 516-773-0971
Fax: (+1) 516-773-0976
E-mail: newyork@brahmakumaris.org

RUSSIA, CIS AND THE BALTIC COUNTRIES

Brahma Kumaris World Spiritual University,
2, Lobachika, Bldg. No. 2,
Moscow 107140 – Russia.
Tel: (+7) 749-9264-6276
Fax: (+7) 495-261-3224
E www: brahmakumarisru.com
www: spiritual-development.ru
mail: moscow@brahmakumaris

HAPPINESS UNLIMITED BY BK SHIVANI

The book is a conversational adaptation of the TV series –
Awakening with Brahma Kumaris, where **Sister BK Shivani** is
in conversation with the veteran movie actor **Suresh Oberoi**.
The discussion sheds light on what happiness is, how to find
it and what has fundamentally been wrong in our pursuit for
it. Happiness is only possible when we accept everyone as they
are, at every moment, in every situation. That means an end
to judging or resisting others, an end to complaining, an end
to criticising or controlling and an end to competing. It means
the awakening of self-responsibility.

One can then create a life of joy, contentment and bliss, as the
choice and power lie with the self. The book explores ways
to defeat negative mental outlook, stroll through day-to-day
challenges and experience lasting happiness, rather than the
fleeting kind felt today. Happiness is a Decision.